LITTLE GIANT® ENCYCLOPEDIA

The

ZODIAC

D0173360

LITTLE GIANT® ENCYCLOPEDIA

The ZODIAC

THE DIAGRAM GROUP

Sterling Publishing Co., Inc.
New York

Library of Congress Cataloging-in-Publication Data

The little giant encyclopedia of the zodiac / the diagram group.
               p.   cm
      Includes index.
      ISBN 1-4027-4731-4
        1. Houses (Astrology) 2. Zodiac 1. Diagram Group.
BF1716.L58   1997
133.5'2 - dc21   96 - 48341
                                            CIP

10 9 8 7 6 5 4 3 2

Published by Sterling Publishing Company, Inc.
387 Park Avenue South, New York, N.Y. 10016
A Diagram Book first created by Diagram Visual Information
195 Kentish Town Road, London NW5 2JU, England
© 1999 by Diagram Visual Information Limited
Distributed in Canada by Sterling Publishing
c/o Canadian Manda Group, 165 Dufferin Street,
Toronto, Ontario, Canada M6K 3H6
Distributed in the United Kingdom by GMC Distribution Services,
Castle Place, 166 High Street, Lewes, East Sussex, England BN7 1XU
Distributed in Australia by Capricorn Link (Australia) Pty Ltd.
P.O. Box 704, Windsor, NSW 2756, Australia

Manufactured in China

Sterling ISBN-13: 978-1-4027-4731-1
ISBN-10: 1-4027-4731-4

Foreword

The Little Giant Encyclopedia of the Zodiac is a fascinating introduction to Western astrology, based on the tropical zodiac, and Chinese astrology, based on a 12-year lunar calendar.

The positions of the signs of the tropical zodiac are determined by the timing of the four seasons, each of which is then subdivided into three equal sections, making the 12 signs of the zodiac. The first half of the book is devoted to the 12 signs of the zodiac, detailing aspects of life, love, work, friends, likes, and dislikes. For added interest, each chapter ends with a list of famous people born under that sign.

Section 2 is devoted to the Chinese system based on a 12-year cycle. Each year of the cycle is a lunar year and each year is named after an animal. Tables of dates are included so the reader can find which animal rules the year of his or her birth. Once you have identified your animal sign, read the chapter devoted to that animal. Each chapter also includes a brief look at how Western and Chinese zodiacs can be combined to give more detailed readings, as well as a list of famous people born in the same animal year and their zodiac sign. A detailed index is included for all signs.

6

Contents

SECTION 1 ZODIAC TYPES

	Introduction	8
	Astrological symbols	15
♈	1. Aries: the Ram	16
♉	2. Taurus: the Bull	36
♊	3. Gemini: the Twins	56
♋	4. Cancer: the Crab	76
♌	5. Leo: the Lion	96
♍	6. Virgo: the Virgin	116
♎	7. Libra: the Scales	136
♏	8. Scorpio: the Scorpion	156
♐	9. Sagittarius: the Archer	176
♑	10. Capricorn: the Goat	196
♒	11. Aquarius: the Water Carrier	216
♓	12. Pisces: the Fishes	236

SECTION 2 CHINESE ASTROLOGY

Introduction   256

	1. The Rat	278
	2. The Ox	297
	3. The Tiger	316
	4. The Rabbit	335
	5. The Dragon	354
	6. The Snake	373
	7. The Horse	392
	8. The Goat	411
	9. The Monkey	430
	10. The Rooster	449
	11. The Dog	468
	12. The Pig	487

Index   506

Section 1

ZODIAC TYPES

Introduction

Zodiac Types is a clear and concise introduction to
the signs of the zodiac and the behavioral
characteristics they are believed to endow. Each
sign and its attributes have been detailed within
separate chapters. Many different aspects – from a
Scorpio's personality and reactions to situations in
the workplace and at home, to a Taurean's behavior
when in love – are described with the help of lists,
panels, and illustrations.

What is a sign of the zodiac?

Each of the 12 signs of the zodiac is a name given to
a 30-degree arc of the sky, as viewed from Earth. As
the Earth moves around the Sun, the Sun appears to
pass from one 30-degree arc to the next, completing
the journey through all 12 zodiac arcs in one year.
For example, a person whose birthday is on
January 1 is born when the Sun is in the zodiac sign
of Capricorn. This is referred to as a person's sun
sign (see "zodiac band," opposite) Hence, a person
born a month later, when the sun is passing through
the next 30-degree arc, would have the next zodiac
sign, Aquarius, as his or her sun sign.

1

**Zodiac band showing
zodiac position**

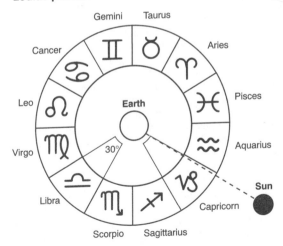

Characteristics of the zodiac signs

The popular view is that a person will display the
characteristics associated with his or her sun sign.
For example, characteristics typical of Capricorn
include ambition, faithfulness, weak knee joints, and
a long life span. In reality, however, many people
born with the Sun in Capricorn may well have little
ambition, be unfaithful, have perfect knees, or may
have died young.

What is astrology?

Astrology is the study of apparent coincidences
between certain events on Earth and the positions of
the Sun, Moon, and eight planets. In traditional
terms, the Sun, Moon, and planets (often loosely
called "the stars") are said to influence events on
Earth. The modern view, first suggested by the
psychologist Carl Gustav Jung, is that events
coincide with a particular pattern of the stars. This
phenomenon is known as synchronicity.

The personal birth chart

When studying synchronicity between personality
and the stars, a complete horoscope or birth chart
must be made. This shows the positions of the Sun,
Moon, and planets at the time of birth, relative to the
place of birth. The birth chart indicates many
features, only one of which is the position of the Sun
at birth.

A sample birth chart

The symbols on the chart are the standard ones used
to indicate the zodiac signs, the Sun, Moon, and
planets. The chart opposite is for a person born on
May 25, 1931; therefore, the Sun is in the zodiac

sign of Gemini. The position of the Moon at birth, the positions of all the eight planets of the solar system, and several other important features, such as geographical location, are all taken into account when interpreting the chart. For example, in the sample chart, the Moon is in Virgo, i.e., the moon sign is Virgo. The Moon is linked with mood and

A birth chart

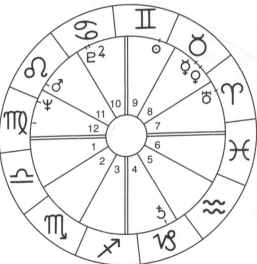

See "Astrological Symbols," p.15, for the meanings of the symbols shown.

emotion, so astrologically this person's moods would be Virgoan, rather than Geminian. A person who had been born on the same day, in a different year and location, however, would have a chart that was oriented differently, although it would have several similar features.

In very broad, general terms, this is the basis of personal astrology.

Finding your sun sign

The approximate dates of when the Sun moves into each sign are listed below. They will be correct for most years, but incorrect for others. For example, if your birthday is July 22, some lists will say your sun sign is Cancer, as shown below; others will say Leo.

Sign	Dates
Aries	March 21 – April 19
Taurus	April 20 – 20 May
Gemini	May 21 – June 20
Cancer	June 21 – July 22
Leo	July 23 – August 22
Virgo	August 23 – September 22
Libra	September 23 – October 22
Scorpio	October 23 – November 21
Sagittarius	November 22 – December 21
Capricorn	December 22 – January 19
Aquarius	January 20 – Febuary 18
Pisces	February 19 – March 20

The cusp

The exact time when the Sun moves from one sign to the next is known as the cusp or beginning of the sign. Because the movement of the Earth around the Sun is not exactly regular each year, the precise date when the Sun moves from one sign to the next sometimes differs.

Predictions

Future events cannot be predicted. Professional astrologers read trends by comparing a person's birth chart with the day-to-day movements of the Moon and the small planets (Mercury, Venus, Mars), and the longer-term movements of the larger planets (Jupiter, Saturn, Neptune, Uranus, Pluto).

Astrology and free will

In general, astrological interpretations are descriptions of how a person may behave rather than what he or she might actually do. Every characteristic has its positive and negative sides, the interpretation of which is a matter for personal choice; for example, one Taurean characteristic is never to change without very good reason. This could be interpreted either as undying loyalty or as stubborn resistance.

How to enjoy this book

The information about each zodiac sign is a summary of the main characteristics associated with it. If you find that you happen to be typical of your sun sign, it is probably because several planets are in your sign or are linked with it in positive ways.

If you have few or none of the characteristics of
your sun sign, it could be for one or more of the
following reasons:
1 Other signs are stronger in your chart
2 Your full potential has not yet emerged
3 The characteristic has negative "influences" in the
orientation of your chart, which you have controlled
4 Your birth date is the day of a cusp, and the exact
time of birth may indicate that your sun sign is
actually in the next, or previous, sign
Reading the sun signs is fun and may be revealing.
If, however, you wish to investigate astrology
further, the best course of action is to have a full
chart made and interpreted by a qualified astrologer.

Astrological symbols

The symbols used to represent the signs and their ruling planets are depicted below.

Sign	Symbol	Ruling planets	Symbols
Aries	♈	Mars	♂
Taurus	♉	Venus	♀
Gemini	♊	Mercury	☿
Cancer	♋	Moon	☽
Leo	♌	Sun	☉
Virgo	♍	Mercury	☿
Libra	♎	Venus	♀
Scorpio	♏	Mars; Pluto	♂♇
Sagittarius	♐	Jupiter	♃
Capricorn	♑	Saturn	♄
Aquarius	♒	Saturn; Uranus	♄♅
Pisces	♓	Jupiter; Neptune	♃♆

1. Aries: the Ram
March 21 – April 19

The first sign of the zodiac is concerned with
- self-assertion, initiation, new beginnings
- action, daring, challenge, adventure
- exploration, pioneering, discovering
- aggression, creativity, personal goals
- personal control of everything
- competition, winning, being first
- courage, honesty, nobility, openness

Elemental quality

Aries is the cardinal fire sign of the zodiac. It can be
likened to a fire which gives direction, such as in
a rocket, a gun, or an engine. Superman and
Superwoman, who can propel themselves in any
direction, are good metaphors of Aries energy.
Fire is a process that causes change and Aries uses
energy to bring about changes. Being a cardinal
sign, Aries is the most energetic of the fire signs and
usually takes the initiative.

Spiritual goal

To learn the meaning of selfless love.

THE ARIES PERSONALITY

These are the general personality traits found in people who are typical of Aries. An unhappy or frustrated Aries may display some of the not-so-attractive traits.

Characteristics

Positive	Negative
• Is a leader	• Must be the boss
• Is energetic	• Brashness
• Helps others to achieve their dreams	• Blind to his or her effect on others
• Accepts challenges	• Intolerance
• Believes the best of others	• Jealousy
• Takes risks for others	• Doesn't listen
• Defends the vulnerable	• Selfishness
• An Aries life is an open book	• Impulsiveness
• Will give life for the loved one	• Poor judge of character
• Continues action even if others give up	• Dislikes being told what to do

Secret Aries

Inside anyone who has strong Aries influences is a person who thinks that he or she is more interesting than others and better than those with whom they are in competition.

It is patently obvious to all that Aries is interested in winning, whoever or whatever the challenge.

A fight, a race, a bit of physical or verbal sparring, or an opportunity to do things in new ways are what keep the Aries' fires burning bright. Aries is an original, and being first lights him or her up.

Aries has to be number one in every respect. The secret fear of a typical Aries is that he or she won't be liked or valued, even though a winner. However, failure is never a problem because Aries doesn't know the word . . . every outcome is seen as a part of the winning process, which is why warnings of impending disasters are usually ignored.

Ruling planet and its effect

Mars rules the zodiac sign of Aries, so anyone whose birthchart has a strong Aries influence will tend to look for challenges to overcome. In astrology, Mars is the planet of aggressive energy and creative action. Like Mars, Aries is the knight in shining armor, an inspiration to friends, and a conquering hero to the underdog.

Arien lucky connections

Colors	red, black, white
Plant	tiger lily
Gemstones	ruby, diamond
Metal	iron
Tarot card	the magician
Animals	ram and lamb

THE ARIES LOOK

People who exhibit the physical characteristics distinctive of the sign of Aries are tall and bold. Usually lean, they have strong bodies and may even be quite athletic. They are usually concerned to project a physical image of success. They need to be winners and generally do their very best to look the part. Appearances are important to Aries.

Physical appearance

- Body: lean and strong, with large bones, thick shoulders, and a long neck
- The face is usually long and the eyes are steady and somewhat piercing – not looking through you, but certainly looking at you, as if to challenge
- There may be a scar on the face or the body from a past fight – if so it will be "worn" with a certain pride like a winner's trophy

THE ARIES MALE

If a man behaves in a way typical of the personality associated with the zodiac sign of Aries, he will have a tendency toward the characteristics listed below, unless there are influences in his personal birthchart that are stronger than that of his Aries sun sign.

Appearance

The typical Aries man

- has a strong body
- is extremely energetic
- has a dominating sex appeal
- walks with an air of nobility

- dresses in clothes appropriate to the current challenge

Behavior and personality traits

The typical Aries man

- is fiercely competitive
- is honest
- appears to be self-assured
- takes initiative and expects others to follow
- is enterprising
- dreads physical disability
- has very clear goals
- will put his partner on a pedestal
- needs to win
- uses wit and brains to get what he wants

THE ARIES FEMALE

If a woman behaves in a way that is distinctive of the personality associated with the zodiac sign of Aries, she will have a tendency toward the characteristics listed below, providing there are no influences in her personal birthchart that are stronger than that of her Aries sun sign.

Appearance

The typical Aries woman

- is slim and strong
- is very active and glows with energy
- has strong, luxurious hair
- wears sophisticated colors and perfume
- dresses in clothes appropriate to the occasion

Behavior and personality traits

The typical Aries woman
- looks you in the eye and gives a firm handshake
- is enthusiastic and optimistic
- talks back and often gets hurt because of it
- expects loyalty
- is fearless
- has interests outside the home or has a career
- expects to win in any situation
- is direct, open, and honest
- can make miracles happen

YOUNG ARIES

If a child behaves in a way that is distinctive of the personality associated with the zodiac sign of Aries, he or she will have a tendency toward the characteristics listed below.

Behavior and personality traits

The typical Aries child
- has a strong, active body and mind
- has a temper when thwarted
- usually walks and talks early
- wants attention and to be in charge
- can be lazy until someone claims to be better
- is generous with toys
- has a vivid, practical imagination
- can achieve much in a short time
- is normally very affectionate
- has an inexhaustible curiosity
- gets over childhood fevers very quickly

Bringing up young Aries

Most Aries children are very direct about their likes and dislikes. They are also very determined to do things their way. Saying "No" doesn't work, nor does persuasion, coaxing, or using other obedient children as examples.

Young Aries children of any age respond best to a challenge. Tell him he's probably just slow at organizing his toys or tell her that it isn't her fault that she can't do something very well and young Aries goes into action, to prove he or she is better than anyone else at anything – including doing the things they don't like.

Young Aries needs Adventure, opportunities to find out, to try things, take charge, solve problems, and be a winner. Above all, Aries needs to know that he or she is loved and valued. Big hugs and reassurance, especially after emotional bumps, are essential, despite the brave face they put on.

What to teach young Aries At school, Aries children take the lead in every way and will react against authority. So teach them when to obey by making it a challenge.

Because Aries youngsters are so adventurous, they ignore dangers, so parents need to be extra vigilant about hot pans and fires. As they become old enough, show them how to handle dangerous situations. Don't forbid them to do things, or they will take it as a challenge.

They need to be guided gently, with logic and praise, not ordered about. Ask them with a smile and they will respond with increasing confidence.

Teach Aries to handle their own money from a very early age. Explain the rights of others too, as young Aries dominates without knowing it.

They will have a few falls and show their fiery temper often, but they recover very quickly from both and come out smiling.

ARIES AT HOME

If a person has the personality that is typical of those born with an Aries sun sign, home is a place to come back to after many adventures, and she or he will have a tendency toward the characteristics listed below.

Typical behavior and abilities

When at home, an Aries man or woman

- wants to be the top dog
- makes a substantial and secure home
- doesn't like to feel tied down or restricted
- will generously give money, goods, and space to those who need it
- can turn a hand to anything but doesn't enjoy those little jobs needed to run and repair a home

Aries as parent

The typical Aries parent

- won't spoil the children
- will give plenty of hugs and praise
- can create a magical fantasy world for children
- usually insists on strict discipline
- will raise children to be successful
- may try to dictate the future careers of offspring
- will fight to the death if anyone hurts the kids
- will be a devoted dad and an affectionate mom

Two Aries in the same family

Aries can be comfortably married to each other
providing they each have separate challenging
situations in their lives to confront and win. Two
Aries need to converse regularly as neither likes
being left out.

A parent and child who are both Aries will clash
many times, so the parent must recognize that young
Aries also hates being told what to do. Families with
two or more Aries can be exciting with plenty of
affection and challenge to keep them all going.

ARIES AT WORK

At work, the person who has a typical
Aries personality will exhibit the
following characteristics.

Typical behavior and abilities

A typical Aries at work

- is loyal and enthusiastic about the company
- will work all hours and is not a clock-watcher
- will look elsewhere for an opening if bored
- is highly creative and can initiate
- has very strong willpower
- is not suited to political work

Aries as employer

A typical Aries boss (male or female)

- is idealistic and needs the faith of his or her
  employees and expects their loyalty
- believes he/she can make the future a success
- needs others but will go it alone when necessary
- wants to be recognized as the boss
- can pull a business up from near bankruptcy

- is generous with rewards for hard work
- expects everyone to drop everything to solve a crisis

Aries as employee

A typical Aries employee (male or female)
- works best when answerable only to the boss
- can promote anything
- tends to work late rather than early
- looks for opportunity to learn and progress
- intends to succeed but is careless with details
- knows he or she can do well
- will move to another job if he or she feels the challenges in the current job have run out; security is not a priority, although Aries workers usually make their way under the most difficult circumstances

Working environment

The workplace of a typical Aries man or woman
- will have people and machines to take care of the details
- may be almost anywhere that is exciting
- must be stimulating and allow freedom of movement
- will support an important-seeming image
- must be accessible at all times: day, night, and weekends

Typical occupations

Aries is associated with work which inspires activity in others – for example, leaders, directors, supervisors, or any job that has authority. Aries must be in command or they will lose interest. Aries works best at the initiation of a project, leaving the

consolidation to other people. Typical jobs are in
recruitment and training, work in the theater,
business enterprises, politics, sports, and the military
in any position that has power.

ARIES AND LOVE

To Aries, love is a conquest. Male Aries
love the chase and seem to have little
difficulty attracting women, while female
Aries also love the challenge of the hunt but go
about it a little more subtly. Aries of both sexes are
attractive because of their natural energy. Aries in
love will have many of the characteristics listed
below.

Behavior when in love

The typical Aries
- is very romantic and believes in courtly love
- will insist on doing the chasing and cannot bear to
  be chased by anyone
- can be extremely possessive of the lover but
  cannot understand if the lover is possessive
- places the loved one on a pedestal
- will be jealous of any attention the loved one gives
  to others
- will defend the loved one to the death

Expectations

The typical Aries expects
- total faithfulness from the partner
- the lover to respond as if he or she is the first and
  best lover ever known
- to be loved exclusively
- never to be criticized

The end of an affair

Boredom is the death of most Aries love affairs. Like the knight in a crusade, it is the winning that is the peak of excitement. Once the fair lady (or fair gentleman) is won, there may be nothing left to stimulate the affair further. At this point the Aries will get itchy feet and want to be off to find new conquests.

It isn't that love itself is merely a conquest, it is the joy of overcoming obstacles to reach love. The partner of an Aries must always keep a little mystery in reserve and must always believe in every new Aries dream. If all fails – and Aries will try and try before leaving a relationship – then the Aries passion cools and there remains only a lack of interest.

A lover who hurts Aries very deeply can expect to be totally frozen out and ignored.

ARIES AND SEX

In many ways the excitement is in the chase not the conquest. It isn't that Aries lovers aren't faithful – they are, as long as the excitement of new challenges in love are always there to stimulate them. Aries may appear to want to dominate, but does not want a submissive partner in sex. Routine is what brings boredom to lovemaking for Aries. Aries woman may have difficulties in love because she may see her partner as a fellow contestant in the world.

ARIES AND PARTNER

The person who contemplates becoming the marriage or business partner of a typical Aries must realize that Aries will want to be in control of all the major decisions. He or she will be happy to leave the day-to-day details to a partner, but will always expect to be in overall control. Given this, the person who partners Aries can expect an exciting, creative relationship with unexpected surprises and plenty of affection.

Aries man as partner

He will want a partner of whom he can be proud, yet who will never do anything better than he can. A clever partner would be wise to be modest about personal abilities and to put effort into supporting and encouraging the sensitive Aries partner in his own dreams.

In marriage, the Aries husband will regard his wife as the queen of his domain and she must behave accordingly, never failing in her loyalty to him and keeping surprises up her sleeve to stimulate his interest.

Aries woman as partner

Like her male counterpart, the Aries partner must always come first. This makes life difficult for the typical Aries wife in a male-dominant situation. She needs a husband who will recognize and accept her powers. A man must have self-respect and tact to partner an Aries woman.

In return, both male and female Aries will bring bountiful energy, enthusiasm, and loyalty to any partnership.

Opposite sign

Libra, the scales, is the complementary opposite sign to Aries. Although relationships between Aries and Libra can be difficult, Libra can show Aries how to cooperate, share, and bring people together in harmony. Libra can intervene diplomatically where Aries will bound in and make demands forcibly.

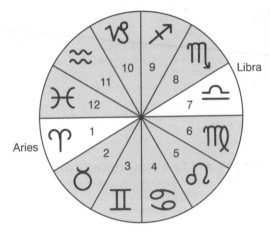

ARIES AND FRIENDS

In general Aries likes a friend who is special in some particular way and who will regard Aries as his or her best friend (never the second best!).

Positive factors

Aries friends are warm and hospitable but they are not usually interested in entertaining for its own sake; they usually have a reason for inviting friends around. Many Aries prefer to go out to dinner, to find an unusual eating place. Both male and female Aries usually get along better with male friends.

Negative factors

Because Aries are very jealous of other people's abilities and achievements, Aries friendships often don't last very long.

However, a person who will admire his or her Aries friend and remain interesting, though not ambitious, can enjoy an enduring friendship with Aries. Aries can become harsh and nasty if his or her fragile ego is under threat.

A compatibility chart, opposite, lists those with whom Aries is likely to have the most satisfactory relationships.

 ARIES LEISURE INTERESTS

Most typical Aries enjoy some physical activity that allows them to display their prowess. Aries may also enjoy board games that give them the opportunity to demonstrate their superior mental and tactical power.

On the whole, typical Aries pursue the following leisure interests (continued on p. 32):

● competitive sports, e.g. football, tennis
● driving a car which has a great image
● racing by car, bicycle, or on foot

Compatibility chart

In general, if people are typical of their zodiac sign, relationships between Aries and other signs (including the complementary opposite sign, Libra) are as shown below

	Harmonious	Difficult	Turbulent
Aries	●		
Taurus	●		
Gemini	●		
Cancer		●	
Leo	●		
Virgo			●
Libra		●	
Scorpio			●
Sagittarius	●		
Capricorn		●	
Aquarius	●		
Pisces	●		

- risky physical activities, such as sailing around the world alone or climbing a new peak
- military pastimes
- theatrical activities

Aries likes and dislikes
Likes

- being liked
- the best wines
- a unique license plate on the car
- money to burn
- new clothes
- red roses
- food in bright colors
- personalized gifts
- presents wrapped in intriguing paper
- books
- sparkling gems

Dislikes

- being ignored
- physical restriction
- being placed less than first
- feeling hungry
- anyone who performs better than they
- old things, second-hand stuff
- having to wait for anything
- lingering after food
- bland food

ARIES HEALTH
Typical Aries are healthy and fight every illness that comes their way, staving off attacks of flu with sheer willpower. When Aries pride is hurt or life teaches a hard lesson, Aries may suffer emotionally and need great

comfort. For all their apparent superiority, Aries are
extremely softhearted and vulnerable to emotional
hurts.

Types of sickness

Fevers and accidents are typical of all fire signs, and
especially so with the highly strung Aries character.
If ill, Aries will expect constant attention to his or
her needs, but recovery is usually very quick.
Typical Aries may suffer from acne, epilepsy,
neuralgia, headaches, migraines, and baldness.
Accidents due to physical activities are common,
accompanied by bangs on the tough Aries head.
Sinuses, eyes, and ears are also vulnerable.

Aries at rest

Rarely is a typical Aries seen to rest during the day.
They seem to have an inexhaustible supply of
energy and a considerable willpower. However,
when eventually tired, at perhaps three in the
morning, the typical Aries will usually sleep well
and may either sleep late or take a long time to get
started again in the morning.

The typical Aries doesn't rest like most other
people; both male and female Aries are too busy
with some project or other to stop for long. The
enthusiasm with which they do things is as good as a
rest to them. When enthusiasm wanes, they still
don't want to rest but are impatient to be off on a
new venture.

Parts of the body linked to Aries
Traditionally, the parts of the body linked with a
strong Aries influence are as shown in the
diagram below. Only the individual birth chart will
show if one or more of these parts of the body
have inherited a strength or a vulnerability. Any
generalization would be misleading.

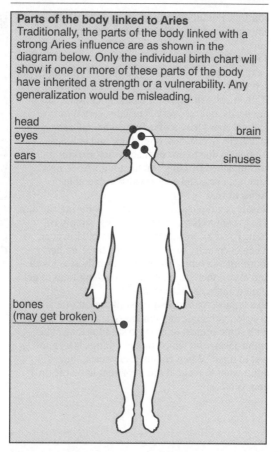

head
eyes
ears

brain

sinuses

bones
(may get broken)

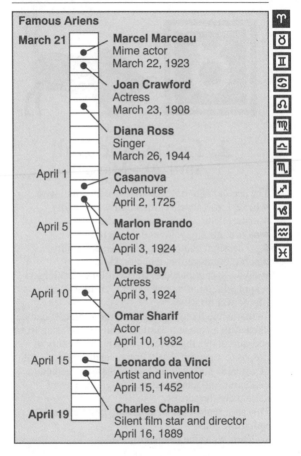

Famous Ariens

March 21

Marcel Marceau
Mime actor
March 22, 1923

Joan Crawford
Actress
March 23, 1908

Diana Ross
Singer
March 26, 1944

April 1

Casanova
Adventurer
April 2, 1725

April 5

Marlon Brando
Actor
April 3, 1924

Doris Day
Actress
April 3, 1924

April 10

Omar Sharif
Actor
April 10, 1932

April 15

Leonardo da Vinci
Artist and inventor
April 15, 1452

April 19

Charles Chaplin
Silent film star and director
April 16, 1889

2. Taurus: the Bull
April 20 – May 20

The second sign of the zodiac is concerned with
- beauty, romance, sentimentality, sensuality
- materialistic values, wealth, prosperity
- nature, harmony, love of living things
- possession, control, security, dependability
- habit, organization, tenacity, kindness
- shyness, cautiousness, trustworthiness, calmness
- appreciation of values, talents, abilities

Elemental quality

Taurus is the fixed earth sign of the zodiac. It can be likened to an ancient rainforest full of enduring trees and rare plants that is teeming with the beauty of life, or to a beautiful, old French château that is full of valuable antiques, and which has established vineyards and gardens that offer all manner of delights to the senses.

This sign represents an enduring, practical reality.

Spiritual goal

To learn the value of insight.

THE TAUREAN PERSONALITY

These are the general personality traits found in people who are typical of Taurus. An unhappy or frustrated Taurus may display some of the not-so-attractive traits.

Characteristics

Positive	Negative
• A careful and conservative outlook	• A tendency to be self-indulgent
• Dependable and offers enduring loyalty	• Can be stubborn, obstinate, and get stuck in a rut
• Calm and patient	• Materialistic
• Artistic	• Slow-moving
• Thorough	• Little to say
• Attentive	• Delays action by lengthy pondering
• Values the talents of others	• Easily embarrassed
• Very loving	• Boring
• Resourceful	• Insensitivity
• Gentle and placid	
• Excellent cook	
• Good sense of time and is orderly	

Secret Taurus

Inside anyone who has strong Taurus influences is a person who takes the long-term view and proceeds slowly but surely, because Taurus is only interested in the very best of everything. Taurus's view is that the best is worth waiting for.

Taurus loves to luxuriate in sensual delights and
desires secure material prosperity. The two secret
fears of Taurus are of being disturbed or of being left
wanting. Taurus will wait for anything, even to get
angry. When Taureans do eventually have to express
anger, it can be devastating and is so disturbing to
themselves that it takes a while for them to recover
both their composure and their self-esteem.

Ruling planet and its effect

Venus rules the zodiac sign of Taurus, so anyone
whose birth chart has a strong Taurus influence will
tend to have a strong set of personal values. In
astrology, Venus is the planet of love, affection,
values, and sensuality.

Like Venus, Taureans can be very affectionate and
fond of the good life, as long as it is a peaceful,
secure life. Taureans rarely detract from their
personal code of what is right.

Taurus, like the mythical Venus, has an idealized
concept of beauty, and may, especially in early life,
be very self-conscious about his or her body.

Taurean lucky connections	
Colors	pastel shades and blues
Plant	mallow
Perfume	storax
Gemstone	topaz
Metal	copper
Tarot card	hierophant (High Priest)
Animal	bull

THE TAUREAN LOOK

People who exhibit the physical characteristics distinctive of the sign of Taurus look as if they are well rooted and in touch with the Earth. They may be plump or slim, but either way they will walk with a slightly ponderous gait, as if each step has been carefully considered. All typical Taureans have a presence which emanates solid reliability.

Physical appearance

- Body compact and sturdy, often with thick, muscular legs and thighs
- Face rounded with a clear, often beautiful complexion
- Neck short and may appear rather thick if the shoulders are high and square, which is typical of those with a very strong Taurean influence
- Typical Taurean feet are large or broad
- Eyes are usually large and offer a steady gaze

THE TAURUS MALE

If a man behaves in a way typical of the personality associated with the zodiac sign of Taurus, he will have a tendency toward the characteristics listed below, unless there are influences in his personal birth chart that are stronger than that of his Taurus sun sign.

Appearance

The typical Taurus man

- has a stocky body, which is muscular if he does a lot of physical activity
- may be plump

- will bear the discomfort of an injury or disability with extreme stoicism
- has very clear skin
- is likely to have plenty of hair and can grow a substantial beard
- walks with determination

Behavior and personality traits

The typical Taurus man

- rarely changes his point of view
- works hard to build security
- is astute and can evaluate a situation very quickly in financial terms
- is quiet and has a low-key charm
- is unpretentious
- enjoys comfort
- can be defensive and suspicious in a new or unexpected situation
- is wary of others taking advantage of him
- dresses to create an image of respectability
- uses influential connections to get what he wants

 THE TAURUS FEMALE

If a woman behaves in a way that is distinctive of the personality associated with the zodiac sign of Taurus, she will have a tendency toward the characteristics listed below, providing there are no influences in her personal birth chart that are stronger than that of her Taurus sun sign.

Appearance

The typical Taurus woman

- tends to have a rounded body

- has a beautiful complexion and hair which always looks in excellent condition
- may live by a very strict diet to attain slimness
- has an air of mystery about her because she does not flaunt her sexuality
- wears clothes which give her sensual pleasure
- has a strong body capable of hard work

Behavior and personality traits

The typical Taurus woman

- is an introvert
- has considerable moral and emotional courage
- takes people as they come
- is very loyal to her friends and sticks by them if they are in trouble
- has practical common sense
- is deeply sensual
- prefers the real to the artificial, e.g., real flowers, real silk, and genuine, high-quality antiques

YOUNG TAURUS

If a child behaves in a way that is distinctive of the personality associated with the zodiac sign of Taurus, he or she will have a tendency toward the characteristics listed below.

Behavior and personality traits

The typical Taurus child

- is usually a quiet baby with rare outbursts
- is stubborn and wants his or her own way
- has a strong little body and can often be found clenching his or her fists when opposed
- is usually calm, pleasant, and a little shy

- is cuddly and affectionate
- dislikes being the center of attention
- responds to common sense and affection
- usually works slowly but steadily at school

Bringing up young Taurus
Never try to force a young Taurus to do something
because the Taurean child will turn stubborn and
will always hold his or her ground longer than
anyone else, except perhaps a Taurean parent. Harsh
commands will never discipline the young Taurus,
but a loving hug will melt all the resistance out of
that obstinate little bull.

Both girls and boys are usually competent little
people and open to practical, common-sense
explanations. Both can charm adults, especially of
the opposite sex.

Young Taurus's needs   Physical affection given
freely and without smothering is essential to the
healthy growth of any Taurean child. Young Taurus
also needs harmonious surroundings. Colors and
sound will affect these children quite deeply.
Harmonious blues, shades of pink and rose, and soft
sounds will be calming and reassuring.

What to teach young Taurus   Most children who
are typically Taurean will have soft, melodious
voices so they should be introduced to singing or
other forms of music from an early age. Usually
these children will prefer melodious music to noisy
modern pop; and nursery rhymes won't satisfy them
for long. Let them hear a wide selection of classical
music which they can absorb into their souls.
Drawing, coloring, and other artistic activities –

such as collage with materials lovely to the touch –
will please and stimulate young Taurus.

In general, Taurean children will take a clear,
practical, and orderly approach to school and
homework. They need to be given time to learn, but
things once learned are not forgotten. Taureans
should be encouraged to communicate through
words, pictures, and music as they tend to hide their
true feelings behind silent obstinacy.

TAURUS AT HOME

If a person has the personality that is
typical of those born with a Taurus sun
sign, home is a place to feel absolutely
secure and comfortable. The person who has strong
Taurean influences will have a tendency toward the
characteristics listed below.

Typical behavior and abilities

When at home, a Taurus man or woman

- hates anything to be moved around
- enjoys comfort and luxury
- has well-tried habits and likes a well-ordered
  household
- prefers to own his or her home
- makes his or her home a castle and usually fills it
  with furniture that will increase in value

Taurus as parent

The typical Taurus parent

- is affectionate
- has seemingly endless patience
- can be dominant and possessive
- may find it hard to relax and play with the children

- will support, encourage, nurture, and protect the children with unswerving faith in their own abilities as a parent
- will teach self-respect
- will save for the future
- expects high standards

Two Taureans in the same family

Taureans can get along well together providing they have similar personal values. If they disagree about fundamental issues, their obstinacy could lead to a permanent impasse as neither will give an inch. On the other hand, their mutual serenity and response to physical affection should overcome any serious disagreements.

TAURUS AT WORK

At work, the person who has a typical Taurean personality will exhibit the following characteristics.

Typical behavior and abilities

A typical Taurus at work

- will work steadily toward achieving what he/she values
- cannot bear interference
- has great respect for institutions
- requires work that gives respectability

Taurus as employer

A typical Taurus boss (male or female)

- patiently tests out the employees
- doggedly sticks to stated principles
- will give everyone more than a fair chance but fire anyone who breaks his or her trust

- is often a self-made person and will make money
- does not make hasty judgments
- wants things done his or her way
- is kind and patient but expects total loyalty
- likes plain facts and hates flattery

Taurus as employee

A typical Taurus employee (male or female)

- needs a regular salary
- is an excellent person to handle money
- is honest and dependable
- is practical, sensible, and down-to-earth
- enjoys sensible routines
- displays foresight
- is rarely thrown off balance
- can handle emergencies

Working environment

The workplace of a typical Taurus man or woman

- must be calm and well-ordered
- any noise or color scheme must be low key, if it is an office
- should be at a fixed location – rural or park settings suit Taurus well

Typical occupations

Taurus is associated with banking, farming, floristry, interior design, architecture, food, engineering, construction, general medical practice, executive secretarial positions, stable occupations in established institutions, and any occupation that involves the shrewd acquisition of land, investments, or goods.

TAURUS AND LOVE

To Taurus, love is a physical, sensual romance which can be expected to last forever. Taureans are attracted by physical beauty and are very sensitive to perfume, color, light, and sound. Taurus in love will have many of the characteristics listed below.

Behavior when in love

The typical Taurus

- is devoted and steadfast
- settles quickly into a stable affair
- loves glamour
- is extremely vulnerable to people who accept his or her affection but only want a flirtation
- will never forgive a betrayal
- the male is generally the strong silent type
- the female is usually an earth mother/Venus

Expectations

The typical Taurus expects

- his woman to be very feminine
- her man to be all male
- a promise to be kept and never broken
- a wholesome, natural approach to physical love
- to be pampered
- to wait for a commitment to be made

The end of an affair

It takes a long time for a Taurean to decide to leave a relationship. Taurus finds it extremely difficult to be convinced he or she was wrong about a person. However, once the Taurean mind is made up, there is never any turning back. He or she will walk away forever.

Being a good judge of character is not one of Taurus's strengths, so some will assume all is well, even when a lover is being deceitful. When a deceit is revealed, Taurus will be very hurt but will still hang on to hope.

Some Taurus men can be macho, so when a relationship is ending, the macho Taurus can lose his normally gentle approach, becoming harsh and domineering. This usually indicates the hurt to his ego, which at heart is very trusting and naive.

The lover who walks out on a Taurean will leave behind a bewildered, disbelieving person, who may suffer one vague illness after another as the hurt and rage slowly come to the surface.

TAURUS AND SEX

When a typical Taurus makes love it is the most physical and natural pleasure in the whole world. Sex is never a power game for a Taurean; it is something very natural to be enjoyed. Taureans, especially females, are sometimes embarrassed about their bodies if they feel they are being criticized. On the whole, Taurus regards nudity as natural and wholesome.

TAURUS AND PARTNER

The person who contemplates becoming the marriage or business partner of a typical Taurus must realize that Taurus will expect absolute loyalty through thick and thin and will probably want to establish a routine way of doing things his or her way.

Given this, the person who partners Taurus can expect honest devotion, a long-term relationship, and a partner who can keep his or her head in any emergency.

Taurus man as partner

He will want a partner who enjoys his way of doing things. The partner should be prepared to take the responsibility for good public relations while Taurus works quietly away ensuring that money and power come their way.

The Taurean husband wants a marriage partner whom he can possess, body, soul and dowry. He needs a woman who enjoys physical love, since to Taureans there is no division between love, sex, and marriage.

Taurus woman as partner

She will want a partner who is attentive and appreciative. Common sense is essential in any partner of a Taurean. She, like her male counterpart, will look for a business partner who will bring prestige to the business.

The Taurean wife wants to be given gifts and treated with gentleness. She does not want to be patronized, but she does want her man to remember her birthday and other anniversaries.

She needs a husband who will let her organize at least a part of his life and who will never give her cause for jealousy.

Opposite sign

Scorpio is the complementary opposite sign to Taurus. Although relations between Taurus and Scorpio can be difficult because they are both stubborn signs, Scorpio can show Taurus how to gain insight into the needs and motives of other people, and thus also into his or her own life. In this way, Taurus can use his or her natural sensitivity to help in the service of others.

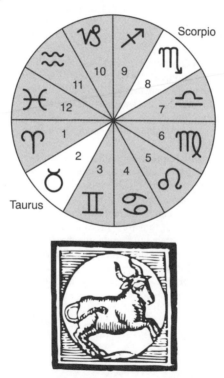

TAURUS AND FRIENDS

In general Taurus likes a friend who is reliable, unchanging, and not given to sudden excitement or changes of plans.

Positive factors

Taureans are very warm and affectionate toward their friends. They enjoy friendship with people who have good taste and with whom they can enjoy a quiet conversation or a concert or a football game. They will enjoy people who have strength of character and qualities of endurance like their own. Toward such friends, Taurus will always be gentle, kind, loving, and totally trustworthy.

Negative factors

Taurus can be jealous of any attention a friend gives to someone else.

Taurus does not like signs of weakness, physical or emotional, and can be quite direct about them.

Taurus prizes friends who have some power which they can share and enjoy.

People who wear cheap perfume, artificial fabrics, and have houses that are built to deceive the eye, e.g., not real stone but faced with stone, are unlikely to attract the friendship of a typical Taurean.

A compatibility chart, opposite, lists those with whom Taurus is likely to have the most satisfactory relationships.

Compatibility chart
In general, if people are typical of their zodiac sign, relationships between Taurus and other signs (including the complementary opposite sign, Scorpio) are as shown below

	Harmonious	Difficult	Turbulent
Taurus	●		
Gemini	●		
Cancer	●		
Leo		●	
Virgo	●		
Libra			●
Scorpio		●	
Sagittarius			●
Capricorn	●		
Aquarius		●	
Pisces	●		
Aries	●		

♈ ♉ ♊ ♋ ♌ ♍ ♎ ♏ ♐ ♑ ♒ ♓

TAUREAN LEISURE INTERESTS

On the whole, typical Taureans pursue the following leisure interests:

- collecting things of value
- singing or listening to music
- gardening
- painting
- the quieter sports
- activities that give Taurus a chance to enjoy physical pleasure, such as horseback riding

Taurean likes and dislikes

Likes

- soft, sensual textures
- sensual pleasures
- a good bank balance
- certainty and well-tried routines
- gifts of value, attractively wrapped
- savoring the moments of pleasure at the table
- doing the same thing over and over

Dislikes

- being disturbed
- change
- lending things
- being told to hurry up
- sleeping in strange beds

TAUREAN HEALTH

Typical Taureans are robust people. They may suffer from being a little overweight, but on the whole Taurus is healthy, provided nothing comes along to disturb the status quo. A Taurus who has an unsatisfactory sex life will be rather like a bull with a sore head . . . irritable and prone to grunting and grumbling.

The greatest danger for Taurus comes from the ability to hold back anger and to stubbornly hold on to a redundant point of view. That can lead to melancholy and medical depression.

Types of sickness

Infections of the throat are said to be linked with Taurus, including laryngitis, swollen glands, and croup. Constipation may also bother a Taurean. When sick or if involved (untypically) in a serious accident, Taurus can withstand any amount of discomfort and pain. The Taurean ability to stubbornly refuse to allow anything to get the better of him or her is a great advantage during times of sickness. Similarly, a Taurean will stand by family and any friend who has a misfortune.

Taurus at rest

Extending the metaphor of the fixed earth sign, Taurus at rest is totally relaxed and lazy. In fact, Taurus can rest with feet up in front of the television or listening to music for days and days.

Taureans usually sleep well and wake up slowly. Once they are on the go again, they can keep going for long periods without feeling tired.

Parts of the body linked to Taurus
Traditionally, the parts of the body linked with a
strong Taurus influence are as shown in the
diagram below. Only the individual birth chart will
show if one or more of these parts of the body
have inherited a strength or a vulnerability. Any
generalization would be misleading.

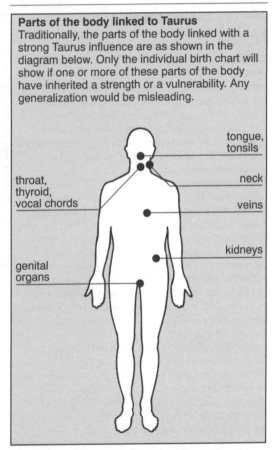

tongue,
tonsils

neck

throat,
thyroid,
vocal chords

veins

kidneys

genital
organs

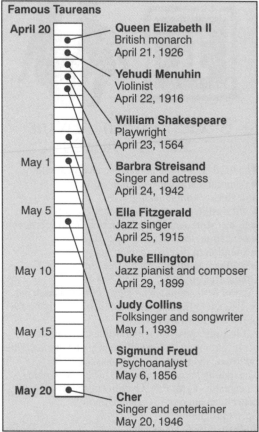

Famous Taureans

April 20

♈ ♉ ♊ ♋ ♌ ♍ ♎ ♏ ♐ ♑ ♒ ♓

Queen Elizabeth II
British monarch
April 21, 1926

Yehudi Menuhin
Violinist
April 22, 1916

William Shakespeare
Playwright
April 23, 1564

Barbra Streisand
Singer and actress
April 24, 1942

May 1

Ella Fitzgerald
Jazz singer
April 25, 1915

May 5

Duke Ellington
Jazz pianist and composer
April 29, 1899

May 10

Judy Collins
Folksinger and songwriter
May 1, 1939

Sigmund Freud
Psychoanalyst
May 6, 1856

May 15

May 20

Cher
Singer and entertainer
May 20, 1946

3. Gemini: the Twins
May 21 – June 20

The third sign of the zodiac is concerned with
- communication, articulation, speech
- dexterity, nimbleness, grace
- wit, instinct, persuasion, change, variety
- movement, curiosity, exploration, short journeys
- education, learning, collecting facts
- attention to details, adaptability
- intellect, intuition, youth, freedom

Elemental quality

Gemini is the mutable air sign of the zodiac. It can
be likened to the wind in that it is constantly on the
move in all its variety.

Air is a metaphor for the invisible thoughts and
ideas that motivate Gemini, such as the intellect, the
intuition, and the natural instincts.

The quality known as mutable means adaptable,
changeable, agreeable. Gemini constantly adjusts
ideas in an attempt to create harmony.

Spiritual goal

To learn how to cooperate.

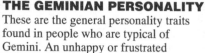

THE GEMINIAN PERSONALITY

These are the general personality traits found in people who are typical of Gemini. An unhappy or frustrated Gemini may display some of the not-so-attractive traits.

Characteristics

Positive	Negative
• Inquisitive	• Restless
• Entertaining and charming	• Quickly bored
• Versatile	• Impractical
• Liberal, broad minded	• Impatient and irritable
• Youthful	• Capricious and fickle
• Quick	• Gossipy
• Stimulating	• Nervous
• Inventive	• Manipulative
• Never prejudiced	• Noncommittal
	• Dual personality

Secret Gemini

Inside anyone who has strong Gemini influences is a person who secretly longs to find his or her true soul mate, the mysterious twin who will make the Gemini feel complete. The more self-aware Geminis will realize in maturity that the wholeness they seek is to be found within, by gathering together their many parts, especially the earthly twin with the spiritual twin.

Few people listening to a confident Gemini talk with that quicksilver, pucklike charm would ever imagine

that the inner Gemini is often feeling desperately
alone and lost.

Communication is a lifeline to Gemini. Contact
through words, ideas, gossip, or philosophy makes
Gemini a happy, inspiring, and devoted person.

Ruling planet and its effect

Mercury rules the zodiac sign of Gemini, so anyone
whose birth chart has a strong Gemini influence will
tend to be on the go, moving to and fro with many
messages like the fleet-footed Mercury of
mythology, who was the eloquent messenger of the
gods.

Mercury wore a winged helmet and carried the
caduceus, a stick around which were entwined twin
snakes. The snakes represent the libido and the
healing powers of the instinctual mind.

In astrology, Mercury is the planet of thought and
communication, and governs all mental and nervous
processes. Mercury is the hermaphrodite of the
zodiac, taking the neutral position of mediator
between the masculine and feminine viewpoints.
Mercury is the planet of duality, the translator, who
speaks in two languages that link body and soul.

Geminian lucky connections	
Color	orange
Plants	orchid and hybrids
Perfume	lavender
Gemstone	tourmaline
Metal	quicksilver
Tarot card	the lovers
Animal	magpie

THE GEMINIAN LOOK

People who exhibit the physical characteristics distinctive of the sign of Gemini are tall and upright.

The youthful look is typical of Gemini. People who always look younger than their actual age, at any stage of life, will have a strong Gemini influence somewhere in their birth chart.

Most typical Geminians are light on their feet, regardless of their body size.

Physical appearance

- Usually slim body (However, if the zodiac neighbors of Gemini, Taurus and Cancer, are present in the birth chart they may affect the body build, because the signs of both Taurus and Cancer can lead to plumpness. A strong Taurus influence, particularly, can lead to a weight problem.)
- Generally tall
- Strong and active
- Long arms and legs
- Fleshy hands

THE GEMINI MALE

If a man behaves in a way typical of the personality associated with the zodiac sign of Gemini, he will have a tendency toward the characteristics listed below, unless there are influences in his personal birth chart that are stronger than that of his Gemini sun sign.

Appearance

The typical Gemini man

- is taller than average

- has a pale, rough complexion that will become
  weather-beaten easily
- is very agile
- has a high forehead and receding hairline
- has quick, darting eyes

Behavior and personality traits

The typical Gemini man

- is eager and always on the move
- is friendly and persuasive
- can sell almost anything to almost anyone
- has a great deal of nervous energy
- can talk himself out of difficulties
- can do two things at once
- likes people
- is adroit, diplomatic, and socially able
- may change his occupation frequently
- is intelligent and witty

THE GEMINI FEMALE

If a woman behaves in a way that is
distinctive of the personality associated
with the zodiac sign of Gemini, she will
have a tendency toward the characteristics listed
below, providing there are no influences in her
personal birth chart that are stronger than that of her
Gemini sun sign.

Appearance

The typical Gemini woman

- is tall and slender, unless there is a strong Taurus
  influence causing plumpness
- has very beautiful eyes
- has long arms and legs

- has exquisitely expressive hands
- moves quickly

Behavior and personality traits

The typical Gemini woman

- is a lively conversationalist
- has many interests
- is a composite of many personalities
- is a great friend, taking an interest in any new subject
- will want to have a career
- seeks true romance but finds it hard to settle down
- is a deep thinker and often very intuitive
- will never turn down a cry for help
- is optimistic
- notices every detail
- can be charming and very persuasive

YOUNG GEMINI

If a child behaves in a way that is distinctive of the personality associated with the zodiac sign of Gemini, he or she will have a tendency toward the characteristics listed below.

Behavior and personality traits

The typical Gemini child

- can seem to be in two places at once
- loves chattering
- will become irritable if cooped up
- needs lots of space to explore
- is friendly
- is bright and alert

- can be quite precocious
- usually learns to read very quickly
- likes to use his or her hands and fingers
- may be ambidextrous
- can often mimic others

Bringing up young Gemini

Most Geminis have an insatiable inquisitiveness
about everything. They like to explore, follow
whatever catches their interest, and literally get their
fingers into everything.

Gemini children tend to live in a world where
imagination and reality are so mixed together that it
is hard for them to learn where one begins and the
other ends.

These children will want to be friends with both
sexes. As they grow up, they will have a variety of
boyfriends or girlfriends. When they actually
become emotionally involved with someone they
will often pretend they are not interested, because
emotional involvement leaves them totally confused.
Children of both sexes will be keenly interested in a
wide variety of sports.

Young Gemini's needs The Gemini child needs the
freedom to explore, investigate, and learn. Frequent
opportunities to change direction, and follow several
lines of interest at once, are essential.

They need to be understood more than anything. The
love that Gemini children need is the attention of
those who accept them for what they are and go
along with them in their dreams.

Confinement and boredom are the worst horrors to a little Gemini.

What to teach young Gemini Young Gemini should be taught how to distinguish between illusion and reality. Encouraging him or her to always tell the truth will help this to happen. Gemini children are naturally honest and will only avoid telling the truth as a defense against feeling misunderstood. These children will enjoy learning to communicate, to read, and to speak several languages. They can easily become bilingual if spoken to in different languages from an early age.

Teaching a Gemini to slow down a little can be difficult but will help the young Gemini to be more selective in later years, as Geminis tend to throw out old ideas and pursuits indiscriminately.

GEMINI AT HOME

If a person has the personality that is typical of those born with a Gemini sun sign, home is a place to return to after yet another period of travel.

The Gemini at home will have a tendency toward the characteristics listed below.

Typical behavior and abilities

When at home, a Gemini man or woman

- likes space to move around in
- will enjoy using gadgets and all the latest technology, especially information technology
- considers a telephone absolutely essential
- will have some form of transport standing by so he or she can take off on the spur of the moment

- will have a bright, cheerful home, surrounded by the evidence of many interests
- enjoys company
- has a deep need for tenderness and emotional warmth for which he or she finds it very hard to ask

Gemini as parent

The typical Gemini parent

- can get on a child's wavelength very easily
- will enjoy playing with and teaching his or her children
- may find it hard to show his or her real emotions
- uses rational arguments to explain things

Two Geminis in the same family

Unless one or both have planets in the earthy or fixed signs, two Geminis in one family means there will be at least four personalities flitting around. Geminis can get along well, provided both have enough space. They will happily talk with each other, absorbing and discussing all the new facts they can find. However, if two Geminis get into an emotional argument, sparks fly because Geminis can be very confused by and feel threatened by strong emotions, especially their own.

GEMINI AT WORK

At work, the person who has a typical Gemini personality will exhibit the following characteristics.

Typical behavior and abilities

A typical Gemini at work

- gets things done

- works better with people around
- can deal with emergencies quickly
- will try anything once
- needs variety

Gemini as employer

A typical Gemini boss (male or female)

- is not dogmatic
- delegates astutely and concentrates on schemes to increase profits and cut costs
- makes changes to improve communication and productivity
- is impatient with mundane administration
- will inspect, notice, and question every aspect of every department
- will classify his or her workers' talents
- enjoys building goodwill and increasing client orders by meeting clients in restaurants, on the golf course, or anywhere out on the road in places near or far

Gemini as employee

A typical Gemini employee (male or female)

- can charm his or her way through an interview
- is good at thinking, new ideas, and details
- makes jokes and small talk, and gets things done
- will get bored and fail to carry through an idea if too much red tape holds up a project
- enjoys fast action and quick returns

Working environment

The workplace of a typical Gemini man or woman

- (if it has to be in a fixed place) must be spacious and stimulating

Typical occupations

Geminis are good in any kind of work that involves
public relations, selling, or getting information and
ideas across to others such as teaching, writing and
work in any of the media. Their quick minds,
combined with dexterous abilities, lead some to
become surgeons, scientific researchers, artists, or
musicians. Because they love words and ideas, they
may become politicians or actors.

GEMINI AND LOVE

To Gemini, love is a romantic ideal
which can only be achieved with the soul
mate. Consequently, many Geminis
may flirt and have frequent affairs, looking for that
perfect romantic love. The characteristics of Gemini
in love are listed below.

Behavior when in love

The typical Gemini
- is overwhelmed by confusing emotions
- may appear cool and distant
- will think things through rather than act
  spontaneously
- needs a rational understanding of love
- tends to repress very strong emotions
- is acutely sensitive and open to hurt
- can become emotionally dependent
- feels very deeply but finds it very hard to express
  love

Expectations

The typical Gemini expects
- to be understood

- the partner to be emotionally telepathic
- sympathy and tenderness
- personal freedom for self and partner
- to enjoy flirting
- faithfulness of partner

The end of an affair

An affair will end when a Gemini gets bored or
when a partner begins to make too many emotional
demands or restrict the Gemini's personal freedom.
The end may seem like a sudden decision, but it
never is; the decision to leave a lover will have been
made only after much mental unhappiness.

Once the decision has been made, Geminis have no
difficulty in communicating that an affair is at an
end; they just cool off, freeze the partner out, or
vanish.

If the partner ends the relationship, Gemini will be
deeply hurt and feel insecure and at a loss. The more
outward Geminis may hide these feelings behind a
sudden outburst of scathing anger, while the quieter
ones will probably try to look cool. Either way,
Gemini will put on a show of confidence and
continue searching for perfect love.

GEMINI AND SEX

When a typical Gemini makes love it is
often a drive to express all their pent-up
emotions at once. Geminis seek variety
in love and enjoy surprises and plenty of light-
hearted romance. Geminis are often not interested in
sex for its own sake; they want more from a partner,
even in a short relationship, such as companionship

and warmth. Love and sex belong together in the
eyes of a Gemini.

The most erogenous zone of a typical Gemini is the
mind. Talk excites, while silence turns off the
Gemini.

GEMINI AND PARTNER

The person who contemplates becoming
the marriage or business partner of a
typical Gemini must realize that Gemini
has probably already had more than one partner and
will not stay long with a person who either clings or
dominates.

Given this, the person who partners a Gemini can
expect the talents of at least six people wrapped up
in the one Gemini.

Gemini man as partner

He will want a partner who will never attempt to
dominate him, nor bore him with endless personal
problems.

He will be drawn either to someone who will help
him climb the professional or social ladder, or a
person who will stimulate him with bright ideas.
Because he loves to travel, he will be delighted by a
partner who will travel with him – or accept his
absences without question.

Gemini woman as partner

She will be attracted to a person who can give her
emotional security so that she can relax and enjoy
expressing her many talents and her
"multipersonality." Often the partnership will be
short-lived because the restless Gemini nature

always wants to be on the move. Many partners fail to understand the need of the mercurial butterfly to have a partner who will fly with her, helping her to find the peace she truly desires.

Opposite sign

Sagittarius is the complementary opposite sign to Gemini. From Sagittarius, Geminis can learn to take a broader view of things and to give some structure to the mass of information they collect – and so eventually find the truth.

Sagittarius

Gemini

GEMINI AND FRIENDS

In general, Gemini likes a friend who is curious about the world and enjoys lively, intelligent conversation.

Positive factors

Geminis generally enjoy people who respond to, or suggest, spontaneous activities.

They will run to help you when you are in need.

A Gemini friend is full of life, often a Peter Pan, and always eager to be off on a new adventure.

They will keep friends amused with endless stories, bits of information, or network gossip.

Negative factors

Gemini never wants to miss a thing, and so may be inclined to be early or late for meetings.

Stretching or elaborating the truth is not uncommon; Geminis can hardly resist adding extra spice to make it more interesting.

A compatibility chart, opposite, lists those with whom Gemini is likely to have the most satisfactory relationships.

GEMINIAN LEISURE INTERESTS

Most typical Geminis like communication, such as conversation, radio, television, the telephone, letter writing, sending postcards, and faxes.

On the whole, typical Geminis pursue the following leisure interests (continued on p. 72):

- "light" sports, e.g., table tennis, archery, darts, pool, bowling

Compatibility chart

In general, if people are typical of their zodiac sign, relationships between Gemini and other signs (including the complementary opposite sign, Sagittarius) are as shown below

	Harmonious	Difficult	Turbulent
Gemini	●		
Cancer	●		
Leo	●		
Virgo		●	
Libra	●		
Scorpio			●
Sagittarius		●	
Capricorn			●
Aquarius	●		
Pisces		●	
Aries	●		
Taurus	●		

- travel, short or long journeys
- newspapers, magazines, quizzes, crosswords
- public-speaking, variety shows, dancing
- discovering and exploring something new
- learning and using languages
- using hands and fingers for crafts, etc.

Geminian likes and dislikes

Likes

- being free to move around
- the excitement of travel
- talking
- telephones, gadgets, instant food
- acting as devil's advocate
- doing several things at once
- knowledge, information
- acting quickly on decisions
- variety, novelty, change
- company; being among people
- pseudonyms
- getting to the bottom of things

Dislikes

- listening to endless complaints
- regimentation
- not knowing what's going on
- wasting time
- being kept waiting
- making irrevocable commitments
- being defeated
- fixed ideas
- having to concentrate on only one thing for a long time

GEMINIAN HEALTH

Typical Geminis are healthy as long as they have plenty of room to breathe and space to explore. They are liable to collapse from nervous exhaustion if they don't find a personally satisfying way to relax. Geminis are not often heard to complain. On the rare times when sickness strikes them down, they may get irritated when well-intentioned people ask how they are. They much prefer to be amused by some interesting news than have to relate the details of their infirmity.

Types of sickness

Coughs, colds, bronchitis, speech problems, and other chest/lung complaints are most typical of Geminian ill health. Whenever physical misfortune strikes, the person who behaves in the way typical of Gemini is likely to hide the most serious side of things and make even less of the least serious aspect. Geminis usually hate being confined to bed and are restless until they finally exhaust themselves. At this point they become still, silent, and heavy, like the closeness that occurs before the thunderstorm breaks and all is well again.

Gemini at rest

There is no such animal as a Gemini at rest. Even when apparently relaxed by a winter's fire after playing in the snow with the children all afternoon, the Gemini mind will be at work, inventing a new gadget to make, thinking up a new idea, working over a problem, or rehearsing a conversation to be held with a colleague.

Parts of the body linked to Gemini
Traditionally, the parts of the body linked with a strong Gemini influence are as shown in the diagram below. Only the individual birth chart will show if one or more of these parts of the body have inherited a strength or a vulnerability. Any generalization would be misleading.

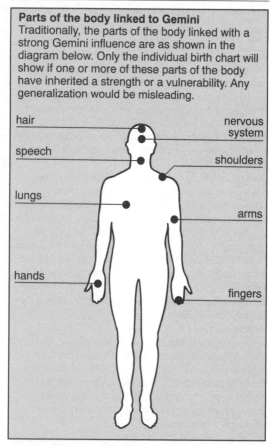

hair

nervous system

speech

shoulders

lungs

arms

hands

fingers

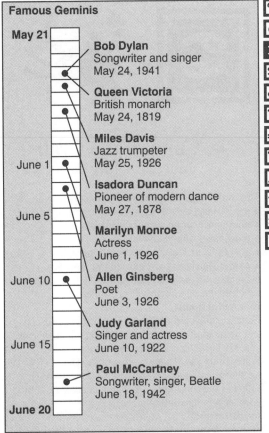

Famous Geminis

May 21

Bob Dylan
Songwriter and singer
May 24, 1941

Queen Victoria
British monarch
May 24, 1819

Miles Davis
Jazz trumpeter
May 25, 1926

June 1

Isadora Duncan
Pioneer of modern dance
May 27, 1878

June 5

Marilyn Monroe
Actress
June 1, 1926

June 10

Allen Ginsberg
Poet
June 3, 1926

Judy Garland
Singer and actress
June 10, 1922

June 15

Paul McCartney
Songwriter, singer, Beatle
June 18, 1942

June 20

4. Cancer: the Crab
June 21 – July 22

The fourth sign of the zodiac is concerned with
- receptivity, sensitivity, defense
- home, protection, comfort, domesticity
- food, nurturing instincts
- nostalgia, sentiment, roots, antiques
- money, business, response to public need
- dreams, the psychic, telepathy
- family, history, memory, patriotism

Elemental quality

Cancer is the cardinal water sign of the zodiac. It can be likened to a safe harbor in which boats can take shelter from the dangers on the sea of life. Water finds its own level – it settles. The metaphorical harbor is the way Cancer provides a safe and organized place for human activity, setting each ship in its allotted place.

Spiritual goal

To learn how to take a balanced view of things.

THE CANCERIAN PERSONALITY

These are the general personality traits found in people who are typical of this sign. An unhappy or frustrated Cancerian may display some of the not-so-attractive traits.

Characteristics	
Positive	Negative
• Tenacious	• Possessive
• Shrewd and intuitive	• Too easily hurt
• Kind	• Moody
• Compassionate	• Crabby
• Domesticated	• Matriarchal
• Good memory	• Holds on to insults
• Helpful	• Selfish
• Caring	• Manipulative
• Sensitive to need	• Introspective
• Protective	• Overpowering

Secret Cancer

Inside anyone who has strong Cancerian influences is a person who was very shy when young and who still tends to use a hard outer shell in defense against what are perceived as hurts from other people. The most vulnerable part of the Cancerian personality is an inner fear of nameless dangers that often reduce a wonderful dream to a pessimistic worry. The fear is of becoming lost in the dark of outer space. This indefinable fear of insecurity is often what drives the typical Cancerian personality to invest much time and effort in activities which will enhance a feeling of security and self-preservation.

Ruling planet and its effect

The Moon rules the zodiac sign of Cancer, so anyone
whose birth chart has a strong Cancerian influence
will absorb and accurately reflect every emotion that
is experienced.

In astrology, the Moon's cycle of waxing and waning
is a metaphor for the cycle of changing moods of the
Cancerian personality, who can experience periods
of wondrous elation and of crabby depression.

The Moon is also associated with oddities and, when
in the mood, Cancerian humor can be quite crazy –
almost lunatic. Cancerian humor provides some of
the best comedy in the world of entertainment,
because it is always based on an accurate
observation of human nature.

Cancerian lucky connections	
Colors	yellow, orange, and indigo
Plants	lotus, moonwort, and almond
Perfume	onycha
Gemstones	pearl, amber, and moonstone
Metal	silver
Tarot card	the chariot
Animals	crab, turtle, and sphinx

THE CANCERIAN LOOK

People who exhibit the physical characteristics distinctive of the sign of Cancer are of three facial types. Whichever type they are, they have very expressive faces. Every mood, emotion, and fleeting response shows in the changing features of the Cancerian face.

Physical appearance

- Body: usually top heavy; can be slim, but often on the plump side
- Face 1: crablike with a large head, high cheekbones and prominent brows; eyes small and far apart
- Face 2: moonlike and baby-faced, round with soft skin, a wide mouth, and a charming grin; eyes are usually round
- Face 3: a combination of the two above, but distinctive, with especially strong cheekbones

THE CANCER MALE

If a man behaves in a way typical of the personality associated with the zodiac sign of Cancer, he will have a tendency toward the characteristics listed below, unless there are influences in his personal birth chart that are stronger than that of his Cancer sun sign.

Appearance

The typical Cancer man

- has a fairly bony structure
- may have remarkable teeth, perhaps prominent, irregular, or in some way unusual

- if crab-faced, he will have a prominent lower jaw
- may have broad shoulders
- even if slim, may appear broad or plump
- may be plump or tend to put on weight very easily

Behavior and personality traits

The typical Cancerian man

- is extremely sensitive
- wears clothes with a conservative cut
- does not like to be conspicuous
- has some favorite old casual clothes which he always wears; he would be very cranky if anyone threw out his precious old sweater
- does not push himself into the limelight
- enjoys the limelight if it turns on him for a while
- dislikes discussing his personal life
- loves security, money, food, and children
- uses roundabout tactics to get what he wants
- has an uncanny business sense
- is usually very attached to his mother

THE CANCER FEMALE

If a woman behaves in a way that is distinctive of the personality associated with the zodiac sign of Cancer, she will have a tendency toward the characteristics listed below, providing there are no influences in her personal birth chart that are stronger than that of her Cancer sun sign.

Appearance

The typical Cancer woman

- has a face that is typically round and soft but may be a crab type as described above

- may be flat-chested or have a large bust
- has hips that are often slimmer than her bust
- puts on weight easily in middle age
- has a strong bone structure
- has very expressive eyes
- has long arms and legs compared with body
- has large and long or small and chubby hands and feet

Behavior and personality traits

The typical Cancer woman

- is introspective and emotional
- uses her intuition more often than logic
- will use all her nurturing instincts to care for and protect friends and family
- wants material security and comfort
- never does anything impulsively
- is shy but very sexual
- easily takes offense at minor insults
- is patient, subtle, and often unconsciously manipulative

YOUNG CANCER

If a child behaves in a way that is distinctive of the personality associated with the zodiac sign of Cancer, he or she will have a tendency toward the characteristics listed below.

Behavior and personality traits

The typical Cancer child

- changes mood frequently
- loves delicious food and drinks but almost always dribbles even when past babyhood

- is fascinated by colors and pictures
- will remember every experience right into adulthood
- longs to be hugged, loved, and encouraged
- withdraws inwardly from any kind of rejection
- can play alone for hours
- often invents invisible playmates
- may cry a lot and use tears to get what he or she wants
- when older, Cancerian children seek any kind of job to earn money and save it

Bringing up young Cancer
Most Cancerians are delightful, fascinating children whose faces show every changing mood. They love to use their imaginations and are easy to manage and discipline when young, providing they are given a lot of warmth, approval, and attention.

Parents should laugh and cry with a Cancerian infant and give constant reassurance when he or she is fearful, which is likely to be often.

Cancerian children are usually docile and well mannered, but prefer to be the leader rather than the follower.

Young Cancer's needs Cancerian children are very sensitive to emotional hurts and rejections and must have parental support at these times. If they feel rejected and unloved they will grow up to be reclusive, withdrawing permanently inside their shell in self-protection.

What to teach young Cancer A Cancerian child needs to feel free to express his or her emotions in poetry, painting, story making, music making, acting, or any other form of creative activity. Thus, young Cancer should be taught the basic techniques and given the space and materials to enable him or her to express things adequately.

The parents of a Cancerian child must find a middle way between too much firmness and too much spoiling. Teaching the young Cancerian to use his or her natural instincts to care for others is a very good way of achieving this.

A clear and quick punishment will do no harm when it is necessary, providing it is balanced with much physical affection at other times.

When Cancerian children use their vivid imaginations to exaggerate the truth, they should be taught to distinguish between reality and imagination. They need plenty of outlets for their imagination.

CANCER AT HOME

If a person has the personality that is typical of those born with a Cancer sun sign, home is a place which must offer complete security, and he or she will have a tendency toward the characteristics listed below.

Typical behavior and abilities

At home, a Cancerian man or woman

- is capable of most kinds of home improvement jobs
- can cook and will keep a well-stocked kitchen
- feels safe and secure and so can relax
- will tend the garden
- may have collections of antiques
- spoils all visitors

- will hoard anything seen as potentially valuable

Cancer as parent

The typical Cancerian parent

- may worry too much about their offspring
- will protect and support the children
- may be over-possessive
- will enjoy looking after and playing with the babies
- will do anything to help and encourage the children's creative development
- remembers every birthday and anniversary

Two Cancerians in the same family

If the mutual need for security and reassurance can be satisfied, two Cancerians can get along well. Their greatest conflicts will arise when they disagree about intuitive matters. Together they can work very well at a money-making activity. The Cancerian sensitivity may result in some highly emotional moments, but as long as each person has a creative outlet, all will be well.

The Cancerian sense of humor should be encouraged and will relax any stressful moments that arise from Cancerian selfishness.

 CANCER AT WORK

At work, the person who has a typical Cancerian personality will exhibit the following characteristics.

Typical behavior and abilities

A typical Cancerian at work

- is there to make money
- takes work seriously and works hard

- will take responsibility
- responds to affectionate appreciation
- works steadily and is reliable

Cancer as employer

A typical Cancerian boss (male or female)

- expects his or her people to be neatly dressed
- takes work seriously and does not like frivolity
- has one aim: to make money
- drives a hard bargain but is fair
- rarely forgets anything
- generously rewards hard work

Cancer as employee

A typical Cancerian employee (male or female)

- will work hard for money because a good bank balance makes him or her feel secure
- will accept discipline calmly
- expects the rate of pay to increase steadily in response to increased output and responsibility
- enjoys taking responsibility

Working environment

The workplace of a typical Cancerian man or woman

- must be comfortable and secure
- will have family photos displayed
- will be organized for hard work
- should be furnished with the best quality tools
- a location near water would be an added bonus

Typical occupations

Occupations that attract typical Cancerians are the food industry, such as baking, candy making, catering, nutrition, hotel or domestic work; animal breeding; horticulture; gardenings; anything

connected with boats, water, ponds, rivers,
fountains, pools, fishing; any kind of trading;
counseling; psychotherapy; social work; nursing;
obstetrics; political work connected with any of
these.

CANCER AND LOVE

For a Cancerian, love thrives when there
is a combination of constant affection with
a healthy bank balance and substantial
assets.

A Cancerian in love will have many of the
characteristics listed below.

Behavior when in love

The typical Cancerian

- will rarely make the first move
- fears he or she will be rejected
- will retreat, deeply hurt, at the first sign of ridicule
  or criticism
- will respond to honest warmth and affection
- can become tenaciously attached to the loved one
- is a romantic at heart
- will put the loved one first in all things

Expectations

The typical Cancerian expects

- to be loved forever
- to have his or her cooking appreciated
- to work hard for money and security
- the family to come first in all things
- to be needed as a tower of strength and refuge
- unshakable loyalty and devotion

The end of an affair

The confusion between emotional hunger and love can lead to relationship problems. Cancerians often feel they are not loved enough, and so make draining demands on any partner who seems to have become uninterested. The Cancerian will cling more tightly as a relationship deteriorates, making separation very difficult.

If the partner has been unfaithful, the Cancerian will become very jealous and may react aggressively because the hurt is so great.

On the other hand, a Cancerian who feels unloved may secretly wander off to find someone else to satisfy their strong emotional needs. Even so, they will resist divorce, no matter how unpleasant the marriage becomes as a consequence.

CANCER AND SEX

Love and sex are synonymous to the typical Cancer, as are love and marriage. The Cancerian does not want a complicated sex life. The place where a Cancerian makes love must be secure and help him or her to relax.

Cancerians tend to dramatize love and can become very strongly attached to someone who never intended to make a commitment and therefore cannot reciprocate their feelings.

CANCER AND PARTNER

The person who contemplates becoming the marriage or business partner of a typical Cancerian must realize that Cancer will want to be the dominant partner and will expect total devotion.

Given this, the person who partners Cancer can expect consideration, prosperity, and a strong sense of belonging to family or company. The contented Cancerian will never let the partner down.

Cancerian man as partner

He will want a partner who will nurture him and take care of all the domestic details, making sure he has a comfortable nest to return to after a day's work.

In marriage or business, he will want others around him. If the marriage proves to be childless, adoption or fostering are likely.

A business is itself seen as a family. He will not usually enjoy working freelance.

Cancerian woman as partner

She will seek a partner as soon as she leaves the parental home – someone who will luxuriate in her protective caring.

She will devote herself completely to the partner, even taking subtle control of him or her.

In business, she will be an excellent manager.

A Cancerian woman will want a family, and if denied the joy of children will acquire a household full of animals instead.

The Cancerian wife is never a dependent when it comes to earning money. She will take a job outside the home to enhance the family's financial security.

Opposite sign

Capricorn is the complementary opposite sign to Cancer, and forms the paternal complement to Cancerian maternalism. From Capricorn the Cancerian can learn how to distinguish reality from imagination, thus getting things into the right perspective and consequently making better judgments.

Capricorn

Cancer

CANCER AND FRIENDS

In general, Cancer likes friends who will support his or her emotional and financial needs when necessary – and Cancer will reciprocate.

Positive factors

Friends are, in many ways, regarded as family possessions themselves and are treated as such, with loving care, protective hospitality, sensitive consideration, and great tenderness.

Although some friends may come and go, friends from younger days are the most precious.

Negative factors

When he or she is hurt by a friend, the Cancerian anger may last for a long time and the friend may be abandoned. However, if the friend is an old friend, then the emotional attachment will finally lead to reconciliation.

Cancerians do tend to set their own standards by the progress their friends are making.

A compatibility chart, opposite, lists those with whom a Cancerian is likely to have the most satisfactory relationships.

CANCERIAN LEISURE INTERESTS

Not fond of heavy exercise, Cancerians may join clubs or causes that allow an outlet for making complaints and putting their nurturing instincts to good use.

Consumer affairs rouse their interest, and they will follow popular interests in the arts.

Compatibility chart

In general, if people are typical of their zodiac sign, relationships between Cancer and other signs (including the complementary opposite sign, Capricorn) are as shown below

	Harmonious	Difficult	Turbulent
Cancer	●		
Leo	●		
Virgo	●		
Libra		●	
Scorpio	●		
Sagittarius			●
Capricorn		●	
Aquarius			●
Pisces	●		
Aries		●	
Taurus	●		
Gemini	●		

On the whole, typical Cancerians pursue the
following leisure interests:
- boating, sailing, swimming
- water sports that are played in teams
- fishing and gardening
- keeping and breeding animals
- building collections
- keeping in contact with family members

Cancerian likes and dislikes

Likes

- anyone who loves his or her mother
- sentimental and family keepsakes
- gourmet food
- shopping trips
- history, especially family genealogy
- any demonstration of affection such as flowers
- a birthday card on the right date
- the company of other people
- a calm working atmosphere
- physical contact

Dislikes

- any tiny criticism of the home
- having to handle a crisis
- pressure to take part in conversation
- anyone who refuses their cooking
- people who forget names and dates (Cancerians have excellent memories themselves)

CANCERIAN HEALTH

Typical Cancerians are calm, docile people able to withstand sickness as long as they have material security, plenty of affection, and are needed by several people. Their greatest problems can arise from worries caused by a lack of these things.

Types of sickness

Some Cancerians are complainers when they feel not enough affectionate attention is coming their way, yet when an illness slowly creeps up on them, they are remarkably tough and complain less and less. A melancholy or full depression may then be evident.

Typical illnesses often arise from the upper digestive tract, especially the stomach. Indigestion, coughs, anemia, and lowered vitality are common.

Cancerians may also suffer from eating disorders.

Cancer at rest

Extending the metaphor of Cancer as the cardinal water sign, it follows that emotion in action is the key to understanding how Cancerians relax.

Although they do enjoy lounging around, preferably on or near water, they are at their most relaxed when their busy emotional sensors are satisfied by being surrounded by the warmth of a contented family atmosphere.

When on vacation, Cancerians most enjoy a home away from home, which may mean a luxurious trailer or RV. They can also relax in the peace of a comfortably furnished period house, and generally prefer old buildings to modern styles.

Parts of the body linked to Cancer
Traditionally, the parts of the body linked with a
strong Cancer influence are as shown in the
diagram below. Only the individual birth chart will
show if one or more of these parts of the body
have inherited a strength or a vulnerability. Any
generalization would be misleading.

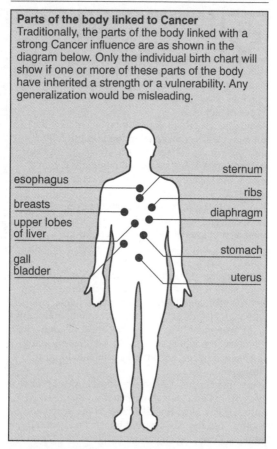

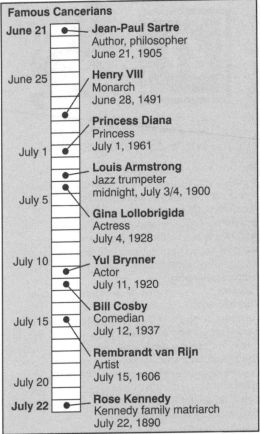

Famous Cancerians

June 21 — **Jean-Paul Sartre**
Author, philosopher
June 21, 1905

June 25

Henry VIII
Monarch
June 28, 1491

Princess Diana
Princess
July 1, 1961

July 1

Louis Armstrong
Jazz trumpeter
midnight, July 3/4, 1900

July 5

Gina Lollobrigida
Actress
July 4, 1928

July 10 **Yul Brynner**
Actor
July 11, 1920

Bill Cosby
Comedian
July 15 July 12, 1937

Rembrandt van Rijn
Artist
July 15, 1606

July 20

July 22 **Rose Kennedy**
Kennedy family matriarch
July 22, 1890

5. Leo: the Lion
July 23 – August 22

The fifth sign of the zodiac is concerned with
- pleasures, fun, playfulness, entertainment
- creativity, recognition, compliments
- romance, love affairs, sex, offspring
- children, childlike activities, childishness
- taking risks, gambling, sports, games
- performance, drama, limelight, applause
- hospitality, appreciation

Elemental quality

Leo is the fixed fire sign of the zodiac. It can be
likened to a fire burning in its appropriate place,
such as a campfire, a blazing log fire, or a bonfire
around which everyone can gather.

Fire changes substances, and Leos like transforming
things with their energy. Being a fixed sign, Leos
may be loyal, stubborn, and proud of their
achievements.

Spiritual goal

To learn the true meaning of love.

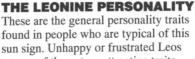

THE LEONINE PERSONALITY
These are the general personality traits found in people who are typical of this sun sign. Unhappy or frustrated Leos may display some of the not-so-attractive traits.

Characteristics

Positive	Negative
• Honesty and loyalty	• Stubborness or willfulness
• A sunny disposition	• Contempt or arrogance
• A sense of dignity	• Sulkiness
• Pride in the home	• Smugness or boasting
• Attractive liveliness	• Indifference or an uncaring attitude
• Friendliness and kindness	• A tendency to take undue credit
• Generosity and hospitality	• A tendency to cut others down to size
• Acceptance of people at face value	• A tendency to keep up appearances
• A mature sense of responsibility	• Coldhearted when hurt
• Courageousness to the point of self-sacrifice	

Secret Leo
Inside anyone who has strong Leo influences is a person who wants to be on top. Potential competitors should remember this. Leo is not interested in winning, but in being king or queen of a particular castle.
Privately, the typical Leo craves love more than

anyone would ever guess. Love, adoration, appreciation, recognition: these are what keep Leo's generous, fun-loving nature burning brightly. While typical Leos may appear to be confident, especially when they take center stage in the limelight, they have secret doubts about their true worth and may seriously undervalue themselves.

Ruling planet and its effect

The Sun rules the zodiac sign of Leo, so anyone whose birthchart has a strong Leo influence may expect things in life to orbit around them.

In astrology, the Sun is the life giver and the source of creativity. Like the Sun, Leos can be a source of life-enhancing warmth, joy, and pleasure to friends and family.

Leonine lucky connections	
Colors	yellow and orange
Plants	sunflower and laurel
Perfume	olibanum
Gemstones	cat's-eye and olivine
Metal	gold
Tarot card	fortitude
Animal	lion

THE LEONINE LOOK

People who exhibit the physical characteristics distinctive of the sign of Leo look majestic. They may seem tall if (typically) they are proud of their appearance. They are either very particular about their looks or apparently somewhat careless. Either way their appearance catches the attention of others – a usual Leo trait.

Physical appearance

- Body: slim and graceful in movement
- Hair: long or short, bushy and curly or straight – a feature of pride which they emphasize by stroking, running their fingers through their locks, or playing with a curl
- Baldness: a Leo will either wear a well-made hairpiece or make the bald head a feature!
- Face: oval with large eyes
- Voice: strong

THE LEO MALE

If a man behaves in a way typical of the personality associated with the zodiac sign of Leo, he will have a tendency toward the characteristics listed below, unless there are influences in his personal birth chart that are stronger than that of his Leo Sun sign.

Appearance

The typical Leo man

- has a well-proportioned body
- is slim and athletic if he takes care of himself
- if disabled, will fight to regain prowess in some sports-related aspect

- has sex appeal and may be a playboy when young
- walks tall with a noble bearing
- dresses to impress

Behavior and personality traits

The typical Leo man

- likes to show off
- is trusting
- appears to be in control of himself
- gives and expects loyalty
- likes everything he does to be exciting
- is generous with affection and money
- likes an elegant environment
- is popular
- needs to be adored
- uses charm to get what he wants

 THE LEO FEMALE

If a woman behaves in a way that is distinctive of the personality associated with the zodiac sign of Leo, she will have a tendency toward the characteristics listed below, providing there are no influences in her personal birth chart that are stronger than that of her Leo sun sign.

Appearance

The typical Leo woman

- is slim and elegant
- if disabled, will use the disability to advantage, making it attractive
- has sex appeal
- appears to possess an inner sense of royalty
- is well dressed

- looks attractive even in adverse circumstances
- exudes dignity and class

Behavior and personality traits

The typical Leo woman
- likes to show off in subtle ways
- is trusting and loyal
- is never docile or adoring in affairs of the heart but gives respect, warmth, and real emotional commitment
- likes everything she does to be exciting
- is generous with affection and hospitality
- likes an elegant environment
- is a social leader
- needs to be admired
- uses courtesy to get what she wants

YOUNG LEO

If a child behaves in a way that is distinctive of the personality associated with the zodiac sign of Leo, he or she will have a tendency toward the characteristics listed below.

Behavior and personality traits

The typical Leo child
- is sunny and friendly
- has a bottomless well of energy
- is more often on the move than still
- loves games and physical play
- when tired often falls fast asleep for a while
- loves to be the center of attention
- is adventurous and sometimes reckless
- likes to be waited on

- dislikes menial tasks
- loves parties
- is generous with whatever is seen as his or hers

Bringing up young Leo

Most Leos enjoy the limelight at school and often take the lead. As they grow up, they will be attracted to the opposite sex and fall in and out of love. Their emotions will be turbulent and often dramatic.

To be able to grow and experiment, both sexes need freedom, which they will use well if they have become used to a discipline that is tempered with love.

Leo girls are naturally happiest when doing something physical.

Young Leo's needs Young Leo needs plenty of love and honest compliments. Lies, even flattering ones, are very hurtful to the trusting Leo child. He or she also needs a good balance of affection and discipline: plenty of hugs and praise for their achievements.

What to teach young Leo Young Leo should be taught from early on that too much boasting is undignified. This explanation will probably work because even in the messiest situations, Leo likes to keep his or her dignity.

The friendly Leo nature endears Leo children to everyone, including strangers. Leo children should be watched over very carefully until they are old enough to understand that not everyone is as warm-hearted as they are.

Young Leo needs to be trained to take a share in the

jobs around the home. If not, doting parents may find a little tyrant on their hands. If the jobs are given special titles, little Leos will enjoy doing even menial tasks.

He or she needs to be taught about the importance of regular study and given an understanding of the rights of others.

He or she should be taught to handle money, including the need to save it, as they are likely use it generously.

LEO AT HOME

If a person has the personality that is typical of those born with a Leo sun sign, home is the most natural territory, and he or she will have a tendency toward the characteristics listed below.

Typical behavior and abilities

At home, a Leo man or woman

- is head of the household
- creates an elegant, comfortable home
- offers superb hospitality
- expects others to respect his or her territory
- is able to fix most practical things
- enjoys entertaining
- shows courage and strength in emergencies

Leo as parent

The typical Leo parent

- is conscientious about bringing up children
- wants to be proud of offspring
- may put too much pressure to succeed on children
- expects to be loved and appreciated by offspring

- is capable of giving great warmth
- knows how to play with children
- is generous with pocket money
- insists on honesty
- makes every effort to teach children many things

Two Leos in the same family

Leos can be happily married to each other once they realize they both have similar needs for love and adoration. Two Leos in the same family, whether parents or children, can get along well together if they each have a castle of their own on which they can stand and be admired. Each needs to be a leader in their own field.

If one feels he or she is receiving less praise than the other, there could be some very dramatic quarrels. Otherwise, a home with Leos in it will be a happy, exciting, and relaxing place.

LEO AT WORK

At work, the person who has a typical Leo personality will exhibit the following characteristics.

Typical behavior and abilities

A typical Leo at work
- gives a good first impression at interviews
- is able to act a part or exaggerate when necessary
- must be in charge of something
- can work very hard
- finds it difficult to apologize

Leo as employer

A typical Leo boss (male or female)
- has huge self-confidence

- can get everyone working hard for him or her
- loses confidence if his or her authority is undermined
- is thoughtful toward workers and their families
- is generous with praise and compliments
- enjoys showing people how to do things
- tends to take the credit for everyone's success
- cannot tolerate failure
- can charm people into working devotedly

Leo as employee

A typical Leo employee (male or female)

- needs to have his or her superiority recognized
- works hard
- is very loyal
- can keep customers happy
- makes a good showperson
- responds to genuine praise of his or her efforts

Working environment

The workplace of a typical Leo man or woman

- is convenient and comfortable
- has an air of luxury
- usually has pictures on the wall
- often has status symbols displayed
- is a place that inspires admiration

Typical occupations

Leo is often associated with leadership, promotion and sales, any job which has a special title, acting, directing, teaching, politics, public relations, management, the law, or a self-employed skill or business. Leo often shows his or her inner strengths when under great pressure or when a crisis occurs.

LEO AND LOVE

To Leo, love is a dramatic ideal. Male Leos seem to have no trouble attracting women, while female Leos attract many men with their natural beauty and liveliness. The typical Leo in love will have many of the characteristics listed below.

Behavior when in love

The typical Leo

- is romantic and proud of it
- becomes more regal and noble
- is very generous to the person who is loved
- is attentive and loyal to the loved one
- is radiant with happiness
- is caring, protective, and supportive
- will make great sacrifices for love
- will fight to the death for the loved one

Expectations

The typical Leo expects

- to be adored by the loved one
- to be the envy of others
- to be treated like royalty
- his or her love to be seen as very special
- total commitment from the loved one
- the partner to be dependent in some way

The end of an affair

If Leo's passions cool, the partner is still needed, but more as a friend than a lover, which may cause problems and lead to parting or divorce if the partner does not like this arrangement. When a Leo wants to end an affair of the heart, pride may make it very difficult for the Leo to say straight out that things

are finished. Consequently, some Leos deal with this
problem by withdrawing from contact or even by
behaving badly toward the partner. If the partner
does not confront the Leo and continues to cling, he
or she can become quite psychologically cruel,
treating the discarded partner with disdain.

The partner who is unfaithful to Leo, or who walks
out on a serious love affair, will leave behind a very
wounded person. It will take Leo months to recover
from such a deep hurt and may make him or her
very wary of risking serious love again.

LEO AND SEX

When a typical Leo makes love it is
regarded as a many-splendid thing. In
fact, Leos can often forget about their
partners as they wander through their personal,
playful world of lovemaking. Leos are unrestrained
lovers and can make the partner feel very special.
Any idea of failure is alien to both male and female
Leos. If sexual problems arise, a typical Leo is
mortified and often will not seek the help that is
needed. The sexual partner is also required to be a
friend. In fact, the Leo wants love, sex, and
friendship from his or her spouse or lover.

LEO AND PARTNER

The person who contemplates becoming the marriage or business partner of a typical Leo must realize that Leo will believe that he or she is superior in some way or other. Given this, the person who partners a Leo can expect warmth, loyalty, support, generosity, and undying devotion. Only lazy, foolish Leos look for a partner who will worship them.

Leo man as partner

He will want a partner who enhances his own image and who enjoys being in the spotlight as much as he does. The partner must be good-looking but should not outshine Leo himself. Leo man wants a marriage partner who will place him at the head of the table and believe in his dreams. She will be a woman of good manners who will never do anything to tarnish her own, and therefore his, reputation and she will be a devoted mother to their children.

Leo woman as partner

The typical Leo woman looks for a partner who will install her as queen of the whole neighborhood. He must provide her with a house she can make into a welcoming place, where she can entertain with enthusiasm and generous hospitality.

With the right partner, a lady Leo will rise in social status due to her boundless strength and persistence. Consequently, her light will shine on her partner too. Leo woman will take the responsibility of motherhood in her stride and will expect her partner to be as devoted to the children as she is.

Opposite sign

Aquarius, the water-carrier, is the complementary
opposite sign to Leo. There may be tough relations
between them, but Aquarius can show Leo how to
share without needing appreciation, and give the
center stage to others. In this way Leos can learn to
stand alone and value themselves.

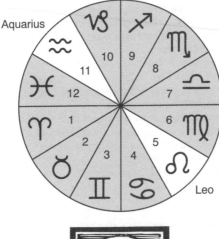

LEO AND FRIENDS

In general, Leos like their friends to be successful, but not so successful as to completely outshine and detract from Leo!

Positive factors

Leos are friendly, warm, and often playful. They enjoy their friends and are proud of them; they are generous to their friends, but the friends are expected to show their gratitude, either in kind or by performance, putting Leo's support to good use.

Negative factors

A friend who in some way fails a Leo, perhaps by seeming to criticize or failing to appreciate something Leo sees as very important, may be dropped without explanation.

A friend, partner, or business associate who has personal aspirations may find it increasingly impossible to take second billing to a Leo, and so may end the relationship.

A compatibility chart, opposite, illustrates those with whom Leo is likely to have the most satisfactory relationships.

 LEONINE LEISURE INTERESTS

Most typical Leos like to follow an exercise routine. Done sensibly, this will strengthen any weak points. As Leos always want to be outstanding in anything they do, they should beware of overdoing exercise – it may make them vulnerable to stress reactions.

Compatibility chart

In general, if people are typical of their zodiac sign, relationships between Leo and other signs (including the complementary opposite sign, Aquarius) are as shown below

	Harmonious	Difficult	Turbulent
Leo	●		
Virgo	●		
Libra	●		
Scorpio		●	
Sagittarius	●		
Capricorn			●
Aquarius		●	
Pisces			●
Aries	●		
Taurus		●	
Gemini	●		
Cancer	●		

On the whole, typical Leos pursue the following
leisure interests:
- any sport that offers skill with grace
- tennis, diving, running, dancing
- driving, rallying, cycling
- theater and dramatic activities
- family party games
- eating out

Leonine likes and dislikes

Likes

- activity
- anything that
  promises pleasure
- being creative, e.g.
  gourmet cooking
- receiving birthday
  cards
- beautifully wrapped,
  personalized gifts
- silks, satins, gold
- receiving thanks

- an appreciative
  audience
- sincere compliments
- children and pets
- unusual food and
  new recipes
- exotic drinks
- luxury furnishings
- top-quality,
  fashionable clothes

Dislikes

- physical hurt
- sedentary activities
- being ignored
- being backstage
- lies and deceit

- being laughed at
- being told something
  they don't know
- one-upmanship

LEONINE HEALTH

Typical Leos are happy, healthy, energetic people as long as they are loved. Only when seriously deprived of affection or appreciation will a Leo tend to look haggard and be heard complaining about life.

Types of sickness

High fevers, sudden illnesses, and accidents are typical of Leonine ill health. Whatever physical misfortune strikes, the person who behaves in a way typical of Leo will enjoy only a brief period of being spoiled in the sickbed before he or she is up again and on the go. To be incapacitated for long is a sign of weakness to a Leo. This desire to get up too soon after an illness may mean that a health problem recurs.

Leo at rest

Extending the metaphor of Leo as the fixed fire sign, it follows that the fire in the grate will sometimes burn brightly and be a center of warmth and delight to everyone who gathers around it. However, fires do go out and have to be relit. So it is with typical Leonine energy. The Leo will sometimes need to rest, relax, and have catnaps. This should not be mistaken for incipient sickness or laziness. Once revitalized, the typical Leo will be on the go again for hours.

Parts of the body linked to Leo
Traditionally, the parts of the body linked with a strong Leo influence are as shown in the diagram below. Only the individual birth chart will show if one or more of these parts of the body have inherited a strength or a vulnerability. Any generalization would be misleading.

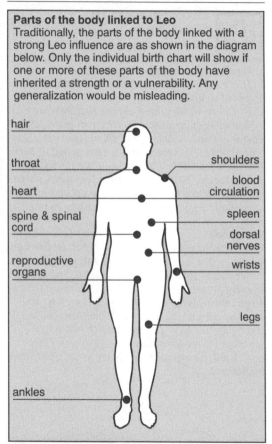

hair

throat

heart

spine & spinal cord

reproductive organs

shoulders

blood circulation

spleen

dorsal nerves

wrists

legs

ankles

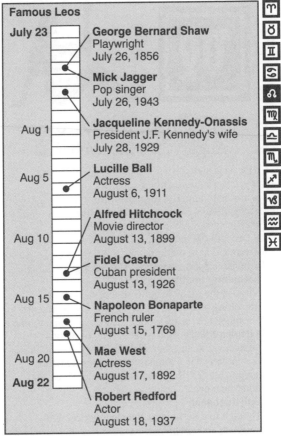

Famous Leos

July 23

George Bernard Shaw
Playwright
July 26, 1856

Mick Jagger
Pop singer
July 26, 1943

Jacqueline Kennedy-Onassis
President J.F. Kennedy's wife
July 28, 1929

Aug 1

Aug 5
Lucille Ball
Actress
August 6, 1911

Aug 10
Alfred Hitchcock
Movie director
August 13, 1899

Fidel Castro
Cuban president
August 13, 1926

Aug 15
Napoleon Bonaparte
French ruler
August 15, 1769

Mae West
Actress
August 17, 1892

Aug 20

Aug 22

Robert Redford
Actor
August 18, 1937

6. Virgo: the Virgin
August 23 – September 22

The sixth sign of the zodiac is concerned with
- self-perfection, critical faculties
- altruism, honesty, responsibility
- cleanliness, hygiene, health, healing
- efficiency, daily routines, reliability
- strength of character, veiled sensuality
- service, hard work, passivity, modesty
- incisive communication, shrewd logical thought

Elemental quality

Virgo is the mutable earth sign of the zodiac,
indicating adaptable practicality. It can be likened to
a semi-shaded patio which has been adapted to make
a garden filled with a great variety of plants,
climbers, and an arbor. Half hidden, here and there,
are garden chaise longues with rich patchwork
covers, bottles of homemade organic wines, and
other unexpected practical delights.

Spiritual goal

To learn to discriminate between destructive
criticism and simple wisdom.

THE VIRGOAN PERSONALITY

These are the general personality traits found in people who are typical of Virgo. An unhappy or frustrated Virgo may display some of the not-so-attractive traits.

Characteristics

Positive	Negative
• Gentleness with the helpless	• Scathing criticism of the lazy
• Sympathetic	• Cranky and irritable
• Humane and helpful	• Dogmatic
• Organized	• Untidy
• Knowledgeable about good health	• Tendency to be a hypochondriac
• Witty and charming	• Nervous and worried
• Physically sensual	• Prudish
• Painstaking	• Eccentric
• Emotionally warm	• Undemonstrative
• Dedicated	• Overdemanding

Secret Virgo

Inside anyone who has strong Virgo influences is a person who worries too much about every personal imperfection and is never satisfied with his or her own standards. Virgo may appear to know it all and be a compulsive worker; both these behaviors hide a deep fear that he or she cannot be good enough for, say, the job or the partner.

Virgos crave the opportunity to serve others and take charge of the many apparently mundane matters that, collectively, are the bedrock of success.

One of the least suspected aspects of a Virgo personality is a strong, almost volcanic sexuality that can lie hidden and dormant for years until the right partner comes along.

Ruling planet and its effect

Mercury rules the zodiac sign of Virgo, so anyone whose birth chart has a strong Virgo influence will have a good and quick mind.

In astrology, Mercury is the planet of the mind and communication. Being more concerned with practicalities than ideas (Gemini, the ideas sign, is also ruled by Mercury), Virgo is usually interested in acquiring information and in communicating by writing.

The other traditional ruler of Virgo is the mythological Vulcan, the lame god of thunder, who had a confident and brilliant mind.

Virgoan lucky connections

Colors	yellow-green, brown, cream
Plants	narcissus, vervain, herbs
Perfume	narcissus
Gemstones	peridot, opal, agate
Metal	mercury
Tarot card	the hermit
Animals	bat, porcupine, mink

THE VIRGOAN LOOK

People who exhibit the physical characteristics distinctive of the sign of Virgo look neat and fastidious and have a pleasant, often quietly beautiful face. Many Virgos look like loners and are not usually noisy people.

Physical appearance
- High forehead
- Cranium may seem too big in comparison with the face
- Eyelids are often veiled
- Nose is straight
- Jaw is broad

THE VIRGO MALE

If a man behaves in a way typical of the personality associated with the zodiac sign of Virgo, he will have a tendency toward the characteristics listed below, unless there are influences in his personal birth chart that are stronger than that of his Virgo sun sign.

Appearance
The typical Virgo man
- has a straight, wedge-shaped nose
- has an extremely large forehead
- has a high hairline
- is upright and has a straight body
- may be quite tall
- often has one foot turned in more than the other

Behavior and personality traits
The typical Virgo man
- is practical and unsentimental

- instinctively has a love of work
- will be devoted to serving those less fortunate than himself
- may relax by working a little less hard than usual
- takes responsibilities seriously
- is subtle and rarely obvious about his intentions
- notices and remembers details

THE VIRGO FEMALE

If a woman behaves in a way that is distinctive of the personality associated with the zodiac sign of Virgo, she will have a tendency toward the characteristics listed below, providing there are no influences in her personal birth chart that are stronger than that of her Virgo sun sign.

Appearance

The typical Virgo woman

- has a pointed chin and a face in repose
- the eyes are often soft and very beautiful
- the hair may be long or short but is normally impeccably groomed
- the mouth and lips are well formed
- is typically clean and very neatly dressed

Behavior and personality traits

The typical Virgo woman

- can analyze situations in detail
- is devoted to her work, usually serving others in some way
- is basically shy
- has incredible strength of purpose
- will pursue happiness wherever it leads

- is pure of mind but not naive
- thinks of herself as more orderly and efficient than other people
- has a delightful, straightforward personality
- does not express her feelings easily
- can be soothing one moment and critical the next

YOUNG VIRGO

If a child behaves in a way that is distinctive of the personality associated with the zodiac sign of Virgo, he or she will have a tendency toward the characteristics listed below.

Behavior and personality traits

The typical Virgo child

- is quick, alert, and an excellent mimic, and so can learn many things in a short time
- gets upset if he or she forgets something that has been learned by heart
- rarely questions authority but frequently questions facts
- is honest and reliable
- is usually shy among strangers
- loves to do jobs around the home imitating an adult
- is sometimes a fussy eater
- is usually tidy, with occasional bouts of disorganization
- gets very upset if teased
- is often an early talker and reader

Bringing up young Virgo

Young Virgos will try very hard to please, as long as they know what is expected.

As they grow up they will often find close relationships with the opposite sex very difficult. Virgos take a lot of convincing that they are attractive people. Lots of genuine praise and encouragement early in life will help to smooth the path to true love in teenage and early adulthood. Parents should never interfere when their young Virgo begins to notice the opposite sex. Even the slightest hint of criticism or teasing may cause Virgos to withdraw and choose the single life.

Young Virgo's needs Young Virgo must have physical affection, in the form of hugs, and sincere compliments every day in order to build the self-confidence that every typical Virgo child lacks.

What to teach young Virgo Myths, fairy tales, make-believe, daydreams, and how to use imagination should all be taught to young Virgos so they have plenty of magical moments to remember in their adult years when they often feel lonely.

On the whole, young Virgos aim for good grades at school, are helpful around the house, and are usually tidy about their own things, almost to a fault. An untidy Virgo will have some other strong influence in the astrological birth chart.

Virgos can be exacting about time, orderliness, and food. They also have a tendency to be critical about everyone else in the family, especially when asked an opinion. They, therefore, need to be taught to accept the little foibles of other people and not to get

upset when someone else leaves the top off the
toothpaste.

VIRGO AT HOME
If a person has the personality that is
typical of those born with a Virgo sun
sign, home is a place to thrive, and he or
she will have a tendency toward the characteristics
listed below.

Typical behavior and abilities

When at home, a Virgo man or woman
- enjoys being head of the household
- is domesticated in most areas, such as cooking,
  managing the household finances, general
  maintenance, health, hygiene, and gardening
- will always be doing or making something
- is usually at his or her most relaxed
- pursues several hobbies at or from home

Virgo as parent

The typical Virgo parent
- encourages children to ask questions
- supports practical activities during free time
- worries about the children's health
- is helpful, especially about detailed work
- can adapt to almost any practical demand
- may find it hard to express affection warmly
- gets upset by children's dirt and untidiness
- will explain demands he or she makes
- will do anything to help their children

Two Virgos in the same family

Married to each other, or as members of the same
family, Virgos can get along very well. But

difficulties will arise if they become too critical of each other and undermine each other's confidence. On the whole, however, Virgos are made of sterner stuff and can adapt their practical arrangements to accommodate any serious differences. Normally their mutual need for cleanliness and tidiness works very well. The Virgo tendency to worry, especially about matters of health, could lead to an air of hypochondria in the home. However, Virgo quick thinking and wit can usually overcome these disadvantages.

VIRGO AT WORK

At work, the person who has a typical Virgo personality will exhibit the following characteristics.

Typical behavior and abilities

A typical Virgo at work
- is best in a supporting role
- is meticulous and self-disciplined
- offers others a sense of stability
- is very helpful to other people
- can enjoy complicated, routine work

Virgo as employer

A typical Virgo boss (male or female)
- is excellent as boss of a small company
- can see the details very clearly
- will call a spade a spade
- expects honesty in all matters
- is kindhearted, honest, and fair
- expects good grooming, good manners, and good habits

- can handle extremely complicated projects
- will reward good work with pay not perks

Virgo as employee

A typical Virgo employee (male or female)

- is good in service work or research, rather than manufacturing
- will become an excellent assistant to the boss
- does good work and expects to be paid well
- is courteous, reliable, and thorough
- is quick-thinking, analytical, and intelligent
- will be cautious, critical, and methodical

Working environment

The workplace of a typical Virgo man or woman

- will not be noisy
- will have the most up-to-date equipment
- is best decorated with subtle, neutral colors
- is organized so that work can have a regular routine

Typical occupations

Any occupation which enables the Virgoan to give service and handle complicated or difficult details will suit most Virgoans.

VIRGO AND LOVE

To Virgo, love is not dramatic, emotional, or sentimental. A Virgo's love is devotion and will include love of family, friends, and those less fortunate than he or she. Virgo in love with another person will have many of the characteristics listed below.

Behavior when in love

The typical Virgo

- looks for quality
- is frightened by overt romance
- may wait for years for the right person
- once in love, loves warmly and steadily
- is devoted to the loved one
- will rarely give cause for any jealousy
- will do anything to avoid breaking up

Expectations

The typical Virgo expects

- devotion from the partner
- a sense of decency
- to enjoy platonic flirtation
- to be fussed over when feeling down
- personal matters to be kept private
- feelings to be handled with great care

The end of an affair

Virgos are typically loyal and will avoid ending a marriage or other permanent relationship whenever possible. However, in the long run, Virgos are sensible, practical people. If the Virgoan sense of fair play has been outraged, the Virgo will make a quick and final break, legally and in every other way.

It is rare for a typical Virgo to linger in a fading marriage. If sensible, intelligent discussion does not solve the problems, the Virgo soon makes up his or her mind to end it.

Reconciliation is not typical of Virgoan behavior. Pleading, tears, sentimentality, or a more aggressive approach will have no effect. Because the Virgoan has good self-discipline, the past is soon put aside. However, if children are involved, the divorced Virgo will want to ensure that the children receive good educations.

VIRGO AND SEX

When a typical Virgo makes love it is a pure-minded, natural, healthy act. Virgo only enjoys sex when it is with someone who has gained Virgo's confidence.

Celibacy, for short or long periods, is not usually difficult for a Virgo. In general, Virgoans are looking for a spouse, not a one-night stand or an affair.

A Virgo who has not had his or her fragile sense of self undermined in youth will enjoy sex. The bedside library may include informative books on sex, because Virgos like to understand the finer details.

Virgo (male or female) tends to seduce with finesse, charm, and subtlety.

The fact that typical Virgoan instincts are chaste does not mean that Virgos are virgins. The Virgin of astrology is a symbol of self-improvement and fertility.

VIRGO AND PARTNER

The person who contemplates becoming the marriage or business partner of a typical Virgo must realize that Virgo will regard the union as permanent, although the finer details can be flexible.

Given this, the person who partners Virgo can expect absolute loyalty. Virgos make strong commitments because they combine duty with devotion.

The Virgo will approach a proposal with great caution and will analyze the pros and cons thoroughly before getting involved. This is an excellent approach to any long-term partnership but may sound rather cold and clinical in the case of a proposed marriage.

Virgo man as partner

He will be thoughtful, considerate, and honest. He will remember dates, anniversaries, and agreements. He can be a wizard when it comes to the sensible balancing of the budget. He will love, honor, and criticize, but will not expect to be obeyed, waited on, or be dazzled by sexy make-up and clothes. However, he will want cleanliness and a lot of warmth and sincere respect.

Virgo woman as partner

She is shy but as tough as nails when the need arises. In business, she will be cool, intelligent, and fully committed.

Slow to love, Virgo woman is not interested in anything less than true love. When it happens, she will love intensely. She will only break a partnership if there has been hypocrisy. She is the most practical romantic in the zodiac.

Opposite sign

Pisces is the complementary opposite sign to Virgo. From Pisces, Virgo can learn to let go a little and float with the tide, giving imagination a chance to develop. In this way, Virgo can begin to accept human imperfections, especially his or her own.

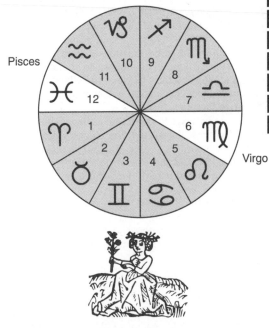

VIRGO AND FRIENDS

In general Virgo likes a friend who is tidy, clean, and intelligent with a broad range of interests. They prefer people who are not given to big shows of emotion and are attracted to those who offer a sense of peace and serenity.

Positive factors

Virgos love any pageantry that gives them an outlet for their tightly controlled emotions. Hence they are delightful companions at these events.

Virgos are discriminating and have a fine artistic taste and a wealth of information on many subjects. They are not coarse and do not waste money.

Virgos are loyal to their friends and will be extremely kind, considerate, and helpful.

Negative factors

Virgos are nervous worriers, and a friend who in some way feeds the worries will reduce Virgo to a nervous heap.

Virgos can be cold and critical, so a friend who softens the barbed remarks with caring laughter will bring out the Virgo wit.

Most Virgos find it almost impossible to admit they are occasionally wrong.

A compatibility chart, opposite, lists those with whom Virgo is likely to have the most satisfactory relationships.

Compatibility chart
In general, if people are typical of their zodiac
sign, relationships between Virgo and other
signs (including the complementary opposite
sign, Pisces) are as shown below

	Harmonious	Difficult	Turbulent
Virgo	●		
Libra	●		
Scorpio	●		
Sagittarius		●	
Capricorn	●		
Aquarius			●
Pisces		●	
Aries			●
Taurus	●		
Gemini		●	
Cancer	●		
Leo	●		

VIRGOAN LEISURE INTERESTS

Most Virgos enjoy intellectual and practical pursuits. While many will take regular exercise for the sake of their health, they are not natural sportsmen and sportswomen.

Virgoan likes and dislikes

Likes

- making lists
- a well-stocked medicine cabinet
- self-improvement courses
- punctuality
- mimicking others
- grooming self, taking showers, using nice soaps
- dealing with details
- tiny animals
- helping others
- wearing well-tailored tailored clothes in muted colors and textures

Dislikes

- crowds and noise; brash people
- slang, vulgarity, slovenliness, and dirt
- people who whine and complain a lot
- sitting still for a long time
- disrupted schedules
- lids left off boxes, or tops off toothpaste
- being obligated to others
- people who move Virgo's personal things
- hypocrisy and deceit
- any admission of weakness or failure
- bright, bold, primary colors

On the whole, typical Virgos pursue the following leisure interests:
- theater, concerts, plays, pageants
- books, magazines, dictionaries, encyclopedias
- detailed crafts, especially weaving
- cults, alternative medicines, psychology
- gardening, health foods, flowers
- computers with all the paraphernalia

VIRGOAN HEALTH

Typical Virgos are healthy although, if very worried or unhappy, they may succumb to the Virgoan tendency toward hypochondria.

Types of sickness

Diseases most usually associated with Virgo are disturbances of the lymph system, or the digestive system such as appendicitis, malnutrition, diarrhea, indigestion, hernia, etc. Normally Virgos look after themselves well, so avoid many upsets.

When Virgo is sick, he or she needs to have a little fuss made while being encouraged to get well.

Virgo at rest

Extending the metaphor of Virgo as the mutable earth sign, it follows that adaptability (the mutable quality) can sometimes work for Virgo, who finds it easy to change position if the body or mind are under stress. However, Virgo is also nervously restless, so Virgo needs plenty of interesting, practical things to keep him or her occupied. Making detailed models or doing needlework can be very soothing and relaxing.

Parts of the body linked to Virgo
Traditionally, the parts of the body linked with a
strong Virgo influence are as shown in the
diagram below. Only the individual birth chart will
show if one or more of these parts of the body
have inherited a strength or a vulnerability. Any
generalization would be misleading.

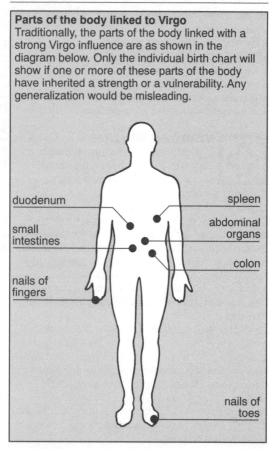

duodenum

spleen

small
intestines

abdominal
organs

colon

nails of
fingers

nails of
toes

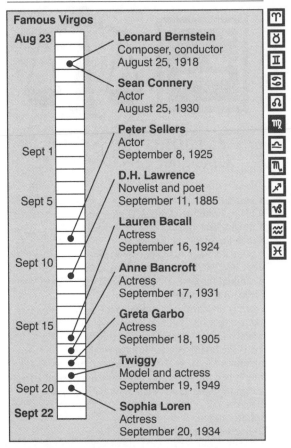

Famous Virgos

Aug 23

Leonard Bernstein
Composer, conductor
August 25, 1918

Sean Connery
Actor
August 25, 1930

Peter Sellers
Actor
September 8, 1925

Sept 1

Sept 5

D.H. Lawrence
Novelist and poet
September 11, 1885

Lauren Bacall
Actress
September 16, 1924

Sept 10

Anne Bancroft
Actress
September 17, 1931

Greta Garbo
Actress
September 18, 1905

Sept 15

Twiggy
Model and actress
September 19, 1949

Sept 20

Sophia Loren
Actress
September 20, 1934

Sept 22

7. Libra: the Scales
September 23 – October 22

The seventh sign of the zodiac is concerned with
- partnership, relationships
- ideas, opinions, politics, diplomacy
- music, harmony, balance, romance
- tact, argument, self-control
- good manners, personal appearance
- refinement, sophistication, good taste
- rational thought, ideas for social well-being

Elemental quality

Libra is the cardinal air sign of the zodiac. It can be likened to a finely tuned wind instrument, producing powerful, moving music in perfect harmony.

Air is the breath of life, and cardinal air is a metaphor for ideas put into action. Libras are doers rather than thinkers, although they may spend a long period thinking about a situation before making a decision and acting upon it.

Spiritual goal

To learn the meaning of selfless love.

THE LIBRAN PERSONALITY

These are the general personality traits found in people who are typical of Libra. An unhappy or frustrated Libra may display some of the not-so-attractive traits.

Characteristics

Positive	Negative
• Cooperative	• Narcissistic
• Good companion	• Indolent or sulky
• Artistic	• Fearful
• Refined	• Indecisive
• Has clear opinions	• Manipulative
• Good negotiator	• Overbearing
• Very strong beliefs	• Flirtatious
• Loving and romantic	
• Sense of fair play	
• Able to lead on behalf of good causes	
• Uses intellect when going into action	
• Sincere	
• Charming	
• Communicative	
• An excellent mediator	

Secret Libra

Inside anyone who has strong Libran influences is a person who is terrified of being alone. The fear is usually well controlled so the typical Libra always looks calm, collected, and in charge of the situation. Good-natured and loving, Libras can also be petulant, and even objectionable, when asked to take orders. Similarly, they are extremely intelligent, yet sometimes gullible; they enjoy talking to people, yet can also be very attentive listeners.

The Libra symbol (the scales) is a clue to understanding this apparent inconsistency in behavior. In attempting to gain an even balance, the scales first tip one way and then the other. This is how the typical Libra behaves – constantly trying to attain that perfect balance.

Ruling planet and its effect

Venus rules the zodiac sign of Libra, so anyone whose birth chart has a strong Libran influence will tend to be a gentle, loving peacemaker – until the scales tip too far and need to be adjusted.

In astrology, Venus is the planet of values, self, possessions, beauty, and love. Libras tend to express these attributes in words and action.

Libran lucky connections

Colors	green, purple, pink
Plants	aloe, myrtle, rose
Perfume	galbanum
Gemstone	emerald
Metal	copper
Tarot card	justice
Animal	elephant

THE LIBRAN LOOK

People who exhibit the physical characteristics distinctive of the sign of Libra are not easy to describe, since there is no typical Libran feature, except for the dimple. It is a Libran habit to spend time deciding what to wear each morning and to change clothes during the day if the occasion demands it.

Physical appearance
- Features are generally well balanced
- Face is pleasant, even when angry
- There may be a dimple in the chin or in the cheeks or knees
- Charming smile

THE LIBRA MALE

If a man behaves in a way typical of the personality associated with the zodiac sign of Libra, he will have a tendency toward the characteristics listed below, unless there are influences in his personal birth chart that are stronger than that of his Libra sun sign.

Appearance
The typical Libra man
- is usually handsome, but is never ugly
- has a fine bone structure and balanced features
- has a clear and very charming voice
- dresses with discrimination in subtle colors
- is usually graceful and athletic
- likes to check his appearance in mirrors or as he passes a store window

Behavior and personality traits

The typical Libra man

- wants to make a visual impression that is appropriate to the task at hand, whether it be an international conference, a romantic assignation, or a day on the beach
- gives advice freely
- is interested in the opposite sex, at all ages
- is a master in the art of romance
- is very trustworthy
- can be fickle and change his mind often
- is interested in the facts of a situation so that he can come to a balanced decision
- enjoys art and needs harmony
- can be lavish with money, spending it on things that will bring happiness
- has financial abilities

 THE LIBRA FEMALE

If a woman behaves in a way that is distinctive of the personality associated with the zodiac sign of Libra, she will have a tendency toward the characteristics listed below, provided there are no influences that are stronger than her Libra sun sign.

Appearance

The typical Libra woman

- is usually slim but curvy
- has large eyes
- has delicately flared nostrils
- has a large, well-shaped mouth
- has even teeth, often a gap between the front two

Behavior and personality traits

The typical Libra woman

- is very aware of her looks
- takes care of her body and appearance
- uses her natural attraction to get what she wants
- presents her opinions with diplomacy and tact
- is excellent at partnership and teamwork
- loves luxurious clothes and perfumes
- has excellent powers of analysis
- will create a beautiful home

 YOUNG LIBRA
If a child behaves in a way that is distinctive of the personality associated with the zodiac sign of Libra, he or she will have a tendency toward the characteristics listed below.

Behavior and personality traits

The typical Libra child

- is a really beautiful baby
- hates having to decide between two things
- does not like to be hurried
- likes candy
- always seems to know more about things than seems likely for someone of that particular age
- is kindhearted
- likes to be fair and to be treated fairly
- can wheedle almost anything out of adults
- will obey rules if they are seen to be fair
- is usually neat and clean
- teenage Libras are romantics; they love warm water, bubble baths, and lazy days in the sun

Bringing up young Libra

Most young Libras quickly learn how to argue about everything with total conviction. They use this natural ability to make their needs and wants known. It is difficult for a parent to avoid complying with such reasonable, fair-minded demands. To always give in is to risk spoiling young Libra. But to refuse their requests too often may injure the child's developing sensibilities – so the parents of a Libra need to keep their wits about them and aim for a balance in these matters.

Young Libra's needs A harmonious environment and fair treatment are essential to the developing Libra. Privacy is regarded as sacred. Similarly, Libra will respect the privacy of others and will keep confidences.

Affection and, especially, attention are crucial. While Libras can pursue their interests alone, they also need company. It is from close contact with others that they learn who they are.

What to teach young Libra At a very early age, young Libra needs to be given direction and told, gently and firmly, what to do and when to do it. What may appear to be reluctance to do something is often a sign that young Libra is giving extensive thought to the matter in hand.

Most young Libras seem to know more about everything than anyone else. This can be irritating, especially when they are right. Parents need to take an optimistic view of this tendency and should provide plenty of sound information. Young Libra absorbs information readily from books.

Libras do not usually need to be strongly
disciplined, as they are good at disciplining
themselves. But it is important not to spoil them or
fuss over them too much, or they will become
impossible to handle and make their own and
everyone else's life miserable.

 LIBRA AT HOME
If a person has the personality that is
typical of those born with a Libra sun
sign, home is a place to retire to for rest
and recuperation, ready for the next period of
sustained activity. The Libra will have a tendency
toward the characteristics listed below.

Typical behavior and abilities
When at home, a Libra man or woman
- will spend time just lounging around listening to
  music or reading pleasant books
- will enjoy arguing about almost everything with
  all the family – just for the sake of it
- uses good taste to create a place of harmony
- will be a very gracious host, offering good food
  and wines while making interesting conversation
- will keep the place tidy and clean, unless he or she
  has become resentful due to unfair treatment

Libra as parent
The typical Libra parent
- is often quite permissive
- may spoil the children
- likes to be proud of the children's appearance
  and behavior
- will show his or her children much affection

- gives the children the best possible education
- will try to be just and fair
- will probably dominate the family

Two Libras in the same family

Two Libras are likely to understand each other's
need for a peaceful, pleasant home. Providing they
both have similar tastes in music, life will be
smooth, although their other interests may be
different. If there are children, they may eventually
follow very different careers. Two Libras may be
quite convinced that they are not at all alike. Anyone
listening to them saying this will actually be struck
by how similar they are. Libran twins will be
extremely attached to each other, although one will
usually tend to dominate the other.

LIBRA AT WORK

At work, the person who has a typical
Libran personality will exhibit the
following characteristics.

Typical behavior and abilities

A typical Libra at work
- takes time to get things right
- is usually honest in business
- is more often than not in a partnership
- is a great promoter of ideas
- builds a good network of contacts

Libra as employer

A typical Libra boss (male or female)
- is unhurried but extremely restless
- takes note of everyone's opinion before making
  decisions

- often suggests unusual answers to problems
- is an expert at the rational analysis of situations
- believes his or her policy is the best
- has strong opinions about finance

Libra as employee

A typical Libra employee (male or female)

- belongs to a union
- expects and gives a fair deal
- never gossips, although he or she talks a lot
- mediates effectively in personality tiffs
- can be moody, but is not rude or mean
- needs periods of rest

Working environment

The workplace of a typical Libra man or woman

- must be harmonious – Libras can get migraines just because the walls are the wrong color
- should be peaceful
- if there is music, it must be classical or refined
- should be free from anything upsetting
- will have a calm but purposeful atmosphere

Typical occupations

Libras are liable to be involved with any aspect of the law, politics, or diplomacy. Their eye for design may lead them into areas such as fashion, art dealership, or graphics. They will also enjoy working in jobs that involve talking and presentation, such as promotional work. Many Libras are good at planning business ventures.

LIBRA AND LOVE
To Libra, love is all. He or she tends to
fall in love with love itself and is eager to
share life with the partner. The Libran
ideal is a life that is filled with the peaceful, rosy
glow of romance. Libra in love will have many of
the characteristics listed below.

Behavior when in love

The typical Libra

- is emotionally dependent upon the partner
- is casual and easygoing
- enjoys romantic settings
- will ignore the partner's shortcomings in return for
  love
- does not want a partner who is overly
  demonstrative
- glows with love for the whole world
- will do anything to avoid hurting the loved one
- gives the loved one complete attention

Expectations

The typical Libra expects

- to be supported and cared for
- faithfulness and loyalty
- to be free to get on with his or her work
- a partner to have his or her own separate interests
- to be amused
- to be admired and even exalted

The end of an affair

If a Libra is rejected, he or she is initially
demoralized. However, the Libra quickly takes
action to try to redress the balance that has been lost.
Often the Libra will do everything to charm the

loved one again, courting the partner as if for the first time.

If the rejection is final, the hurt Libra will disguise the pain he or she feels by searching once more for true love.

A Libra is most likely to reject a partner who makes too many demands on the Libran emotions. If this happens, the break will be as orderly and as well mannered as possible.

LIBRA AND SEX

When a typical Libra makes love it is not always a passionate experience, unless there are more passionate signs in the Libra's chart.

Libras may appear to be calm, confident, and in control, but they are often very uncertain about their sexual identity. They are usually very influenced by images of sexual attractiveness in the media, and no matter how beautiful or handsome they are (and they often are) Libras can feel sexually very insecure and uncertain. All this does not, however, lessen Libra's interest in sex.

LIBRA AND PARTNER

The person who contemplates becoming the marriage or business partner of a typical Libra must realize that Libra forms partnerships to avoid the terrible sense of loneliness which is always present at the heart of a Libra.

Given this, the person who partners Libra can expect

the marriage or the business to be happy and successful. Libra is the zodiac sign of partnerships, and typical Libras cannot imagine life without a relationship. The Libra will work hard and thoughtfully to make the partnership a harmonious balance of two personalities.

Libra man as partner

He will want a partner who has some good social or business connections. The young or immature Libra sees himself as the ugly duckling of the fairy tale. He will want his partner to be his personal mirror, reflecting back to him a self-image that is mature and confident. The developed Libra will indeed grow into a swan, but most Libras need plenty of encouragement on the way.

In a partnership, Libra will generally take charge of the finances, making sure that there is always a good bank balance. Libras tend to have very strong views about money.

Libra woman as partner

The young, inexperienced Libran female will see a partner as the provider of all that she needs. As she matures, she will want to share herself with her partner. She will have plenty of talent and energy, and her aim is to be successful in every field.

She will bring logic and sophistication to any business and a calm beauty to her home – where she will help her loved one to relax and renew himself.

Opposite sign

Aries is the complementary opposite sign to Libra. Although relations between them can be difficult, they can become entirely complementary to each other as they mature. Aries, the sign of self, can inspire Libra to take the initiative alone sometimes. Libra can thus learn to become self-sufficient and also gain a greater sense of personal identity. In this way, Libra, the sign of partnership, may be able to enjoy a separate identity while in a partnership.

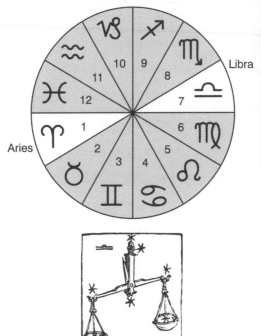

LIBRA AND FRIENDS

Libras are usually very social people who like to be on the go. Life for Libras revolves around keeping in touch with other people; this is what makes them happy. Libras will work hard for a friend, giving of themselves tirelessly for days on end. When they become tired, they will need to rest completely. But friends should not mistake the Libran recuperation periods as a loss of interest.

Positive factors

Libras are loving friends and are unlikely to embarrass anyone with emotional outbursts. A Libran friend is honest and will treat a friend fairly. They make sensitive companions for visits to events concerned with the arts.

Negative factors

Libras can occasionally try the patience of a friend with their indecisiveness.

They can be jealous of a friend who is better looking than they are.

Friends must also be aware of the periodic depressive moods into which Libras seem to plunge. Such moods can be lightened by a genuine compliment.

Friends should never forget that the worst thing for a Libra is to be left alone for too long. If this happens, they can become irritable and sulky, and they can lose their self-esteem.

A compatibility chart, opposite, lists those with whom Libra is likely to have the most satisfactory relationships.

Compatibility chart
In general, if people are typical of their zodiac sign, relationships between Libra and other signs (including the complementary opposite sign, Aries) are as shown below

	Harmonious	Difficult	Turbulent
Libra	●		
Scorpio	●		
Sagittarius	●		
Capricorn		●	
Aquarius	●		
Pisces			●
Aries		●	
Taurus			●
Gemini	●		
Cancer		●	
Leo	●		
Virgo	●		

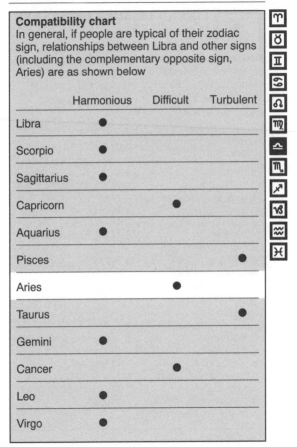

LIBRAN LEISURE INTERESTS
Most typical Libras are not overly fond of vigorous, sweaty exercise. This offends their preference for a harmony of the senses. Whatever exercise they do, it must enable them to stay relatively neat and unruffled. Many Libras have a lasting interest in the arts. Of these, music is a high priority.

Libran likes and dislikes

Likes

- pleasing surroundings
- getting notes, cards, and flowers
- a good, detailed argument
- being fussed over
- being admired
- people running errands for them
- credit cards
- having people around
- attending to the finest details
- very small animals, even ants
- being of service to others
- sensible, tailored clothes
- muted, subtle colors and textures

Dislikes

- loud arguments
- confused situations
- sloppiness, especially in public
- ugly places
- being pressured to make up their mind
- being told it is up to them to make a change
- any criticism of their chosen partner or project

On the whole, typical Libras pursue the following leisure interests:

- listening to music, studying music history, playing an instrument in a group, such as a string quartet or a jazz band, listening to poetry
- dancing, especially graceful styles
- dressing with sophistication
- eating out in romantic settings
- the scientific side of cooking
- computers
- any kind of discussion group

LIBRAN HEALTH

Typical Libras have a tendency to become sick if they are obliged to live or work alone for long periods. Otherwise Libras are generally healthy people and recover from any medical problem very quickly when they are in beautiful, calm surroundings.

Types of sickness

Back problems are typical, as are any diseases of the kidneys, liver, and skin. Whatever the physical problem, a Libra puts on a brave face in public and will respond very positively to a lot of fuss and attention from their loved ones and friends.

The Libra at rest

A typical Libra loves a luxurious bedroom where he or she can lie around in blissful indolence. While at rest, the Libran mind is rarely still, always planning ahead.

Parts of the body linked to Libra
Traditionally, the parts of the body linked with a
strong Libra influence are as shown in the
diagram below. Only the individual birth chart will
show if one or more of these parts of the body
have inherited a strength or a vulnerability. Any
generalization would be misleading.

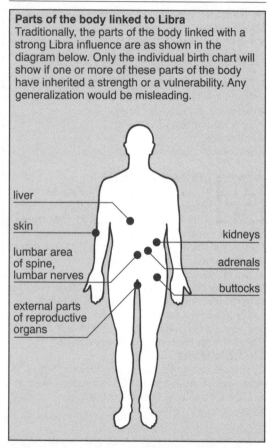

liver

skin

lumbar area
of spine,
lumbar nerves

external parts
of reproductive
organs

kidneys

adrenals

buttocks

Famous Libras

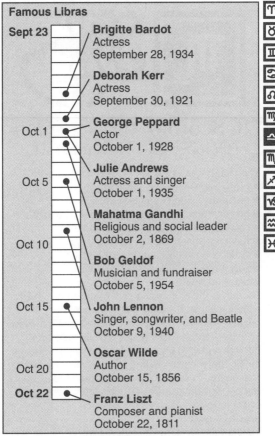

Sept 23

Brigitte Bardot
Actress
September 28, 1934

Deborah Kerr
Actress
September 30, 1921

Oct 1

George Peppard
Actor
October 1, 1928

Julie Andrews
Actress and singer
October 1, 1935

Oct 5

Mahatma Gandhi
Religious and social leader
October 2, 1869

Oct 10

Bob Geldof
Musician and fundraiser
October 5, 1954

Oct 15

John Lennon
Singer, songwriter, and Beatle
October 9, 1940

Oscar Wilde
Author
October 15, 1856

Oct 20

Oct 22

Franz Liszt
Composer and pianist
October 22, 1811

8. Scorpio: the Scorpion
October 23 – November 21

The eighth sign of the zodiac is concerned with
• birth, life, death, sex, sensuality
• passion, pushing boundaries of discovery
• regeneration, transformation, metamorphosis
• finance, investments, wills, inheritance
• hidden matters, secrets, taboos, magic
• collective unconscious, defense systems
• social revolution, reformation, change

Elemental quality

Scorpio is the fixed water sign of the zodiac. It can
be likened to still waters that run deep. The
relentless power of water to penetrate and transform
even the hardest rocks is an excellent metaphor
through which to understand the driving passion of
the Scorpionic personality. Just as stalactites and
stalagmites cannot be prevented from growing, once
started, Scorpio cannot easily be deflected from his
or her purpose.

Spiritual goal

To learn the meaning of selfless love.

THE SCORPIONIC PERSONALITY

These are the general personality traits found in people who are typical of this sign. An unhappy or frustrated Scorpio may display some of the not-so-attractive traits.

Characteristics	
Positive	Negative
• Self-critical	• Self-destructive
• Penetrating	• Ruthless
• Investigative	• Overbearing
• Passionately caring	• Suspicious
• Protective	• Jealous
• Tenacious	• Possessive
• Magnetic	• Dangerous
• Dynamic	• Quick-tempered
• Probing	• Obstinate
• Emotional	• Moody
• Sensual	• Sadistic
• Compassionate	• Insulting
• Concerned	• Secretive
• Unshockable	• Intolerant
• Intense	• Cunning
concentration	• Vindictive
• Understands failings	

Secret Scorpio

Inside anyone who has strong Scorpionic influences is a person who is intractable and impenetrable, so the secret Scorpio usually remains a secret. All

Scorpios like to keep their true nature as hidden as possible. Astrologically, a Scorpio is said to be at one or other of three stages of evolution.

A "stage one" Scorpio exercises power through emotion and instinct. This Scorpio is symbolized by the scorpion, an insect more likely, in the end, to sting itself than others.

The "stage two" type exercises power through the intellect. This Scorpio is symbolized by the golden eagle – a bird that soars higher than any other.

At the final stage of evolution, Scorpio exercises power through love. This Scorpio is symbolized by the dove of peace.

Ruling planet and its effect

Both Mars and Pluto rule the zodiac sign of Scorpio, so anyone whose birth chart has a strong Scorpio influence will tend to have two drives – one influenced by the battling energy of Mars and the other by the hidden depths of Pluto. In astrology, Mars is the planet of aggression, and Pluto is the planet of magnetic forces.

Scorpionic lucky connections	
Colors	deep red, blue-green
Plants	cactus, ivy, oak
Perfume	Siamese benzoin
Gemstones	turquoise, ruby
Metals	iron, steel
Tarot card	Death (regeneration)
Animals	wolf, gray lizard

THE SCORPIONIC LOOK

People who exhibit the physical characteristics distinctive of the sign of Scorpio have eyes that look at the world with almost hypnotic intensity. Eye color and shape can vary widely, but if someone looks at you with deep penetration it is a sign of a personality strongly influenced by Scorpio.

Physical appearance
• broad face with wide forehead and thick neck
• strongly built body of middle stature
• generally slender with broad shoulders
• intense eyes

THE SCORPIO MALE

If a man behaves in a way typical of the personality associated with the zodiac sign of Scorpio, he will have a tendency toward the characteristics listed below, unless there are influences in his personal birth chart that are stronger than that of his Scorpio sun sign.

Appearance
The typical Scorpio man
• has strong features
• has penetrating eyes
• has thick eyebrows
• has hairy arms and legs
• has a well-proportioned figure
• has an athletic body
• has a tendency to be bowlegged

Behavior and personality traits

The typical Scorpio man

- is never self-effacing
- is possessive of what he believes belongs to him
- has to maintain his dignity
- is a law unto himself and is most courageous in adversity
- will give absolutely honest advice, appraisal, or compliments
- will move mountains to help someone
- is intensely loyal to friends
- never forgets a kindness or an injury
- can be a saint or a sinner, but pursues either course with great zeal

 THE SCORPIO FEMALE

If a woman behaves in a way that is distinctive of the personality associated with the zodiac sign of Scorpio, she will have a tendency toward the characteristics listed below, providing there are no influences in her personal birth chart that are stronger than that of her Scorpio sun sign.

Appearance

The typical Scorpio woman

- has a compact and well-proportioned body
- has legs that are often short and thick
- is slender, but has a rather thick waist
- has attractive looks, even when frowning
- inclines her head downward even when looking intensely at a person

Behavior and personality traits

The typical Scorpio woman

- is poised and apparently cool
- never uses flattery
- only smiles when she means it
- wants total freedom of action
- regards flirting and flattery as insulting
- wants to dominate but can accept some restriction in order to win in the end
- has many talents, all used with passion
- is loyal to family and home
- sets and keeps to her own standards

YOUNG SCORPIO

If a child behaves in a way that is distinctive of the personality associated with the zodiac sign of Scorpio, he or she will have a tendency toward the characteristics listed below.

Behavior and personality traits

The typical Scorpio child

- enjoys a good fight and intends to win
- will learn only from a person seen as stronger
- keeps his or her own thoughts secret
- can find out everyone else's secrets easily
- has an instinctive understanding of adult problems
- can often bear pain well
- will be loving and loyal to family and friends
- will take revenge on others who break his/her favorite toys
- knows what he/she wants and attempts to get it
- is suspicious of strangers

Bringing up young Scorpio
Scorpio children are usually active, quick to learn, and intelligent. They have a passionate curiosity which needs satisfying. They should be tactfully guided away from too much interest in forbidden areas, as they are fascinated by anything that is hidden, mysterious, or a private part of someone else's life!

The best way to love a Scorpio child is to always be loyal and to make it possible for him or her to follow an interest in science, medicine, magic, engineering, sports, and literature.

Young Scorpio's needs A private place is essential for Scorpionic children – somewhere they can be alone and undisturbed. It could be a room of their own or even just a closet. It might be a secret hiding place or a little box with a key. A secret hiding place gives the Scorpio child a sense of security.

What to teach young Scorpio Understanding the rights and needs of others is an important lesson for young Scorpio. In this way, Scorpio children learn to forgive the hurts and mishaps of everyday life.

 SCORPIO AT HOME
If a person has the personality that is typical of those born with a Scorpio sun sign, home is a place to be proud of, and he or she will have a tendency toward the following characteristics.

Typical behavior and abilities

When at home, a Scorpio man or woman
- makes the home self-contained
- is protective of children
- is gentle with the sick
- guards home territory jealously
- likes the home kept clean and orderly
- expresses good taste
- enjoys comfort

Scorpio as parent

The typical Scorpio parent
- is strict about rules
- demands high standards
- enjoys the children
- keeps the children busy
- often takes the children out
- finds it hard to change viewpoints and to bridge the generation gap
- cares passionately about the family
- remains his or her child's friend throughout life

Two Scorpios in the same family

They will understand each other only too well. Two Scorpios mean double the passion, and it is essential that both have the facilities to follow their own passionate interests, so that no jealousies arise. Two Scorpios can get along well, provided each has a space of his or her own that is private.

The greatest problems could arise from sexual jealousy if the two are of the same sex and age group. However, in the final analysis, the Scorpionic loyalty to family will overcome all other problems.

SCORPIO AT WORK

At work, the person who has a typical Scorpionic personality will exhibit the following characteristics.

Typical behavior and abilities

A typical Scorpio at work

- will eventually know everyone's secrets
- will sense the moods of other people
- is indefatigable
- will excel as a team leader
- will appear to be calm in all situations

Scorpio as employer

A typical Scorpio boss (male or female)

- will demand total loyalty
- will do anything to help someone he/she likes
- will solve even the most difficult problems
- will never reveal the depth of his or her competitiveness
- confronts problems directly
- will be concerned and compassionate toward the workers' families, regarding them as part of the team

Scorpio as employee

A typical Scorpio employee (male or female)

- is self-motivated
- knows what he/she wants to achieve
- will take any amount of criticism from someone who has something he/she wants
- will accept failure as inevitable only when the odds are overwhelming
- is tenacious, intense, and career minded
- does not waste time and is not a clock-watcher

Working environment

The workplace of a typical Scorpio man or woman

- suggests an air of quiet confidence
- is usually tidy, or at least orderly
- contains nothing superfluous to the job
- contains equipment that helps Scorpio increase knowledge and undertake shrewd analysis

Typical occupations

Scorpios enjoy solving mysteries and penetrating the secrets of life. They love to get to the heart of any problem, human or mechanical.

They may be detectives, pathologists, surgeons, scientists, researchers, undertakers, sewage workers, insurers, market analysts, butchers, members of the armed services, or pharmacists.

Any occupation which Scorpios feel is important and offers the opportunity to investigate and analyze complex problems will satisfy them. Scorpios can run a big business or a small enterprise as long as they feel that they are achieving something.

SCORPIO AND LOVE

To Scorpio, love is an intensely passionate and enduring emotion that may be directed at one person only. Love is central to the life of typical Scorpios and inspires many of their ambitions and actions. Scorpio in love will have many of the following characteristics.

Behavior when in love

The typical Scorpio

- is deeply attached to the loved one
- attracts the loved one like a magnet
- is possessive
- hides emotions in public
- keeps dependence on the loved one hidden
- is faithful when in love
- dominates the loved one
- remains true to his/her own feelings

Expectations

The typical Scorpio expects

- absolute faithfulness and loyalty
- demonstrative love
- no great emphasis on romance
- genuine tenderness
- acknowledgment of how lucky the loved one is
  to be party to Scorpio's secrets

The end of an affair

If a Scorpio has an affair, it is often because the
sexual life within the marriage has serious problems.
Scorpios seem able to attract partners without much
effort, and they will take the upper hand from the
start, so that ending an affair is an easy matter.
However, the Scorpio who is rejected is always very
wounded and may want to take revenge. Some
Scorpios immediately attempt to hurt their ex-
partner. Others take their revenge in more subtle
ways over a period of time. A rejected Scorpio is
unlikely to forgive and will never forget the hurt.

SCORPIO AND SEX

When a typical Scorpio makes love, it is an expression of all the pent-up passion that is hidden inside this most magnetic of personalities. Sex is an important element of life to a Scorpio.

Indeed, Scorpio is the zodiac sign that indicates the greatest interest in sexual matters.

As in other areas of their life, Scorpios are liable to be both inventive and single-minded – but for most Scorpios, sex is very much an expression of love.

SCORPIO AND PARTNER

The person who contemplates becoming the marriage or business partner of a typical Scorpio must realize that Scorpio will expect to dominate the partnership.

Given this, the person who partners Scorpio can expect unwavering loyalty, hard work, and a passionate drive to succeed – whether in business or marriage.

Scorpio man as partner

In business, the Scorpio man will inevitably be in charge of the partnership and is most likely to have initiated the terms of agreement. A Scorpio who accepts orders from a partner is doing so for a particular reason. For example, if money or future progress are the reward, Scorpio will appear to accept even a subordinate position for as long as it takes to achieve the results he wants.

Scorpio will be proud of his partner and his partner's

skills, and he will go out of his way to enable the partner to achieve ambitions, too.

Scorpio woman as partner

A Scorpio woman is often even more subtle than her male counterpart. She happily accepts the subordinate role and plays this part well. Again, however, this is only so that she can achieve her ambition in the end.

Like her male counterpart, she will be loyal to the partner and do everything to help the partner. Scorpios can work very hard, and they often provide the dynamic quality in a business.

It is unlikely that Scorpio and her partner will have an equal footing. The Scorpio will, in reality, have the edge on the partner – but only in ways that the Scorpio sees will be helpful to the joint venture. Scorpio shrewdness is a vital asset in any partnership.

Opposite sign

Taurus is the complementary opposite sign to Scorpio. From Taurus, Scorpio can learn to recognize the talents of other people and appreciate their value. In this way, Scorpio can learn to value his or her own talents more realistically, because Scorpio is more self-critical than critical of others and often reproaches himself or herself.

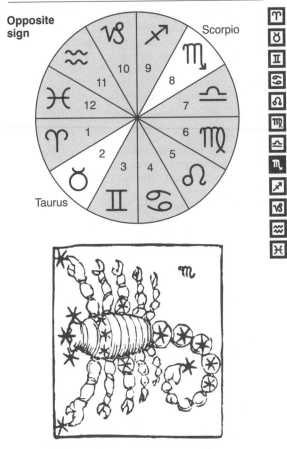

Opposite sign

Scorpio

Taurus

SCORPIO AND FRIENDS

In general, Scorpio likes a friend who recognizes Scorpio's magnetic superiority without fear or undue compliments.

Scorpio chooses only a few friends and expects loyalty from them. Scorpio is not a natural socializer, but will keep close friends for many years.

Positive factors

Scorpios have good memories and enjoy telling jokes. They are generous and hospitable toward friends, and also make strangers welcome when they call for help or advice.

Friends of Scorpios will be treated like family and given every help and consideration. Whenever Scorpio gives a friend advice it will be reliable. A friend can also trust Scorpio never to gossip.

Negative factors

Scorpios are unlikely to visit friends without making arrangements and having a good reason. Scorpios like others to do the visiting. If they are out when a friend comes to visit, their attitude is that it is the friend's loss and that the friend will have to visit again.

Scorpios have an almost psychic insight into the motives and secrets of their friends. Anyone who dislikes someone knowing their secrets should stay away from Scorpios.

A compatibility chart, opposite, lists those with whom Scorpio is likely to have the most satisfactory relationships.

Compatibility chart
In general, if people are typical of their zodiac sign, relationships between Scorpio and other signs (including the complementary opposite sign, Taurus) are as shown below

	Harmonious	Difficult	Turbulent
Scorpio	●		
Sagittarius	●		
Capricorn	●		
Aquarius		●	
Pisces	●		
Aries			●
Taurus		●	
Gemini			●
Cancer	●		
Leo		●	
Virgo	●		
Libra	●		

SCORPIONIC LEISURE INTERESTS

Finding out how things work, taking something apart and reconstructing it, or delving into the mysteries of the human mind are all of interest to Scorpios, who also enjoy a variety of sports. Winning is important to them.

On the whole, typical Scorpios pursue the following leisure interests:

- any sport that demands shrewd tactics
- competitive driving, flying, or cycling
- scientific hobbies
- archeology, anthropology, psychology
- detective novels, treasure hunts, caving
- breeding animals or plants

Scorpionic likes and dislikes

Likes

- activity
- mysteries
- secrets
- winning

- sex
- being acknowledged
- home

Dislikes

- being analyzed
- being asked personal questions
- people who know more than they do

- too many compliments
- having to trust a stranger

SCORPIONIC HEALTH

Typical Scorpios are rarely sick. When they do become ill it is generally serious, but they have the willpower to get well. Scorpios can destroy their own health by allowing themselves to get depressed or by doing too much hard work.

Types of sickness

Some Scorpios are prone to accidents due to their burning desire to finish a job or get somewhere more quickly than anyone else.

Nose and throat problems, hernias, piles, bladder disorders, and problems with the reproductive organs are the most common Scorpio illnesses.

The phoenix symbolizes Scorpio's activities, and in matters of health, it seems that Scorpio has a tremendous ability to rise from the metaphoric ashes of sickness and fly again.

Scorpio at rest

Scorpios often find it hard to relax. Some Scorpios will even avoid situations where they can relax. When on vacation, they often seem to have a small accident or minor illness in the first days.

Many Scorpios try to relax by continuing to work because of the intense pressure they put on themselves to finish everything before leaving for that much-needed rest. Their best policy is to have an alternative interest or hobby that they can pursue with passion, thus giving them relaxation from their main work. This especially applies to Scorpios who are homemakers and parents caring for children, as they may find it difficult to take even a short break.

Parts of the body linked to Scorpio
Traditionally, the parts of the body linked with a strong Scorpio influence are as shown in the diagram below. Only the individual birth chart will show if one or more of these parts of the body have inherited a strength or a vulnerability. Any generalization would be misleading.

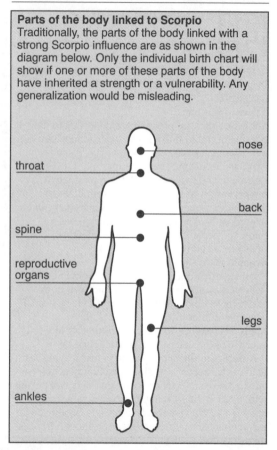

nose

throat

back

spine

reproductive organs

legs

ankles

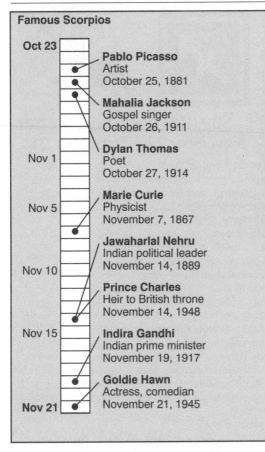

Famous Scorpios

Oct 23

Pablo Picasso
Artist
October 25, 1881

Mahalia Jackson
Gospel singer
October 26, 1911

Dylan Thomas
Poet
October 27, 1914

Nov 1

Marie Curie
Physicist
November 7, 1867

Nov 5

Jawaharlal Nehru
Indian political leader
November 14, 1889

Nov 10

Prince Charles
Heir to British throne
November 14, 1948

Nov 15

Indira Gandhi
Indian prime minister
November 19, 1917

Goldie Hawn
Actress, comedian
November 21, 1945

Nov 21

9. Sagittarius: the Archer
November 22 – December 21

The ninth sign of the zodiac is concerned with
- philosophy, idealism, religion, spiritual growth
- optimism, positive outlook, forward planning
- travel, freedom of movement, the outdoors
- honesty, justice, morality
- imagination, aspirations, open-mindedness
- wit, intellect, flashes of intuition
- generosity, pleasure, romance

Elemental quality

Sagittarius is the mutable fire sign of the zodiac. It
can be likened to stars, a thousand lighted candles,
the sparks rising from a rapidly spreading grass fire,
or the reflectors marking the route along the center
of a major road.

Fire changes substances and Sagittarians have a
knack of transforming negative situations with their
optimism. Mutable means adaptable. Sagittarians
can adapt to almost any situation, whether earthly or
spiritual.

Spiritual goal

To learn to use their talents to guide others.

2 THE SAGITTARIAN PERSONALITY

These are the general personality traits found in people who are typical of Sagittarius. An unhappy or frustrated Sagittarius may display some of the not-so-attractive traits.

Characteristics

Positive	Negative
• Frank and open	• Argumentative
• Optimistic	• Impatient to be
• Sees the best in	moving
people	• Critical of those who
• Honest and	deny their talents
fair-minded	• A gambler at heart
• Spiritual	• Can be a fanatic
• Enthusiastic	• Hotheaded
• Inspiring	• Fails to plan
• Disarmingly happy	adequately
• Stimulating	• Tends to preach
• Happy-go-lucky	• Denies sadness
• Holds no grudges	• Uncommitted
• Sensual	• Fears any
	responsibility that
	curtails freedom
	• Blundering and inept
	• Indulgent

Secret Sagittarius

Inside anyone who has strong Sagittarian influences is a person who wants to be free. Possessive partners, conservative thinkers, and bureaucrats with

whom Sagittarius comes into contact should be
aware of this.

No matter who or what the cause, the Sagittarian
who is held back in life, in love, or in opportunity
for spiritual growth will be unhappy, even though he
or she will keep smiling through all adversities.

Like the centaur, one of the Sagittarian symbols, the
Sagittarian personality experiences conflict between
mind and body. The Sagittarian purpose is to
overcome this conflict so that they may guide others.

Ruling planet and its effect

Jupiter rules the zodiac sign of Sagittarius, so
anyone whose birth chart has a strong Sagittarius
influence will tend to be expansive, pleasure-loving,
benevolent, and have a strong sense of justice.

In astrology, Jupiter is the planet of beneficence.
Psychologically, Jupiter is linked with wisdom and
is the guide to the psyche.

Sagittarian lucky connections	
Colors	blue, royal blue, purple, white
Plants	rush, oak, fig, hyssop
Perfume	lignaloes
Gemstones	jacinth, lapis lazuli
Metal	tin
Tarot card	temperance
Animals	horse, dog

THE SAGITTARIAN LOOK

People who exhibit the physical characteristics distinctive of the sign of Sagittarius look strong and active. They are often taller than average and have handsome faces. Since a typical Sagittarius is an optimist, the face often appears about to break into a smile – and regularly does.

Physical appearance

- Body: strongly built and energetic; movement is normally quick, although not always graceful
- Head: large, well-shaped skull with a high, broad forehead
- Uses hands and arms to make broad, sweeping gestures
- Bright, intelligent, and sparkling eyes which often twinkle with good humor
- Either tall and athletic in appearance, or shorter with a sturdier body. Excess weight can be a problem, as Sagittarius is ruled by expansive, jovial, life-loving Jupiter

THE SAGITTARIUS MALE

If a man behaves in a way typical of the personality associated with the zodiac sign of Sagittarius, he will have a tendency toward the characteristics listed below, unless there are influences in his personal birth chart that are stronger than that of his Sagittarius sun sign.

Appearance

The typical Sagittarius man

- can be likened to a lively horse and often has a

mane of hair that falls over the forehead and has to
be tossed away. In later life, the Sagittarius may
become bald, yet still retain a youthful look

- is physically noticeable because of his strong
  sense of confidence
- will retain his physical faculties to a very old age

Behavior and personality traits

The typical Sagittarius man

- is a risk taker
- says exactly what is on his mind
- enjoys physical danger
- has an unerringly accurate wit
- has a good memory for facts, but often forgets
  where he has left everyday objects such as keys
- is trusting until let down
- can tell really funny jokes, but often fluffs the
  punch line – which makes the joke even funnier
- may be tactless but is never deliberately cruel
- likes learning, study, and creative interpretation

 THE SAGITTARIUS FEMALE

If a woman behaves in a way that is
distinctive of the personality associated
with the zodiac sign of Sagittarius, she
will have a tendency toward the characteristics listed
below, providing there are no influences in her
personal birth chart that are stronger than that of her
Sagittarius sun sign.

Appearance

The typical Sagittarius woman

- has an oval face, a high forehead, and a
  pointed chin

- has a tall and slender body
- has eyes that are steady, bright, open, and honest
- has movement that is purposeful and even graceful

Behavior and personality traits

The typical Sagittarius woman

- is honest
- enjoys freedom of thought and travel
- will laugh about her misfortunes and mistakes, even while she is upset or in pain
- is angry if her integrity is questioned
- is kindhearted, though sometimes tactless
- can be deceived in romance, but is rarely misled in other areas of life
- enjoys taking risks, both physical and intellectual
- is often unconventional in relationships
- sticks by her own very clear moral standards
- can be cuttingly sarcastic when hurt
- regards herself and all others as equals

YOUNG SAGITTARIUS

If a child behaves in a way that is distinctive of the personality associated with the zodiac sign of Sagittarius, he or she will have a tendency toward the characteristics listed below.

Behavior and personality traits

The typical Sagittarius child

- is a happy, playful little clown
- greets everyone and is despondent if others don't say "Hello"
- acts on impulse

- is active, interested in many things, and usually adores animals
- tends to get more bumps, bruises, and cuts than many children because he or she is so adventurous and rarely sits still
- gives and expects total honesty
- enjoys company
- when left on his or her own will hug a teddy bear or a blanket
- asks endless questions
- expects to be trusted

Bringing up young Sagittarius

Most young Sagittarians enjoy learning but dislike being held back by what they see as needless rules. They are capable of setting their own standards and should be encouraged to do so. A frustrated Sagittarian child can turn from being a happy-go-lucky optimist into an angry, sarcastic adult; therefore, it is important that the child be allowed to take any opportunities for learning and socializing. Sagittarian children question adult values and poke fun at adult hypocrisy. The best thing that the parents of a Sagittarian can do is to be totally honest.

Young Sagittarius's needs Love is essential to all children, but the way it is given varies. In the case of young Sagittarius, there should be no pressure or possessiveness, but love should be given by way of encouragement and by showing pleasure. Young Sagittarians hide their hurts, disappointments, and sorrows behind a spirited belief that everything must get better. The clown who laughs while his or her heart is breaking is behaving in a very Sagittarian way.

What to teach young Sagittarius These restless, freedom-loving children need to be taught that there are some social rules that must be obeyed for their own good.

Handling money is another Sagittarian weakness, so a few practical lessons should be given: for example, not supplementing an allowance that has been rashly spent. Economy does not come naturally to generous, expansive Sagittarians.

Wise parents will teach their Sagittarian offspring the facts of life from an early age, so that they are well prepared when their adventures become romantic.

SAGITTARIUS AT HOME

If a person has the personality that is typical of those born with a Sagittarius sun sign, home is a place to rest the mind and body before moving off on the next trip. He or she will have a tendency toward the characteristics listed below.

Typical behavior and abilities

When at home, a Sagittarius man or woman
- could be almost anywhere; Sagittarians make their home wherever they happen to be; some have, or would like, several homes, while others may be permanent travelers. It is not unusual for Sagittarians to spend time living abroad, or to divide their time between two different countries
- is usually planning for the next journey
- is not naturally domesticated
- enjoys making and receiving social visits

- does not enjoy formality, but loves informal
  gatherings where he/she is free to roam

Sagittarius as parent

The typical Sagittarius parent

- has very clear moral standards
- has faith in the children
- may expect too much intellectually
- will provide a very stimulating home
- will be eager to play with children, talk with them,
  and take them on travels
- enjoys the children and is great fun as a parent
- will always answer questions honestly
- will encourage the children to leave home
  when grown up

Two Sagittarians in the same family

Sagittarians are not usually very good at family
relationships because they are natural wanderers and
resume contact sporadically. Hence, two typical
Sagittarians in the same family should get along
perfectly well; each will understand the other's need
for freedom of thought and action. Two Sagittarian
children are apt to get into more physical scrapes,
since they are both risk takers.

SAGITTARIUS AT WORK

At work, the person who has a typical
Sagittarian personality will exhibit the
following characteristics.

Typical behavior and abilities

A typical Sagittarian at work

- needs a challenge, so even in the dullest, most
  routine job, he or she will seek challenges

- is versatile
- needs to do several things at once
- may have two jobs
- needs intellectual and physical exercise
- gets tired only when bored

Sagittarius as employer

A typical Sagittarian boss (male or female)

- is rarely naturally tactful and may be quite blunt
- has a sense of overall planning, although they may overlook details
- expects people to be straightforward
- can be erratic and hard to tie down
- can promote anything extremely well
- can boost morale and will fight for what he/she believes is right
- is generally cheerful
- is kind and understanding

Sagittarius as employee

A typical Sagittarian employee (male or female)

- works best when allowed to get on with the job at their own speed – which is usually fast
- is cheerful and does not complain
- is enthusiastic, willing, and generally ahead of everyone else
- enjoys praise and will promise almost anything
- is interested in current pay but not in long-term career plans
- will boost everyone's spirits when they are depressed

Working environment

The workplace of a typical Sagittarian man or woman

- is wherever they are – they take their tools with them
- will be open and airy
- may be decorated imaginatively

Typical occupations

Anything in sales and promotion that involves travel and knowledge of foreign languages; anything that allows Sagittarius to perform; and any career that involves learning and the use of the intellect such as teacher, lawyer, or writer. A Sagittarius will be attracted to work that combines intellect and physical activity, such as veterinary practice, or indeed any kind of work with animals.

 SAGITTARIUS AND LOVE

To Sagittarius, love is a romantic adventure. Sagittarius in love will have many of the characteristics listed below.

Behavior when in love

The typical Sagittarius

- enjoys love on the move in foreign places
- is inventive
- needs good intellectual compatibility
- is totally honest with the loved one
- enjoys the physical pleasures of love
- is happy when he or she is loved
- is very generous and good-natured

Expectations

The typical Sagittarius expects

- not to be tied down
- to feel secure in love
- the loved one to be honest
- to retain freedom of movement
- never to be falsely accused of philandering
- to stimulate, amuse, and be enjoyed by the loved one

The end of an affair

If a partner is possessive or jealous of Sagittarius, the relationship will begin to crack. Eventually, these pressures will cause Sagittarius to simply pack up and move on.

Sagittarians enjoy meeting people and may indulge in the occasional affair. On the whole, the attraction of the affair will be its excitement, rather than true romance. Sagittarius is prone to look elsewhere if an existing relationship becomes routine.

SAGITTARIUS AND SEX

A typical Sagittarius regards love as another adventure to be enjoyed and explored. Sagittarians tend to take a chance on love, and they enter a relationship with the same recklessness that they display in other activities. In the relationship, he or she will be warm and loving and a wonderful companion.

Sagittarians normally enjoy a lot of touching and cuddling – a good, warm, loving hug is their form of security blanket. Common intellectual interests are equally essential to the success of any long-term sexual relationship.

SAGITTARIUS AND PARTNER

The person who contemplates becoming the marriage or business partner of a typical Sagittarius must realize that Sagittarius will value his or her freedom above everything. Given this, the person who partners Sagittarius can expect honesty and plenty of creative ideas.

Sagittarian man as partner

He will want a partner who enjoys spontaneity and who will appreciate his grand gestures and courageous outbursts of enthusiasm. He will also want a partner who will not try to control him.

In business, a person who has a sound understanding of financial matters would make the perfect partner.

Sagittarian woman as partner

Frank and friendly, she wants a partner who can love her for her outspoken charm, not wilt under it. Her words and actions will always show what she is thinking and feeling, so a potential partner should be quite clear about his own feelings. Sagittarian women are neither coy nor evasive, and will want a partner who does not play silly games. In marriage or in business, a partner must always ask her to do something, never tell her. However, she will respond to hints.

Opposite sign

Gemini is the complementary opposite sign to Sagittarius. Although relationships between the two may have some difficulties, Sagittarius can learn from Gemini how to notice and take account of details. In this way, Sagittarians can become inspiring guides, lighting the way for others, rather than leading them by preaching what the route should be.

Sagittarius

Gemini

SAGITTARIUS AND FRIENDS

In general, Sagittarius likes a friend who is open-minded, ready for an adventure, and trusting.

Positive factors

Sagittarians are friendly, gregarious people who accept any friend who matches up to their personal standards. They will defend a friend with great loyalty, but they will also say exactly what they think.

Sagittarians have friends from many walks of life. Among those are likely to be both men and women, straight and gay people, a range of ages, and a mixture of ethnic groups; they will all be treated as equals.

Sagittarians respond to all calls for help. They will lend a friend money without expecting it to be repaid; they take in stray animals and stray people and will support any cause in the name of friendship.

Negative factors

Close friendship with just one or two people is not the Sagittarian norm. In fact, anyone who tries to get too familiar with or who takes advantage of the Sagittarian natural friendliness, may be struck by the fiery rocket of Sagittarian temper. They generally fight with words, as sharp as darts, but some may also use their fists.

Sagittarians can be eccentric and may find it difficult to keep a secret.

A compatibility chart, opposite, lists those with whom Sagittarius is likely to have the most satisfactory relationships.

 ## SAGITTARIAN LEISURE INTERESTS

Sagittarians are versatile and like to kick against authority, so their leisure interests may be both varied and radical. Sports are natural activities for Sagittarians, who enjoy them for the social contact as much as for the competition.

A Sagittarian who has not traveled is unusual.

Compatibility chart

In general, if people are typical of their zodiac sign, relationships between Sagittarius and other signs (including the complementary opposite sign, Gemini) are as shown below

	Harmonious	Difficult	Turbulent
Sagittarius	●		
Capricorn	●		
Aquarius	●		
Pisces		●	
Aries	●		
Taurus			●
Gemini		●	
Cancer			●
Leo	●		
Virgo		●	
Libra	●		
Scorpio	●		

Long-distance travel to foreign places is one of the main Sagittarian interests. Some may prefer to "travel" in the world of literature or religion, but their travels will also be far and wide.

On the whole, typical Sagittarians pursue the following interests:

- gambling, gaming, racing cars, skydiving, and other risk-taking sports
- travel, exploration, cracking codes, tracking down mysteries, solving problems, speaking foreign languages, breeding animals, keeping pets
- religions, belief systems, new ways of being

Sagittarian likes and dislikes

Likes

• freedom of action	• perfumes and beauty aids
• alternative ideas	
• being on the move	• raffles and lotteries
• food and drink	• parties, flirting

Dislikes

• disapproval from others	• administration
• making promises	• tight clothes
• being too safe, secure, or confined	• having their honesty doubted

SAGITTARIAN HEALTH

Typical Sagittarians are healthy, energetic, and able to keep going in adversity. They hate to be confined to bed, unless it is to dream a little; any kind of routine will tax the Sagittarian optimism. However, their positive outlook helps them to overcome illnesses quickly and keeps them going if serious illness strikes.

Types of sickness

Diseases often linked with a Sagittarian influence in the chart are the whole range of arthritic and rheumatic problems, diseases that attack the hips and legs, and problems arising from the Sagittarian tendency to fall over, trip over, or collide with things.

Asthma is linked with Sagittarius, as are sicknesses caught from animals – Sagittarians are very fond of animals and like to be closely involved with them. Sagittarians tend to take physical risks, so accidents arising from dangerous sports can be expected from time to time. The jovial Jupiter influence is said to lead many a Sagittarian into indulgence in food or drink, and this may lead to health problems.

Sagittarius at rest

A typical Sagittarian never rests. A Sagittarius who lounges around looking bored is one who feels restricted and needs to break free again. The way that typical Sagittarians rest is by sleeping, thinking, and dreaming – and then moving off somewhere new.

Parts of the body linked to Sagittarius
Traditionally, the parts of the body linked with a
strong Sagittarius influence are as shown in the
diagram below. Only the individual birth chart will
show if one or more of these parts of the body
have inherited a strength or a vulnerability. Any
generalization would be misleading.

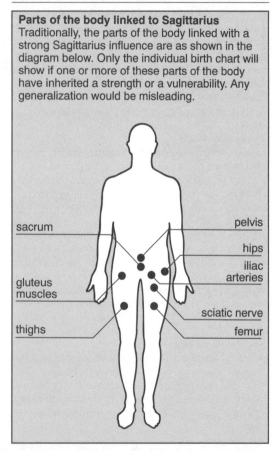

sacrum

pelvis

hips

iliac
arteries

gluteus
muscles

sciatic nerve

thighs

femur

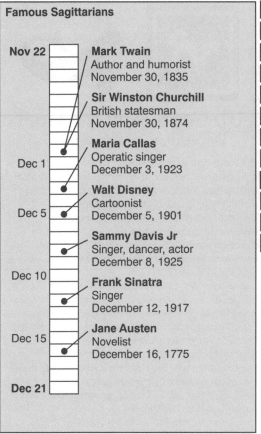

Famous Sagittarians

Nov 22

Mark Twain
Author and humorist
November 30, 1835

Sir Winston Churchill
British statesman
November 30, 1874

Maria Callas
Operatic singer
December 3, 1923

Dec 1

Walt Disney
Cartoonist
December 5, 1901

Dec 5

Sammy Davis Jr
Singer, dancer, actor
December 8, 1925

Dec 10

Frank Sinatra
Singer
December 12, 1917

Jane Austen
Novelist
December 16, 1775

Dec 15

Dec 21

10. Capricorn: the Goat
December 22 – January 19

The tenth sign of the zodiac is concerned with
- practicality, realism, hard work, accomplishment
- planning, determination, persistence, success
- high status, good quality, reputation
- responsibility, difficulties, problems
- paternalism, authority, discipline
- money, wealth, long-term projects
- wisdom, loyalty, sensitivity to beauty

Elemental quality

Capricorn is the cardinal earth sign of the zodiac. It can be likened to the oldest and most valuable tree in the forest.

Surefooted and thoroughly practical, in the end the Capricorn goat always reaches the heights, beating others who are faster but less determined.

The cardinal signs must put their resources to good use. Earth resources represent practical skills: material, financial, and social resources that can be used to further an ambition.

Spiritual goal
To learn to understand the feelings and needs of other people.

THE CAPRICORNEAN PERSONALITY

These are the general personality traits found in people who are typical of Capricorn. An unhappy or frustrated Capricorn may display some of the not-so-attractive traits.

Characteristics

Positive	Negative
• Good organizing skills	• Tendency to believe their way is always the best
• Cautious and realistic	• Egotistical
• Hard working	• A slave driver
• Scrupulous	• Unforgiving
• Fearless	• Anxious, allows inner fears to dominate decisions
• Calculates risks but takes them when necessary	• Takes a very critical view
• Is an admiring spectator	• A perfectionist who is never satisfied
• Has high but realistic standards	• Fatalistic
• Conventional	• Status seeking
• Concerned	
• Gives sound advice	
• Loyal to tradition	
• Respects authority	

♈
♉
♊
♋
♌
♍
♎
♏
♐
♑
♒
♓

Secret Capricorn

Inside anyone who has strong Capricornean influences is a person who worries about security – physical, social, and emotional. A typical Capricorn cannot bear to be embarrassed in public. Sometimes, Capricorn longs to let go a little and to allow themselves to join in the fun – let their toes tap in time with the music. But usually a sense of duty and a terrible fear of looking foolish stop them from acting out their desires. Capricorns are also secret romantics who want a perfect and secure love in their lives.

Ruling planet and its effect

Saturn rules the zodiac sign of Capricorn, so anyone whose birth chart has a strong Capricornean influence will tend to take life seriously.

In astrology, Saturn is the planet of fate, time, sorrow, caution, and wisdom. It is often called the great teacher, because Saturn is associated with the life-long task of gently working out our fears and overcoming them. Saturn is also the most beautiful of the planets.

Capricornean lucky connections	
Colors	green, black, gray, indigo, violet
Plants	yew, ash, hemp, weeping willow
Perfume	musk
Gemstones	jet, black diamond, onyx, ruby
Metal	lead
Tarot card	the devil
Animals	goat, ass

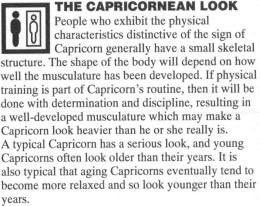

THE CAPRICORNEAN LOOK

People who exhibit the physical characteristics distinctive of the sign of Capricorn generally have a small skeletal structure. The shape of the body will depend on how well the musculature has been developed. If physical training is part of Capricorn's routine, then it will be done with determination and discipline, resulting in a well-developed musculature which may make a Capricorn look heavier than he or she really is.

A typical Capricorn has a serious look, and young Capricorns often look older than their years. It is also typical that aging Capricorns eventually tend to become more relaxed and so look younger than their years.

Physical appearance

- Forehead: narrower than average between the temples, with deep frown lines
- Style of walking: swift and sure because all typical Capricorns take great care of where they put their feet when they take each step

THE CAPRICORN MALE

If a man behaves in a way typical of the personality associated with the zodiac sign of Capricorn, he will have a tendency toward the characteristics listed below, unless there are influences in his personal birth chart that are stronger than that of his Capricorn sun sign.

Appearance

The typical Capricorn man

- is stocky

- has sharp, penetrating eyes
- rarely smiles
- has very strong white teeth
- is conscious of his appearance
- dislikes removing his clothes in public – for example, he will still be wearing a shirt during a heatwave when other men are bare-chested

Behavior and personality traits

The typical Capricorn man

- is dignified in his manner and very polite
- seems unapproachable and self-protective
- is totally reliable in pursuit of an aim
- takes his time sizing up other people before he will relax enough to share his inner warmth
- seeks honors but is not interested in becoming famous; on the contrary, he avoids publicity
- has strong opinions but is not at all vain

THE CAPRICORN FEMALE

If a woman behaves in a way that is distinctive of the personality associated with the zodiac sign of Capricorn, she will have a tendency toward the characteristics listed below, providing there are no influences in her personal birth chart that are stronger than that of her Capricorn sun sign.

Appearance

The typical Capricorn woman

- has a small and well-shaped body with slender neck
- has deep, serious eyes
- has an "earthy" beauty

- has a full mouth and very white teeth
- has shapely legs, slim ankles, small feet

Behavior and personality traits

The typical Capricorn woman
- is very self-conscious
- behaves in a ladylike manner in public
- dresses according to what she intends to achieve that day
- needs to gain recognition for her work
- appears as steady as a rock, but is quite moody inside herself
- runs a well-kept home, although she finds domesticity tedious
- is totally loyal to close family and distant relatives
- cannot bear to be teased
- smiles little, but when she does it is a very beautiful smile

YOUNG CAPRICORN

If a child behaves in a way that is distinctive of the personality associated with the zodiac sign of Capricorn, he or she will have a tendency toward the characteristics listed below.

Behavior and personality traits

The typical Capricorn child
- tends to prefer older company
- often looks very old when still a baby
- is self-contained and strong willed
- is usually even-tempered
- gets what he or she wants by slowly wearing down parental resistance

- likes the security of routine and orderliness
- has just one or two close friends
- enjoys pretending to be grown up
- usually loves reading
- likes to make things that have a practical use

Bringing up young Capricorn

Young Capricorns are not particularly enthusiastic about sports or the outdoors, so they need to be encouraged to spend time outside in the fresh air getting some exercise. Trips to museums, archeological sites, or even rock climbing are likely to satisfy them.

Usually, Capricorns work doggedly at school subjects and aim to get good grades and gain honors. It may be that they need to be encouraged to relax and play. They may seem very serious children, but they have a sense of humor; this needs to be encouraged – but not by teasing.

Young Capricorn's needs A secure, warm home with a regular routine and reliable, appreciative parents are essential to Capricorns. In spite of all their capable maturity, young Capricorns can lose self-confidence very easily.

What to teach young Capricorn Young Capricorn must be taught how to relax and take a rest from his or her responsibilities from time to time, or their life will become joyless. Young Capricorns need plenty of reassurance because they are natural worriers. Their diet and exercise routine should also be carefully handled, as young Capricorns are prone to illnesses. Their resistance to disease improves with age.

Sensitivity to other people's feelings and an understanding of other people's difficulties should be taught in practical situations – but without emotional pressure. Young Capricorns also need to be taught how to express their own very sensitive inner emotions in ways that will not cause them embarrassment.

CAPRICORN AT HOME

If a person has the personality that is typical of those born with a Capricorn sun sign, home is a place for enjoying the family as much as possible, and he or she will have a tendency toward the characteristics listed below.

Typical behavior and abilities

When at home, a Capricorn man or woman
- really enjoys providing for the family and having visits from relatives
- likes having a routine and an organized household
- wants quality furniture and fixtures
- is basically loyal to home and family
- needs home as a safe haven for personal pleasure and business entertaining

Capricorn as parent

The typical Capricorn parent
- is strict but always fair
- takes parenthood seriously
- has an ironic sense of humor
- provides the very best for the children
- is tender and sensitive
- has difficulty relating to young children, but will find it easier as they get older

- will teach the children good manners
- provides plenty of educational stimulation

Two Capricorns in the same family

Since the need for public recognition is basic to
Capricornean well-being, two Capricorns in the
same family will get along quite well, provided they
each have an area of endeavor in which they can
succeed and achieve some adulation from others.
On the whole, Capricorns are not jealous people; nor
are they quarrelsome, unless someone is trying to
give them orders. So Capricorn siblings or spouses
should remember never to try to make the other one
conform to his or her ideas of how things should be
done.

CAPRICORN AT WORK

At work, the person who has a typical
Capricorn personality will exhibit the
following characteristics.

Typical behavior and abilities

A typical Capricorn at work

- works hard and for long hours
- likes to have some home comforts in the
  workplace so he or she can change and go on to
  another appointment, or stay all night if necessary

Capricorn as employer

A typical Capricorn boss (male or female)

- does not neglect family life for business, and
  family members may visit him or her at work
- is kind but expects obedience to the rules
- has a strong sense of duty and works very hard
- is not a good mixer, but others trust him or her

- does not give perks but responds when people are in need
- takes responsibilities very seriously, and so may neglect personal needs
- dresses conservatively and is well organized
- can keep complex operations moving smoothly

Capricorn as employee

A typical Capricorn employee (male or female)

- arrives a little early and leaves late
- is dependable and can carry huge workloads
- minds his or her own business
- works steadily and quietly, staying with the same company a long time
- occasionally reveals a wry sense of humor
- is conscientious and aims high (for power not glory)
- will expect a salary in keeping with the work done
- has respect for superiors, elders, and those more experienced
- enjoys common-sense procedures

Working environment

The workplace of a typical Capricorn man or woman

- must be comfortable, like a home away from home
- must be tidy and well organized
- should have a framed photo of the family on the desk
- must not have money wasted on it unnecessarily

Typical occupations

Any occupation that requires good organization and smart management, but which does not require the

Capricorn to be the front person. Capricorns prefer to work in private. They generally make good bankers, systems analysts, accountants, researchers, dentists, architects, engineers, manufacturers, and politicians. Many Capricorns are jewelers, funeral directors, art dealers, anthropologists, and managers of musicians and other entertainers. They are also to be found on radio and television interview programs; their quiet, unflappable natures are perfect for serious work under pressure.

CAPRICORN AND LOVE

To Capricorn, love is the source of all inspiration. Shy, awkward with the opposite sex, and very much private people, Capricorns are, nevertheless, deeply interested in love and are reputed to be the most capable and loyal of lovers.

Capricorn in love will have many of the characteristics listed below.

Behavior when in love

The typical Capricorn

- is slow to make approaches and never flirts for fun
- only says "I love you" when it is meant and does not see any reason to keep repeating it
- may worry about the emotional aspect of the relationship
- must feel financially secure to enjoy love
- is caring, considerate, and committed to the loved one

Expectations

The typical Capricorn expects

- to be taken seriously
- to make a long-term commitment
- faithfulness
- privacy
- to make a home and family
- to be admired by the loved one

The end of an affair

Typical Capricorns do not have casual affairs. If the relationship begins to fail, it often takes Capricorns a long time to take action, as they have a strong sense of duty to the partner and the family. In general, they dislike divorce.

However, once a Capricorn realizes he or she has made a mistake in choosing a mate, then the parting will be abrupt and final.

If a partner betrays a Capricorn, he or she will try first to organize things so that the partner can be reunited with the family, but if the betrayal continues, Capricorns can turn vengeful.

CAPRICORN AND SEX

When a typical, mature Capricorn makes love, it is lovemaking at its very best: to Capricorn there is no separation between love and sex. Capricorns know by instinct when they have found the right partner for this immensely important ritual. For some people, sex is a release, the satisfying of one of the basic needs in life, but Capricorns want to reach a state of total satisfaction, not only for themselves but also for their partners.

CAPRICORN AND PARTNER

The person who contemplates becoming the marriage or business partner of a typical Capricorn must realize that Capricorn will take over the organization of the partner's working life. Given this, the person who partners Capricorn can expect stability, security, and success.

Capricorn man as partner

He will want a partner who can help him to achieve his ambitions.

He will want to organize the business and will expect absolute loyalty and a disciplined routine. He may assume that the partner is dependent on him.

Capricorn woman as partner

She seeks a partner who has a good, secure position in life already. She is more likely to make a bad choice of partner than the male Capricorn, but she will soon recognize her mistake. In business, Capricorn women do not often choose other women as partners.

If the partner, in marriage or business, is lost through death or similar misfortune, Capricorns of both sexes find it hard to replace the partner and will tend to withdraw into themselves.

Opposite sign

Cancer is the complementary opposite sign to Capricorn. Both are strong willed and may battle for supremacy concerning organization. However, Cancer can teach Capricorn how to sense other people's needs and feelings, and how to express his or her own emotions.

Opposite sign

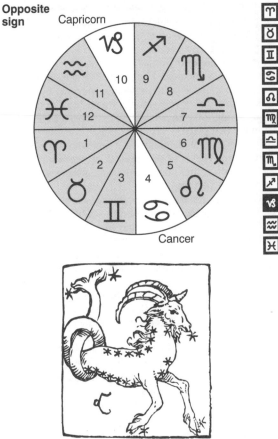

CAPRICORN AND FRIENDS
In general, Capricorn likes a friend who is well bred, good mannered, and not too extroverted.

Positive factors

Capricorns are loyal, kind, and often very generous to friends. They try to prove their sincerity by showing total devotion to the friendship, but this can go wrong if the choice of friend has been a bad one in the first place.

They will continue to love a friend who is old or disabled. They will not desert or neglect a loyal friend, no matter how bad the circumstances.

Negative factors

Capricorns are not very good judges of character. If a friendship goes wrong, because of bad judgment in the first place, Capricorn may turn hateful.

If a Capricorn suspects a friend of deception, he or she will start to suspect all friends. Sometimes Capricorn tests the trustworthiness of friends several times.

Capricorns have an irritating habit of organizing things that they think will be good for a friend, which the friend does not want. At their very worst, Capricorns may use a friend to further an ambition without a word of thanks.

A compatibility chart, opposite, lists those with whom Capricorn is likely to have the most satisfactory relationships.

Compatibility chart

In general, if people are typical of their zodiac sign, relationships between Capricorn and other signs (including the complementary opposite sign, Cancer) are as shown below

	Harmonious	Difficult	Turbulent
Capricorn	●		
Aquarius	●		
Pisces	●		
Aries		●	
Taurus	●		
Gemini			●
Cancer		●	
Leo			●
Virgo	●		
Libra		●	
Scorpio	●		
Sagittarius	●		

CAPRICORNEAN LEISURE INTERESTS

Most typical Capricorns are not much interested in team sports. They will work hard at a hobby and want to make a success of it. Whatever they choose to do, it must be respectable and increase their chances of being admired or honored.

Capricorns are so aware of their duties and responsibilities that they often find it very difficult to allow themselves to enjoy anything for its own

Capricornean likes and dislikes

Likes

- hot, simple food
- antiques, history
- duties and responsibilities
- not being pressured by others, having plenty of time
- sexual love
- privacy
- what is regarded as the best, such as a
- Rolls Royce
- membership of an exclusive club
- home and family
- personalized gifts
- new books
- expensive gemstones

Dislikes

- untidiness
- being teased
- familiarity
- surprises
- new ideas
- loneliness
- being made to feel useless
- being embarrassed in public

sake. As they get older and become grandparents, they tend to let loose a little and enjoy playing with their grandchildren.

On the whole, typical Capricorns pursue the following leisure interests:

- music, listening or playing
- golf, walking, playing chess, tactical games
- visiting museums, galleries, and the theater
- reading, gardening, improving the home

CAPRICORNEAN HEALTH

Typical Capricorns are likely to be less robust than most when they are young, but their resistance to disease increases with age. They are usually sober and temperate, so they often live to a ripe old age.

Worry, heavy responsibilities, gloomy moods, and general pessimism tend to take their toll on Capricornean health, so Capricorns need brightening up sometimes and should learn to relax.

Types of sickness

Many Capricorns seem to have some difficulty thrust upon them. Sometimes that problem may be a chronic illness but, if this is the case, they bear it with great fortitude.

Other sicknesses linked to Capricorn are rheumatism, bone diseases, sterility, damage to leg and knees, skin problems, and depression.

Capricorn at rest

A typical Capricorn likes to be doing something, even when relaxing. Many are to be found doing needlework or knitting while watching television.

Parts of the body linked to Capricorn
Traditionally, the parts of the body linked with a strong Capricorn influence are as shown in the diagram below. Only the individual birth chart will show if one or more of these parts of the body have inherited a strength or a vulnerability. Any generalization would be misleading.

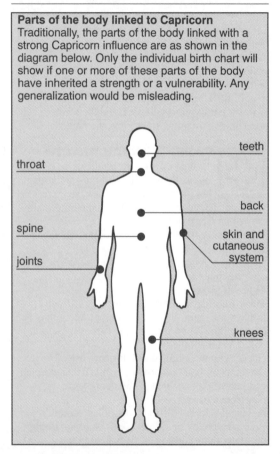

teeth

throat

back

spine

skin and cutaneous system

joints

knees

Famous Capricorns

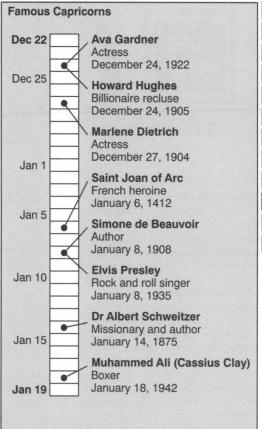

Dec 22

Ava Gardner
Actress
December 24, 1922

Dec 25

Howard Hughes
Billionaire recluse
December 24, 1905

Marlene Dietrich
Actress
December 27, 1904

Jan 1

Saint Joan of Arc
French heroine
January 6, 1412

Jan 5

Simone de Beauvoir
Author
January 8, 1908

Elvis Presley
Rock and roll singer
January 8, 1935

Jan 10

Dr Albert Schweitzer
Missionary and author
January 14, 1875

Jan 15

Muhammed Ali (Cassius Clay)
Boxer
January 18, 1942

Jan 19

11. Aquarius: the Water Carrier
January 20 – February 18

The eleventh sign of the zodiac is concerned with
- scientific analysis, experimentation, detachment
- friendship, courtesy, kindness, tranquillity
- mystery, intrigues, magic, genius, originality
- eccentricity, independence, humanitarian issues
- fame, recognition, politics, creative arts
- electricity, magnetism, telecommunications

Elemental quality

Aquarius is the fixed air sign of the zodiac. It can be likened to a paraglider, jumping off the earth to explore a rainbow, yet aware of the practicalities of thermals and how to ensure a safe landing.

Air represents the mind and the ability to think; Aquarian ideas may be unusual or even original, but once formed, they tend to remain fixed. Fixed air, in brief, is a metaphor for fixed opinions.

Spiritual goal

To learn how to develop true self-confidence.

THE AQUARIAN PERSONALITY

These are the general personality traits found in people who are typical of Aquarius. An unhappy or frustrated Aquarius may display some of the not-so-attractive traits.

Characteristics	
Positive	Negative
• Communicative	• Unwilling to share ideas
• Thoughtful and caring	• Tactless and rude
• Cooperative and dependable	• Perverse and eccentric individuality
• Scientific	• Self-interested
• Strong belief in humane reforms	• Unwillingness to fight for beliefs
• Independence of thought and action	• Uncertainty and lack of confidence
• Intense interest in people	• Voyeuristic curiosity about people
• Loyal friendship	
• Inventive	

Secret Aquarius

Inside anyone who has strong Aquarian influences is a person who is extremely uncertain of his or her true identity. The Aquarius ego is said to be the most precarious in the zodiac, probably because Aquarius is the sign of nonconformity. Intellectual genius, practical eccentricity and mental oddity are all linked with Aquarius.

The typical Aquarius personality has a magnetic and powerful intellect. Putting this to good, practical use is the best way for Aquarius to build an identifiable ego.

Ruling planet and its effect

Uranus and Saturn both rule the zodiac sign of Aquarius, so anyone whose birth chart has a strongly developed Aquarius influence will tend to have original, unexpected ideas. In astrology, Uranus is the planet of the unusual and the unexpected, and Saturn is the planet of applied wisdom and forward planning.

Aquarian lucky connections	
Colors	violet, light yellow
Plants	olive, aspen
Perfume	galbanum
Gemstones	glass, onyx, topaz, sapphire
Metal	lead
Tarot card	the star
Animals	peacock, eagle

 THE AQUARIAN LOOK

People who exhibit the physical characteristics distinctive of the sign of Aquarius often look like nonconformists.

Physical appearance

- There is a distant, dreamy look in the eyes
- Body: taller than average
- Head: in profile always noble with fine features

- Neck: bends to allow head to droop forward or tip to one side when thinking
- Movement is not graceful but has purpose

THE AQUARIUS MALE

If a man behaves in a way typical of the personality associated with the zodiac sign of Aquarius, he will have a tendency toward the characteristics listed below, unless there are influences in his personal birth chart that are stronger than that of his Aquarius sun sign.

Appearance

The typical Aquarius man

- is usually taller than average
- has long bones
- may have broad hips
- is strongly built
- has a distinctive facial profile
- has a high, broad forehead

Behavior and personality traits

The typical Aquarius man

- is unwilling to reveal his feelings
- is friendly toward everyone
- is a group person
- is fair minded and has his own very strong, but personal, moral code
- has wide interests
- is attracted to the mysterious and the secret
- is an intuitive thinker with a very practical streak
- does not usually aim to become rich but to develop his ideas and communicate them

THE AQUARIUS FEMALE

If a woman behaves in a way that is distinctive of the personality associated with the zodiac sign of Aquarius, she will have a tendency toward the characteristics listed below, providing there are no influences in her personal birth chart that are stronger than that of her Aquarius sun sign.

Appearance

The typical Aquarius woman

- may have broad shoulders
- has a large bone structure
- has a long neck
- ignores feminine conventions, but always dresses in such a way that she looks stunning

Behavior and personality traits

The typical Aquarius woman

- has a wide circle of friends from all walks of life
- is concerned about and deeply involved in the community
- is adept at getting people to settle feuds
- can be totally unpredictable
- has a wide variety of interests and a mind of her own
- will have a basic lack of self-confidence
- can be easygoing and accepts the many differences among people

YOUNG AQUARIUS

If a child behaves in a way that is distinctive of the personality associated with the zodiac sign of Aquarius, he or

she will have a tendency toward the characteristics
listed below.

Behavior and personality traits

The typical Aquarius child

- is a quick thinker
- is sensitive and intuitive
- is outwardly calm, relaxed, and delightful
- is unpredictable and full of amazing ideas
- wants to analyze everything and everyone
- does not like emotional demands
- rebels against commands and rules but comes to
  sensible conclusions when allowed to think things
  through for himself or herself
- is generous to friends
- has a huge number of friends of all kinds
- tends to be absentminded

Bringing up young Aquarius

Young Aquarius has an enquiring and analytical
mind and is constantly on the go. He or she needs
plenty of opportunity to make discoveries, try out
inventions and communicate ideas to others. Young
Aquarius tends to be detached and dispassionate,
finding close relationships difficult.

Young Aquarius's needs A peaceful, calm, and
harmonious environment is essential to young
Aquarius, because he or she is so sensitive to
underlying tensions.

Young Aquarius often looks more confident than he
or she is, so parental understanding and genuine
encouragement are needed. Like any child, Aquarius
needs love, especially in the form of respect,
listening, appreciation, and friendship.

What to teach young Aquarius Their minds are always working at lightning speed, so often they get into a mental muddle. Consequently, young Aquarius should be taught how to think logically. In practical terms, they will need to be taught simple methods for remembering things and for finding their way when they get physically lost.

 AQUARIUS AT HOME
If a person has the personality that is typical of those born with an Aquarius sun sign, home is a place where he or she can fully express unconventional ideas.

There are two types of Aquarius: the suave and the messy. He or she will have a tendency toward one of the sets of characteristics listed below.

Typical behavior and abilities
When at home, a suave Aquarius man or woman
- lives in a spacious, elegant apartment filled with interesting items
- eats unusual menus of gourmet food
- enjoys having houseguests from all walks of life

When at home, a messy Aquarian man or woman:
- lives in a tiny, untidy condo filled with oddities
- eats strange mixtures of plain food
- enjoys a wide variety of friends dropping in who feel at home in a creative mess
- leaves inventions lying around
- only washes up when in the right frame of mind

Aquarius as parent
The typical Aquarius parent
- is a friend for life

- encourages independence of thought
- does not concentrate on discipline
- is prepared to discuss even adult problems
- is kind, relaxed, and makes rational judgments
- does not like or encourage emotional arguments
- will want the best of modern education for the children

Two Aquarians in the same family

When married, they usually enjoy a peaceful, friendly relationship. Aquarian parents and children can also get on well, although serious personal problems may be ignored in favor of taking a broad view of humanitarian ideas. Aquarians can be quite crazy together on occasions, as they all have bright minds and are intuitive.

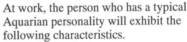

AQUARIUS AT WORK

At work, the person who has a typical Aquarian personality will exhibit the following characteristics.

Behavior and abilities

A typical Aquarius at work
- enjoys working with a group
- usually likes to use his or her mind
- dislikes routine and decision making
- enjoys variety

Aquarius as employer

A typical Aquarius boss (male or female)
- is fair and will pay employees exactly what the job deserves
- will be generous to anyone doing extra special work beyond the terms of a contract

- although not a natural executive, he or she will carry out the role of boss using all the Aquarian skills of quick thinking and shrewd analysis
- will expect a day's work for a day's pay
- dislikes any form of dishonesty
- is unshockable
- will not forgive lies or broken promises
- will give employees all the rope they need (even to hang themselves)

Aquarius as employee

A typical Aquarius employee (male or female)

- is aloof but gathers a large circle of friends
- will regularly go off into a mental exploration of future possibilities – and return with some very creative ideas
- brings a fresh approach to any task
- will frequently change his or her job or type of occupation in the early years; later he or she will settle down and stay with one company
- is conscientious, courteous, and has a knack for sensing what's wrong with machinery

Working environment

The workplace of a typical Aquarius man or woman

- could be almost anywhere in the world
- will have the latest communication technology
- changes frequently
- should be free from emotional tensions and noise

Typical occupations

Anything that involves experimentation, ideas, investigation, analysis, and innovation attracts Aquarius. For example: dancer, scientist, photographer, astrologer, singer, TV or radio

presenter, writer, charity worker, inventor,
archeologist, radiographer, electronics engineer,
humanitarian aid worker.

AQUARIUS AND LOVE

To Aquarius, love is an attitude of caring
for all humanity. Aquarius in love will
have many of the characteristics listed
below.

Behavior when in love

The typical Aquarius

- attracts the opposite sex in the first place by their
  friendly open manner
- may try to seem glamorously aloof
- is afraid of a deeply emotional involvement
- genuinely wants friendship with the loved one
- will guard his or her independence jealously
- enjoys a living-apart relationship

Expectations

The typical Aquarius expects

- his wife to stay at home
- her husband to share or take over the running of
  the home
- personal freedom of movement and action
- loyalty and faithfulness, which Aquarius will give
  in full once happily married
- understanding and tolerance of his or her oddities
- the partner to enjoy frequent visits from a wide
  variety of friends from every walk of life

The end of an affair

The typical Aquarius has only one love affair at a time and is devoted to that partner until curiosity leads them elsewhere.

Aquarius, male or female, likes to dominate the relationship (as a way of controlling the feared emotions). A partner who makes too many demands, becomes jealous, or tries to put limitations on Aquarius's freedom is usually dropped quite suddenly and may be treated like a total stranger. If the partner does not take the hint, Aquarius is quite capable of doing something to make the partner end the affair. Once Aquarius has settled into a marriage, he or she does not like divorce and will often want to remain friends with a past partner.

 AQUARIUS AND SEX

When a typical Aquarius makes love it is more an intellectual experience than an emotional one. He or she will be most assiduous about hygiene and contraception.

Aquarius is likely to do a lot of self-searching, but may not find it easy to listen to the partner's emotional problems.

Aquarian partners often have verbal quarrels which seem to take the place of physical contact.

Affairs do not seem to bother Aquarians, and they are rarely jealous. Many Aquarians make much better friends than lovers. Sometimes Aquarius can be rather modest about sex – even prudish.

AQUARIUS AND PARTNER

The person who contemplates becoming the marriage or business partner of a typical Aquarius must realize that Aquarius will need to have unlimited freedom. Aquarius will also want to dominate the partnership in order to ensure his or her interests in the wider world are not restricted.

Given this, the person who partners Aquarius can expect loyalty, a fair share of the work, and never to have the business taken away from them.

Although Aquarius has no great driving ambition, the typical Aquarius has a very fine mind (one of the best in the zodiac) and can be an asset to any venture. If fame comes their way, the Aquarius partner will happily lap it up.

Aquarius man as partner

He will want a partner who recognizes the ideas and inventiveness that he can bring to the business and who will allow him the freedom to introduce new concepts.

Business partners contemplating asking an Aquarius to join them should first ensure that he has enough knowledge about the business.

Aquarius man wants a marriage partner who will run the home and children and be a loyal, lifelong friend. He wants a woman who is capable of looking after herself and who will not need to lean on him. A woman who wants a good income from a steady breadwinner should look elsewhere.

Aquarius woman as partner

So long as she is left to circulate freely among her
many friends and pursue her dozens of outside
interests, Aquarius woman will be a faithful partner.
Although she can be tender and caring, she inhabits
a world of ideas. She needs a partner who
recognizes her brilliant mind.

In business or marriage, Aquarius woman will be
concerned that her partner is recognized for his
intellectual achievements; she is far less interested in
making money. She will enjoy physical closeness,
but will also be happy with long periods when the
relationship remains relatively platonic.

Opposite sign

Leo is the complementary opposite sign to Aquarius.
Although relations between them can be difficult,
Leo can show Aquarius how to make choices to
please the self, rather than for an ideal. In this way,
Aquarius can build emotional self-confidence.

AQUARIUS AND FRIENDS

Aquarius makes many friends but has very few confidants. In general, Aquarius likes a friend who has intellectual interests and enjoys the unusual and the radical. Aquarius will be friendly toward anyone and will tend to regard any relationship as platonic.

Positive factors

Aquarius rarely passes judgment upon the ethical codes of friends – but will expect them to live by their codes.

Aquarius will put a lot of effort into his or her friendships and make friends with anyone: rich and poor, black and white, good and bad.

An Aquarian friend is a constant source of mental stimulation, information, and practical help.

Negative factors

An Aquarius will take a great interest in his or her friend's ideas, and may eventually adopt some of them as his or her own, using them whenever it is convenient.

Aquarius tends to take over a friendship, slowly but surely, and put the friend in a subordinate role.

Aquarius also pours out troubles to friends, expecting their concerns to be regarded as more important than anything else. However, when friends need help with their own problems, Aquarius tends to draw back and tell them to ignore the problem and it will go away.

A compatibility chart, opposite, lists those with whom Aquarius is likely to have the most satisfactory relationships.

Compatibility chart

In general, if people are typical of their zodiac sign, relationships between Aquarius and other signs (including the complementary opposite sign, Leo) are as shown below.

	Harmonious	Difficult	Turbulent
Aquarius	●		
Pisces	●		
Aries	●		
Taurus		●	
Gemini	●		
Cancer			●
Leo		●	
Virgo			●
Libra	●		
Scorpio		●	
Sagittarius	●		
Capricorn	●		

AQUARIAN LEISURE INTERESTS

On the whole, a typical Aquarius will pursue the following leisure interests:

- radical arts and theater
- music, rhythm, dance, controlled exercise
- clowning, juggling, witty comedy
- flying, parachuting, gliding
- writing his or her autobiography or a personal diary

Aquarian likes and dislikes

Likes

- fame or recognition
- thinking about self
- privacy
- rainbows, dreams, magic
- change, eccentricity, surprises
- credit cards
- telling others what needs to be done – then watching them get on with it
- weird friends
- living within their means

Dislikes

- emotion and intimacy
- people who show off
- being taken for granted
- being pinned down in any way
- any kind of hard sell
- violence and fighting
- making loans or borrowing
- conventional authority
- revealing own motives
- extravagance

- scientific or creative hobbies
- local politics

AQUARIAN HEALTH

A typical Aquarius needs lots of fresh air, plenty of sleep, and regular exercise to stay healthy – alas, they often do not give themselves enough of any of these.

Young Aquarius is usually very healthy, except for the odd complaint which seems undiagnosable and goes away of its own accord.

When mature, Aquarius may suffer from nervous complaints due to their intense mental activity. They may also acquire a series of phobias. Aquarians may respond to hypnosis.

Types of sickness

They have a tendency to suffer according to the weather – which is always too hot, too cold, too humid, or too dry for their comfort. Circulatory problems are linked with Aquarius.

Diseases of the blood and nervous system are common, as are varicose veins and accidents to the calves and ankles.

Aquarius is linked with the extraordinary in every way and that includes sicknesses. Sudden, inexplicable illness can overtake Aquarius and may then clear up equally mysteriously.

Aquarius at rest

Any opportunity to lie in a hammock in the garden and dream the day away is wonderful for Aquarius's well-being.

Parts of the body linked to Aquarius
Traditionally, the parts of the body linked with a
strong Aquarius influence are as shown in the
diagram below. Only the individual birth chart will
show if one or more of these parts of the body
have inherited a strength or a vulnerability. Any
generalization would be misleading.

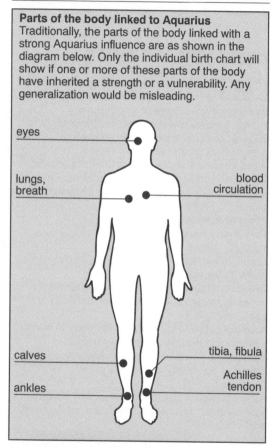

eyes

lungs,
breath

blood
circulation

calves

tibia, fibula

Achilles
tendon

ankles

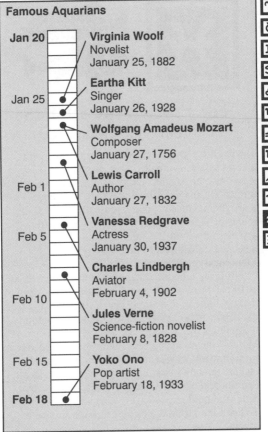

Famous Aquarians

Jan 20

Jan 25

Feb 1

Feb 5

Feb 10

Feb 15

Feb 18

Virginia Woolf
Novelist
January 25, 1882

Eartha Kitt
Singer
January 26, 1928

Wolfgang Amadeus Mozart
Composer
January 27, 1756

Lewis Carroll
Author
January 27, 1832

Vanessa Redgrave
Actress
January 30, 1937

Charles Lindbergh
Aviator
February 4, 1902

Jules Verne
Science-fiction novelist
February 8, 1828

Yoko Ono
Pop artist
February 18, 1933

12. Pisces: the Fishes
February 19 – March 20

The twelfth sign of the zodiac is concerned with
- compassion, sympathy, love, altruism
- dreams, the psychic, clairvoyance, sixth sense
- illusions, magic, film, fantasy, make-believe
- art, drama, music, poetry, prose, dance
- unusual talent, memory, wisdom, versatility
- sensitivity, intuition, humor, satire
- secrets, fulfillment of life, eternity

Elemental quality

Pisces is the mutable water sign of the zodiac. It can
be likened to a warm, turquoise lagoon, twinkling in
the sunshine, or to a strong ocean current rising from
the depths to break over a rocky shore, smoothing
the pebbles for all time.

Mutable means changeable, and water can change its
form in many ways: rain, hail, snow, mist, frost,
clouds, rainbows, warm pools, and puddles; thus,
Piscean feelings can change a dozen times a day.

Spiritual goal

To learn the meaning of peace through service to
others.

THE PISCEAN PERSONALITY

These are the general personality traits found in people who are typical of Pisces. An unhappy or frustrated Pisces may display some of the not-so-attractive traits.

Characteristics

Positive	Negative
• Loving and caring	• Self-pitying
• Trusting, hospitable, and will help all in distress	• Gullible and will give all in a lost cause
• Shy	• Temperamental
• Helpful	• Dependent
• Romantic	• Escapist
• Creative	• Sensationalist
• Mystical	• Depressive
• Gentle and kind	• Can lose touch with reality
• Compassionate	• Too emotionally involved with the problems of others
• Understanding of others	• Tends to blame self for everything

Secret Pisces

Anyone who has strong Piscean influences is a person who has perhaps the most extreme choices of any zodiac sign. Pisces can accept the challenges of life and rise to the top, or can give in to the easy way of oblivion and sink to the bottom. This choice is symbolized by the two fishes.

To help him or her swim to the top, the Pisces must find peace through beauty, music, and harmony. The Pisces needs work which will enable him or her to achieve this. More than any other sign, Pisces has many talents which may be used to develop their character. Many work hard to improve the lot of humanity. Others bring their talents to film and entertainment, enlivening the lives of thousands. Pisces needs to turn his/her private, mystical dream world of love and compassion into a reality. The only other option for Pisces is a life of illusion and, ultimately, a sense of failure.

Ruling planet and its effect

Jupiter and Neptune rule the zodiac sign of Pisces, so anyone whose birth chart has a strong Piscean influence will tend to bring benefit to others through their sensitivity.

In astrology, Jupiter is the planet of expansion, optimism, and generosity. Neptune is the planet of dreams, sensitivity, the unconscious, and the world of unreality.

Piscean lucky connections	
Colors	violet, light green, blue
Plants	opium poppy, lotus, water plants
Perfume	ambergris
Gemstones	pearl, amethyst, beryl, aquamarine
Metal	tin
Tarot card	the Moon
Animals	fish, dolphin

THE PISCEAN LOOK

People who exhibit physical characteristics of Pisces look more clumsy than they actually are. They give off a feeling of otherworldliness, and usually have very sensitive, caring eyes. They may have a trusting, eager look or a quality of empathy and nonjudgment exclusive to those who truly understand human sorrows and failings.

Physical appearance
- Body: usually short and thickset
- Back: may stoop as the person walks
- Eyes: a sleepy appearance with large eyebrows
- Head: oddly shaped
- Limbs: generally short

THE PISCES MALE

If a man behaves in a way typical of the personality associated with the zodiac sign of Pisces, he will have a tendency toward the characteristics listed below, unless there are influences in his personal birth chart that are stronger than that of his Pisces sun sign.

Appearance
The typical Pisces man
- may be tall but is not physically distinctive
- has a somewhat clumsy appearance
- has rather heavy jowls
- has broad or thick shoulders

Behavior and personality traits
The typical Piscean man
- has few prejudices

- is not ambitious for status, fame, or fortune, although he can make good use of opportunities if they come his way
- is very romantic
- cannot easily be fooled
- has few material needs, but needs his dreams
- talks slowly and is knowledgeable on many subjects
- is rarely jealous, but gets hurt all the same
- is emotionally involved in whatever he does, although he may never show it

THE PISCES FEMALE

If a woman behaves in a way that is distinctive of the personality associated with the zodiac sign of Pisces, she will have a tendency toward the characteristics listed below, providing there are no influences in her personal birth chart that are stronger than that of her Pisces sun sign.

Appearance

The typical Pisces woman

- is normally slim, but tends to put on weight easily in later years
- has large eyes and an oval face
- has a clear, soft skin, whatever her color
- has an air of feminine mystery
- has a very warm, charming smile

Behavior and personality traits

The typical Pisces woman

- does not try to dominate her partner in any way
- often appears vague and dreamy

- is subtle and, while appearing to be helpless or incapable, gets things organized and manages the finances extremely well
- protects her emotional vulnerability with humor or a sophisticated exterior
- needs to belong to someone
- has a warm, sympathetic heart

YOUNG PISCES

If a child behaves in a way that is distinctive of the personality associated with the zodiac sign of Pisces, he or she will have a tendency toward the characteristics listed below.

Behavior and personality traits

The typical Pisces child

- has the sweetest, dimpled smiles and the most winning ways of all babies
- lives in a world of make-believe
- dislikes orderliness and routines
- has an amazing imagination
- holds secret conversations with invisible (and sometimes long dead) people
- has a very active sixth sense
- believes in magic, fairies, and Santa Claus, and may reinvent myths
- enjoys the company of adults more than that of other children
- rarely loses his or her temper, and instead just happily goes his or her own way

Bringing up young Pisces

At school, young Pisces avoids the limelight and

does not take leadership positions, so he or she should never be pushed to take such roles. However, Piscean children are the source of wonderful ideas for play and adventure in which Pisces will be happy to let other children take the lead.

Parents would be wise to gently help young Pisces to distinguish between fantasy and reality, without destroying his or her rich imagination. Because of their passive, nonaggressive natures, Piscean children may sometimes be the victims of bullies, so it would be useful to teach them strategies for dealing with such situations.

Young Pisces' needs Young Pisces needs to feel he or she belongs to someone or several someones. Emotional connections with people are absolutely essential to Piscean happiness. He or she is less concerned about places and things, although attachments to animals are often sought as well. Consequently, a Pisces child should be helped to believe in himself or herself and prevented from becoming too clinging. Parents who cling to their Pisces child are doing him or her no good at all.

What to teach young Pisces Piscean children absorb information and ideas like sponges and transform everything into magic. They should be taught to sort their ideas and to distinguish between what is practical and what is not.

Young Pisceans tend to be vulnerable to those who would deceive them. An understanding of human nature and some simple, clear rules will help young Pisces to avoid the dangers – while still developing their precious skills of compassion.

Some simple routines should be taught, otherwise Pisces may become spoilt and will dominate the home with his or her changing desires.

PISCES AT HOME

For a typical Piscean, home is the place where he or she will need to feel loved. Home can be a palace or a hovel, but it must contain people toward whom he or she is drawn emotionally and who love him or her.

Typical behavior and abilities

When at home, a Pisces man or woman

- will often enter a fantasy world
- will feel safe to freely explore his or her imagination
- will probably have no fixed routine
- is likely to be untidy, although he or she may have a sudden urge to tidy everything to avoid confusion: this can happen at any time
- should keep a large, clear clock
- will need a space for personal privacy
- will make the home itself into a wonderful world of art, music, design, and good food and wine

Pisces as parent

The typical Pisces parent

- can happily accommodate all the fantasies of childhood
- will allow a child plenty of imaginative freedom
- may lack discipline
- listens with understanding
- encourages personal development
- may have to teach the children punctuality

- is warm and loving and rarely uses harsh words
- may tend to spoil the children
- will probably have a very personal and unusual set of rules to which the children must adhere

Two Pisces in the same family

Pisces in the same family should get on very well, providing they have an outlet for their vivid, unworldly imaginations. For example, Piscean siblings may build an imaginative world together; or a Piscean parent who makes fictional films will find inspiration in the ideas of his or her offspring.

 ## PISCES AT WORK

At work, the person who has a typical Pisces personality will exhibit the following characteristics.

Typical behavior and abilities

A typical Pisces at work

- is rarely in an executive position, nor does he or she enjoy being tied to working in a team that has a strict routine
- enjoys work that offers freedom of expression, which usually means working alone or in a self-directed position
- if working in a team, Pisces prefers an occupation that allows for frequent changes and adaptations

Pisces as employer

A typical Pisces boss (male or female)

- is more likely to be found in organizations as a director rather than as the boss
- will serve people rather than accumulate power
- uses his or her gifts to make the correct move

- is a shrewd judge of character
- is unconventional and creative
- values those who are conventional and well organized, because they are needed to back up his or her ideas
- will never refuse help to someone in need
- may act tough to hide a deep belief in the mystical

Pisces as employee

A typical Pisces employee (male or female)

- needs work where there is plenty of outlet for either human understanding or creative imagination
- will be depressed, lazy, and useless if neither of these needs are satisfied
- will be very affected by surroundings
- when happy is a loyal worker
- will get the job done, although nobody seems to understand how he or she operates

Working environment

The workplace of a typical Pisces man or woman

- must feel comfortable
- will have a pleasant atmosphere
- should be a large and flexible space
- may be brightly colored

Typical occupations

All kinds of jobs in film, theater, TV, radio, ballet, music, and art will attract Pisces, who is often a good actor. A job that allows travel will be attractive. Advertising, public relations, and any job that is part of the service industry. Helping people to solve their problems and charitable and church work are also very attractive to Pisces.

PISCES AND LOVE

To Pisces, there is no difference between love, affection, and romance. A Pisces needs all three. A Pisces who feels unloved is an unhappy person to whom life seems very gray. Love revitalizes Pisces.

Behavior when in love

The typical Pisces

- is romantic
- eager to please
- adapts to the demands of the relationship
- appears to be helpless, delicate, and vulnerable, but being loved enables Pisces to cope very well with a range of difficulties, problems, and tragedies
- is emotionally involved, to the point of not recognizing when he or she is being deceived or treated badly

Expectations

The typical Pisces expects

- to have his or her dreams valued and to be protected from harsh criticism
- to be cared for romantically
- to have children (Pisces love children)
- to be frequently reassured that they are loved
- all birthdays and anniversaries to be remembered

The end of an affair

Some Pisces tend to drift into another relationship almost without noticing, yet are surprised when they are accused of unfaithfulness. The self-doubt which haunts many Pisces can only be dispelled by repeated reassurance that they are lovable.

Consequently, Pisces may sometimes just leave a
relationship for no clear reason and with no regrets.
It is not that Pisces does not love the abandoned
partner anymore. On the contrary, Pisces will often
show much sympathetic understanding and will try
to retain a friendly relationship with the one he or
she has left.

The worst possible event for a Pisces is to be
rejected by the one who loved them. A partner who
wants to end a relationship with a typical Pisces will
find this a very difficult thing to do. Pisces will
cling, convinced that if they reform in some way,
everything will be all right again. The ex-partner of
a Pisces may have to go to extremes to extricate
himself or herself from the emotional mess that a
hurt Pisces can produce.

PISCES AND SEX

When a typical Pisces makes love it is an
act of romance rather than of carnal
pleasure. Typical Pisces is less interested
in sexual activity than in the expressions of love that
come before and afterward.

Piscean energy is more often used up in the
emotional experiences of love than in the sexual act.
This does not mean Pisces is not interested, indeed
he or she may seek several partners, but this is for
reassurance rather than personal pleasure.

Pisces can be the least prejudiced and most
compassionate of all the zodiac signs. Pisces will
show a deep and real love for a partner who has
problems or physical abnormalities, or who has to

face a tragedy or business disaster. Sex will be one
of the expressions of love given by a caring and
devoted Piscean spouse.

PISCES AND PARTNER

The person who contemplates becoming
the marriage or business partner of a
typical Pisces must realize that Pisces
will expect to be supported – emotionally or
financially. Given this, the person who partners
Pisces can expect loyalty and sensitive
understanding.

Pisces man as partner

He will want a partner who will work for him:
someone to run the household efficiently and who
will entertain his friends and business colleagues.
In return, the married Pisces will bring great joy to a
household with his wonderful imagination. Marriage
gives male Pisces more self-assurance, so he will
become more decisive.

Potential business partners should be prepared to
undertake the practical, administrative side of the
business, leaving the Piscean partner free to exercise
their creativity and understanding.

Pisces woman as partner

She will want a marriage partner who will support
her in every respect. To many men, Pisces is the
perfectly feminine woman. She may appear to be a
helpless, fluffy person but, once married, she will
feel secure, and her reserve of talents and abilities

will pour out in every direction.

In business, a Pisces woman will be best in creative positions and in public relations, but should not be expected to do the routine office jobs.

Opposite sign

Virgo is the complementary opposite sign to Pisces. While Pisces adapts himself or herself to the emotional needs of others, Virgo works hard to serve others by responding to the needs of the moment with practical solutions. From Virgo, Pisces can learn how to translate Piscean sensitivity and understanding into practical action – thus dispelling self-doubt and building confidence in his or her Piscean abilities.

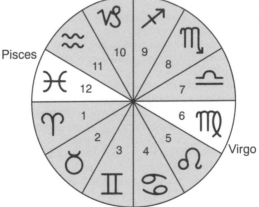

PISCES AND FRIENDS

In general, Pisces likes a friend who is useful and reassuring. In return, they will give unprejudiced understanding and loyalty to their friends.

Positive factors

Pisces are emotionally attached to their friends and will rarely notice if the friend is taking advantage of this involvement.

Pisces are friendly, humorous, and caring friends, even if there are long periods of time between meetings.

Pisces will always think up something interesting to do and will enjoy any kind of artistic ventures.

Negative factors

Pisces can be a confusing person, so arrangements may be difficult to make.

Pisces can sometimes seem to be cool and offhand. This is usually temporary and due to a moment of insecurity.

Pisces needs a hero or heroine to identify with. If a friend happens to be the chosen one, this can be pleasant enough but may become a nuisance when Pisces gives the friend talents he or she hasn't got and expects them to be demonstrated!

Pisces does not find it easy to conform; friends with conservative attitudes may find this a difficulty.

A compatibility chart, opposite, lists those with whom Pisces is likely to have the most satisfactory relationships.

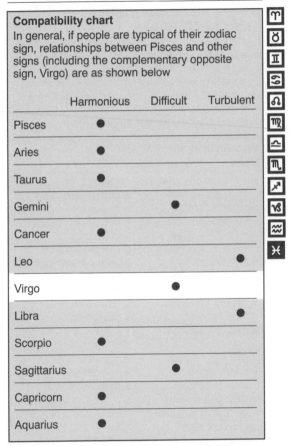

Compatibility chart

In general, if people are typical of their zodiac sign, relationships between Pisces and other signs (including the complementary opposite sign, Virgo) are as shown below

	Harmonious	Difficult	Turbulent
Pisces	●		
Aries	●		
Taurus	●		
Gemini		●	
Cancer	●		
Leo			●
Virgo		●	
Libra			●
Scorpio	●		
Sagittarius		●	
Capricorn	●		
Aquarius	●		

PISCEAN LEISURE INTERESTS

Most typical Pisces love artistic pursuits and anything that has an element of mystery, fantasy, and imagination.

Pisceans love films, theater, traveling entertainers, pantomimes, witches, monsters, elves, gypsies, and mythical creatures.

Team sport is not a natural Piscean activity, but

Piscean likes and dislikes

Likes

- seafood, champagne and organic foods
- romantic places, sunsets over the sea, mountain vistas, waterfalls, ponds and waterlilies
- background music, poetry
- people who need their understanding
- mystical settings,
- candles, incense
- being loved
- freedom to drift along from time to time
- privacy
- colorful food
- personalized gifts
- presents wrapped in magical paper
- new books
- diamonds

Dislikes

- bright, noisy, crowded places
- dirty, ugly objects
- being told to get a grip on things
- stiff clothing
- authorities
- people knowing too much about him or her

Pisceans often love gentle watersports, noncompetitive skiing, and skydiving. Dangerous sports, such as racing cars, can also appeal to the Pisces because they have an unerring instinct in such situations.

PISCEAN HEALTH

Typical Pisces are healthy people so long as they feel loved and have an outlet for their dreams. Unhappy Pisces are vulnerable to problems arising from turning to drink, drugs, or other ways of getting relief from what may seem unbearable emotional insecurities. Pisces often has to work hard to swim against the current that would pull him or her under. The constant effort of avoiding being sucked into oblivion is the cause of much distress to many Pisces, who, consequently, may suffer depression and other emotional problems.

Types of sickness

Troubles with the feet and toes are common among Pisces: bunions, corns, boils and foot deformities may occur.

Pisces may become forgetful when illness is about to strike. They may also suffer from the effects of too much wine or too many drugs. The sensitive Piscean psyche suffers greatly in times of stress and has little to draw on by way of personal resources.

Pisces at rest

A relaxed Pisces is the happiest person on earth. A chance to lie back, sip wine, listen to music and let the imagination wander is perfect bliss to Pisces.

Parts of the body linked to Pisces
Traditionally, the parts of the body linked with a
strong Pisces influence are as shown in the
diagram below. Only the individual birth chart will
show if one or more of these parts of the body
have inherited a strength or a vulnerability. Any
generalization would be misleading.

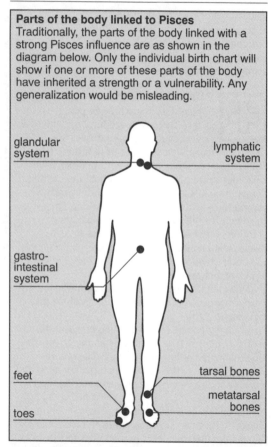

glandular
system

lymphatic
system

gastro-
intestinal
system

feet

tarsal bones

metatarsal
bones

toes

Famous Pisceans

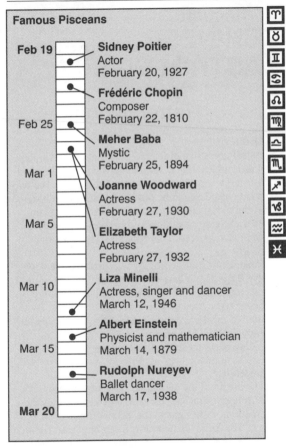

Feb 19

Sidney Poitier
Actor
February 20, 1927

Frédéric Chopin
Composer
February 22, 1810

Feb 25

Meher Baba
Mystic
February 25, 1894

Mar 1

Joanne Woodward
Actress
February 27, 1930

Mar 5

Elizabeth Taylor
Actress
February 27, 1932

Mar 10

Liza Minelli
Actress, singer and dancer
March 12, 1946

Albert Einstein
Physicist and mathematician
March 14, 1879

Mar 15

Rudolph Nureyev
Ballet dancer
March 17, 1938

Mar 20

Section 2
CHINESE ASTROLOGY

Introduction

History

Astrology is one of the most ancient of the Chinese philosophies. It is at least 2,000 years old. Originally, astrology was inseparable from astronomy. The two were considered to be one discipline. China has one of the oldest civilizations in the world, and from very early on practitioners of astronomy/astrology were always present as officials of the imperial court.

In ancient China, astrology was used to reveal what was expected to happen to a nation. It was not until the beginning of the Christian era that astrology began to be used to give individual readings. By the time of the Tang dynasty (618–907 A.D.), a whole encyclopedia had been written about the art of giving personal astrological readings.

Legends

The origin of the 12 animal signs of Chinese astrology is unclear. Chinese legend attributes the creation of the signs to the Yellow Emperor in 2637 B.C. The Yellow Emperor is a semimythical figure in

2

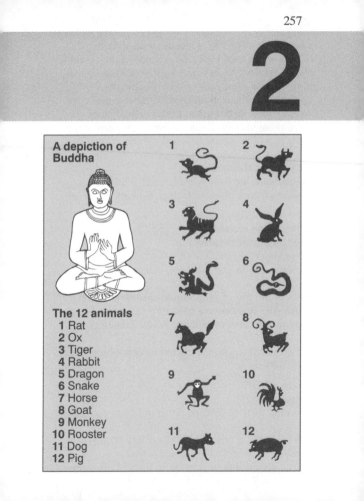

A depiction of
Buddha

The 12 animals
1 Rat
2 Ox
3 Tiger
4 Rabbit
5 Dragon
6 Snake
7 Horse
8 Goat
9 Monkey
10 Rooster
11 Dog
12 Pig

Chinese history. Other legends credit Buddha
(c. 563–c. 483 B.C.) with the creation of the 12-animal
cycle. Apparently, he invited all the animals to visit
him, but, for some reason, only 12 animals showed
up. To thank them, Buddha gave each animal a year
which would be dedicated to that animal alone
throughout history. The years were allocated in the
order in which the animals had arrived.

How to use this book
In this book, we have considered five different
aspects of the Chinese astrological chart. These are:

● the animal sign
● the natural element
● the dominant element
● Yin and Yang
● companion in life

Also, at the end of each animal chapter is a brief look
at how the Western and Chinese zodiacs can be
combined to give even more-detailed readings.

All you need to know to access information about all
these aspects is:

● year of birth
● date of birth
● hour of birth (the nearest hour or two is enough)

For example, if you were born on July 30, 1970
between the hours of 3 P.M. and 5 P.M.:
1 First, using your year of birth, find out your animal

sign from the tables on pp. 260–4. In this instance, the person is a dog.

2 We know that the natural element of all dogs is metal and that they are Yang people (this information is included at the start of each animal chapter and is also shown by the chart on p. 268–9).

3 Also from the year of birth, we know that the person's dominant element is metal (see the sections on elements in the relevant animal chapter). In this case, the dominant and natural element are both metal – but they are not always the same.

4 From the hour of birth, we know that the person's companion in life is the monkey (see the chart on pp. 274–5 to calculate your inner companion).

5 From the date of birth, we can calculate that the person is a Leo (see chart on p. 277 to work this out).

In this example, the person should read the chapters on the dog and the monkey to get a full Chinese astrological reading. Further information on the elements and Yin and Yang forces can be obtained by reading the relevant parts of this introduction.

Animal signs

The animal signs are the most basic aspect of Chinese astrology. The signs are not based on the position of the stars as in Western astrology, but instead on the person's year of birth. Each animal is allocated its own years. There are 12 animals and they always appear in the same order (rat, ox, tiger, rabbit, dragon, snake, horse, goat, monkey, rooster, dog and pig).

The cycle of animals, therefore, repeats itself
every 12 years.

The Chinese calendar is based on the lunar year
(orbits of the Moon around the Earth). The Western
calendar is based on the solar year (orbit of the Earth
around the Sun). The two do not correspond exactly.
Each lunar year, therefore, begins on a slightly
different date of the solar year.

To find your animal sign, look up the year of your
birth in the first column of the following tables. If
you were born in January or February of that year,
however, remember to check the dates that the
Chinese lunar year begins on, as you may find that
you actually belong to the previous animal year.
Once you have identified your animal sign, read the
chapter devoted to that animal.

Jan 31, 1900 – Feb 17, 1912			
1900	Jan 31, 1900	– Feb 18, 1901	Rat
1901	Feb 19, 1901	– Feb 7, 1902	Ox
1902	Feb 8, 1902	– Jan 28, 1903	Tiger
1903	Jan 29, 1903	– Feb 15, 1904	Rabbit
1904	Feb 16, 1904	– Feb 3, 1905	Dragon
1905	Feb 4, 1905	– Jan 24, 1906	Snake
1906	Jan 25, 1906	– Feb 12, 1907	Horse
1907	Feb 13, 1907	– Feb 1, 1908	Goat
1908	Feb 2, 1908	– Jan 21, 1909	Monkey
1909	Jan 22, 1909	– Feb 9, 1910	Rooster
1910	Feb 10, 1910	– Jan 29, 1911	Dog
1911	Jan 30, 1911	– Feb 17, 1912	Pig

Feb 18, 1912 – Feb 4, 1924			
1912	Feb 18, 1912 – Feb 5, 1913	Rat
1913	Feb 6, 1913 – Jan 25, 1914	Ox
1914	Jan 26, 1914 – Feb 13, 1915	Tiger
1915	Feb 14, 1915 – Feb 2, 1916	Rabbit
1916	Feb 3, 1916 – Jan 22, 1917	Dragon
1917	Jan 23, 1917 – Feb 10, 1918	Snake
1918	Feb 11, 1918 – Jan 31, 1919	Horse
1919	Feb 1, 1919 – Feb 19, 1920	Goat
1920	Feb 20, 1920 – Feb 7, 1921	Monkey
1921	Feb 8, 1921 – Jan 27, 1922	Rooster
1922	Jan 28, 1922 – Feb 15, 1923	Dog
1923	Feb 16, 1923 – Feb 4, 1924	Pig

Feb 5, 1924 – Jan 23, 1936			
1924	Feb 5, 1924 – Jan 24, 1925	Rat
1925	Jan 25, 1925 – Feb 12, 1926	Ox
1926	Feb 13, 1926 – Feb 1, 1927	Tiger
1927	Feb 2, 1927 – Jan 22, 1928	Rabbit
1928	Jan 23, 1928 – Feb 9, 1929	Dragon
1929	Feb 10, 1929 – Jan 29, 1930	Snake
1930	Jan 30, 1930 – Feb 16, 1931	Horse
1931	Feb 17, 1931 – Feb 5, 1932	Goat
1932	Feb 6, 1932 – Jan 25, 1933	Monkey
1933	Jan 26, 1933 – Feb 13, 1934	Rooster
1934	Feb 14, 1934 – Feb 3, 1935	Dog
1935	Feb 4, 1935 – Jan 23, 1936	Pig

	Jan 24, 1936 – Feb 9, 1948		
1936	Jan 24, 1936 – Feb 10, 1937		Rat
1937	Feb 11, 1937 – Jan 30, 1938		Ox
1938	Jan 31, 1938 – Feb 18, 1939		Tiger
1939	Feb 19, 1939 – Feb 7, 1940		Rabbit
1940	Feb 8, 1940 – Jan 26, 1941		Dragon
1941	Jan 27, 1941 – Feb 14, 1942		Snake
1942	Feb 15, 1942 – Feb 4, 1943		Horse
1943	Feb 5, 1943 – Jan 24, 1944		Goat
1944	Jan 25, 1944 – Feb 12, 1945		Monkey
1945	Feb 13, 1945 – Feb 1, 1946		Rooster
1946	Feb 2, 1946 – Jan 21, 1947		Dog
1947	Jan 22, 1947 – Feb 9, 1948		Pig

	Feb 10, 1948 – Jan 27, 1960		
1948	Feb 10, 1948 – Jan 28, 1949		Rat
1949	Jan 29, 1949 – Feb 16, 1950		Ox
1950	Feb 17, 1950 – Feb 5, 1951		Tiger
1951	Feb 6, 1951 – Jan 26, 1952		Rabbit
1952	Jan 27, 1952 – Feb 13, 1953		Dragon
1953	Feb 14, 1953 – Feb 2, 1954		Snake
1954	Feb 3, 1954 – Jan 23, 1955		Horse
1955	Jan 24, 1955 – Feb 11, 1956		Goat
1956	Feb 12, 1956 – Jan 30, 1957		Monkey
1957	Jan 31, 1957 – Feb 17, 1958		Rooster
1958	Feb 18, 1958 – Feb 7, 1959		Dog
1959	Feb 8, 1959 – Jan 27, 1960		Pig

	Jan 28, 1960 – Feb 14, 1972		
1960	Jan 28, 1960	– Feb 14, 1961	Rat
1961	Feb 15, 1961	– Feb 4, 1962	Ox
1962	Feb 5, 1962	– Jan 24, 1963	Tiger
1963	Jan 25, 1963	– Feb 12, 1964	Rabbit
1964	Feb 13, 1964	– Feb 1, 1965	Dragon
1965	Feb 2, 1965	– Jan 20, 1966	Snake
1966	Jan 21, 1966	– Feb 8, 1967	Horse
1967	Feb 9, 1967	– Jan 29, 1968	Goat
1968	Jan 30, 1968	– Feb 16, 1969	Monkey
1969	Feb 17, 1969	– Feb 5, 1970	Rooster
1970	Feb 6, 1970	– Jan 26, 1971	Dog
1971	Jan 27, 1971	– Feb 14, 1972	Pig

	Feb 15, 1972 – Feb 1, 1984		
1972	Feb 15, 1972	– Feb 2, 1973	Rat
1973	Feb 3, 1973	– Jan 22, 1974	Ox
1974	Jan 23, 1974	– Feb 10, 1975	Tiger
1975	Feb 11, 1975	– Jan 30, 1976	Rabbit
1976	Jan 31, 1976	– Feb 17, 1977	Dragon
1977	Feb 18, 1977	– Feb 6, 1978	Snake
1978	Feb 7, 1978	– Jan 27, 1979	Horse
1979	Jan 28, 1979	– Feb 15, 1980	Goat
1980	Feb 16, 1980	– Feb 4, 1981	Monkey
1981	Feb 5, 1981	– Jan 24, 1982	Rooster
1982	Jan 25, 1982	– Feb 12, 1983	Dog
1983	Feb 13, 1983	– Feb 1, 1984	Pig

Feb 2, 1984	–	Feb 18, 1996	
1984	Feb 2, 1984 – Feb 19, 1985		Rat
1985	Feb 20, 1985 – Feb 8, 1986		Ox
1986	Feb 9, 1986 – Jan 28, 1987		Tiger
1987	Jan 29, 1987 – Feb 16, 1988		Rabbit
1988	Feb 17, 1988 – Feb 5, 1989		Dragon
1989	Feb 6, 1989 – Jan 26, 1990		Snake
1990	Jan 27, 1990 – Feb 14, 1991		Horse
1991	Feb 15, 1991 – Feb 3, 1992		Goat
1992	Feb 4, 1992 – Jan 22, 1993		Monkey
1993	Jan 23, 1993 – Feb 9, 1994		Rooster
1994	Feb 10, 1994 – Jan 30, 1995		Dog
1995	Jan 31, 1995 – Feb 18, 1996		Pig

Feb 19, 1996	-	Feb 6, 2008	
1996	Feb 19, 1996 – Feb 7, 1997		Rat
1997	Feb 8, 1997 – Jan 27, 1998		Ox
1998	Jan 28, 1998 – Feb 5, 1999		Tiger
1999	Feb 6, 1999 – Feb 4, 2000		Rabbit
2000	Feb 5, 2000 – Jan 23, 2001		Dragon
2001	Jan 24, 2001 – Feb 11, 2002		Snake
2002	Feb 12, 2002 – Jan 31, 2003		Horse
2003	Feb 1, 2003 – Jan 21, 2004		Goat
2004	Jan 22, 2004 – Feb 8, 2005		Monkey
2005	Feb 9, 2005 – Jan 28, 2006		Rooster
2006	Jan 29, 2006 – Feb 17, 2007		Dog
2007	Feb 18, 2007 – Feb 6, 2008		Pig

The five elements

Unlike Western astrology, Chinese astrology has five, not four, elements. These are based on the five planets that were visible to the ancient Chinese astronomers. The elements are:

- water (ruled by Mercury)
- metal (ruled by Venus)
- fire (ruled by Mars)
- wood (ruled by Jupiter)
- earth (ruled by Saturn)

Each of these elements can manifest itself either positively or negatively. In the following tables, the negative and positive characteristics that each of the elements can bestow on a person are listed.

Water	
Positive	Negative
• artistic	• illogical
• expressive	• fearful
• nurturing	• stressed
• sensitive	• nervous
• understanding	• overly sensitive
• sympathetic	• subjective
• gentle	• manipulative
• caring	• fickle
• flexible	• passive
• nonconfrontational	• dependent
• persuasive	• overimaginative

Metal

Positive	Negative
• protective	• inflexible
• visionary	• harsh
• prosperous	• longing
• resolute	• homesick
• inspirational	• self-righteous
• controlled	• single-minded
• determined	• competitive
• romantic	• solitary
• conviction	• cantankerous
• strength	• melancholic
	• opinionated

Fire

Positive	Negative
• cheerful	• destructive
• passionate	• cruel
• honorable	• impatient
• loving	• tempestuous
• charismatic	• excessive
• dynamic	• reckless
• exciting	• demanding
• courageous	• radical
• decisive	• headstrong
• inventive	• exploitative
• optimistic	• ambitious

Wood

Positive	Negative
• compassionate	• frustrated
• resourceful	• bad tempered
• community minded	• impatient
• cooperative	• dissipated
• expansive	• unexpressive
• inspired	• excessive
• sociable	• violent
• extroverted	• angry
• problem solving	• pessimistic
• ethical	• temperamental
• practical	• susceptible

Earth

Positive	Negative
• peaceful	• smothering
• methodical	• confining
• stable	• anxious
• patient	• pessimistic
• enduring	• slow
• just	• narrow-minded
• receptive	• rigid
• supportive	• overly cautious
• practical	• stubborn
• objective	• conservative
• logical	

Dominant element Each year is ruled by a different
element. The element that rules a person's year of
birth is called the dominant element. When you
consider that every year is also ruled by one of the
12 animal signs, you can calculate that each
combination of animal and element occurs only once
every 60 years ($12 \times 5 = 60$). For instance, the year
1901 was an ox/metal year. The next ox/metal year
was 1961 and the next one will be in 2021. This is
referred to as the 60-year cycle. According to the

**The natural elements
and Yin and Yang**

Animal	Yin/Yang	Natural element
rat	Yang	water
ox	Yin	water
tiger	Yang	wood
rabbit	Yin	wood
dragon	Yang	wood
snake	Yin	fire
horse	Yang	fire
goat	Yin	fire
monkey	Yang	metal
rooster	Yin	metal
dog	Yang	metal
pig	Yin	water

Chinese calendar, we are currently in the seventy-eighth cycle.

Natural element In addition, each animal sign is considered to have its own, natural element. This is always the same, regardless of a person's year of birth. The wheel below shows the natural element of each animal, as well as whether the animal is Yin or Yang. Yin and Yang are discussed on the next page. You will notice that only four (water, wood, metal, and fire) of the five elements are natural elements.

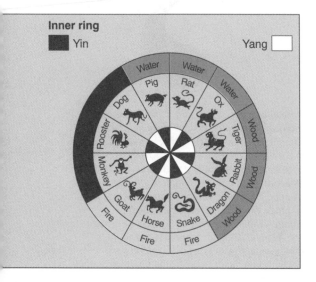

Yin and Yang

According to Chinese philosophy, the whole universe is controlled by two primal forces. These are Yin and Yang. Everything can be categorized according to this system: from people to furniture, and even countries. The balance of the universe, the Earth, a nation, and even the health and moods of individuals are determined by the balance or imbalance of Yin and Yang.

Yin and Yang symbol

The ideal balance of Yin and Yang is depicted by the symbol shown above. As the Yang part (white) decreases, the Yin part (black) increases; when one is at its height, the other is at its lowest ebb. Often people assume that Yang is male and Yin female. This is not quite true. Although they are associated with opposite genders, each contains within itself the seed of the other. So, even though Yang is a masculine force, women can possess it. In such ways, Yin and Yang are opposing yet complementary principles. Neither is more important than the other and only together do they make a whole.

In the table below are listed some examples of Yin and Yang manifestations that show the opposing natures of these forces.

Yin	Yang
● Moon	● Sun
● dark	● light
● feminine	● masculine
● water	● fire
● black	● white
● passive	● active
● negative	● positive
● night	● day
● empty	● full
● cold	● hot
● no	● yes
● left	● right
● south	● north

Everyone has his or her own balance of Yin and Yang. To help you understand what makes you an individual and your compatibility with other people, the tastes, colors, foods, flowers, and plants associated with each animal sign are listed, together with the most auspicious seasons, time of birth, and climate.

Yin and Yang and the five elements

Each of the five elements has a positive and a negative side. Which of these is expressed in people depends on whether their animal sign is Yin or Yang. To work out if your animal sign is Yin or Yang, see the chart on pp. 268–9. For example, the rat is a Yang water animal. So, for rat people, the qualities of the element water are expressed positively. Pigs, on the other hand, are Yin water people. Therefore, the qualities of the element water express themselves negatively in pig people.

In the tables below and right are some of the qualities that are commonly attributed to people of either the Yin or Yang tendency.

Yin people

- average weight or slender
- often tall
- smiling face
- like strong colors
- delicate health
- individualist
- introspective
- responsive
- psychic
- meditative
- intelligent
- independent
- solitary
- spiritual
- rebellious
- nonmaterialistic
- introverted

Yang people

- corpulent
- medium height
- healthy
- serious features
- self-preoccupied
- susceptible
- unstable emotionally
- fear failure
- confident
- conservative

- sociable
- hospitable
- optimistic
- active
- pragmatic
- efficient
- community orientated
- distrustful
- materialistic
- passionate

Companion in life

The Chinese concept of the companion in life does not refer to another person, but rather to an inner person within an individual. This inner companion acts as a guide, guardian, or devil's advocate. Your companion in life is determined by your hour of birth. Every two-hour slot of the day is governed by one of the 12 animal signs.

Identify your inner companion by referring to the table on the next page. Once you have established which of the animal signs is your inner companion, read the chapter devoted to that animal. Do not assume, however, that this means that you have the attributes of both the animal signs. Instead, your companion in life modifies the traits of your animal sign. For example, tigers are usually reckless and unpredictable people. A tiger whose inner companion is the ox, however, will be more stable than would otherwise be expected.

Companion in life
The 24-hour cycle of the animals is shown in the table (right) and the diagrams. The hours given refer to local standard time. If you were born in a month when daylight saving or summer time were in use, you will need to deduct an hour (sometimes two) from your birth time before looking up the sign of your companion.

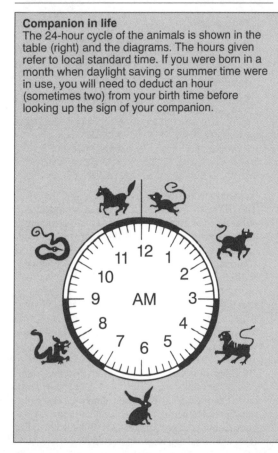

Time of birth Sign of companion

11 pm –	1 am	Rat
1 am –	3 am	Ox
3 am –	5 am	Tiger
5 am –	7 am	Rabbit
7 am –	9 am	Dragon
9 am –	11 am	Snake
11 am –	1 pm	Horse
1 pm –	3 pm	Goat
3 pm –	5 pm	Monkey
5 pm –	7 pm	Rooster
7 pm –	9 pm	Dog
9 pm –	11 pm	Pig

If a person has the same animal sign and inner companion, then they have the potential to balance the negative and positive aspects of their character.

The companion in life and compatibility

The compatibility of different animals can be radically altered by their respective companions in life. For example, horse and rat are naturally antagonistic toward each other. If the rat's companion in life is horse and the horse's companion in life is rat, however, then the reverse can be true.

Western astrology

To add an extra dimension to your Chinese astrological reading, you can consider it in conjunction with your Western zodiac sign.

Use the chart on the right to determine your Western star sign. There is a brief analysis of the effect of each star sign on an animal sign toward the end of each of the animal chapters.

More detailed information on Western astrology can be found in section 1, *Zodiac Types*, which has a chapter devoted to each zodiac sign.

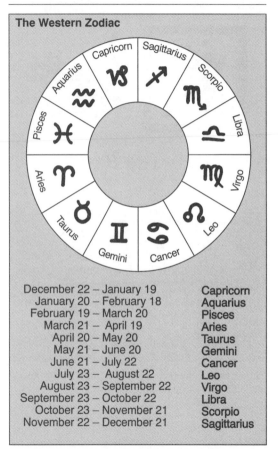

The Western Zodiac

December 22 – January 19	Capricorn
January 20 – February 18	Aquarius
February 19 – March 20	Pisces
March 21 – April 19	Aries
April 20 – May 20	Taurus
May 21 – June 20	Gemini
June 21 – July 22	Cancer
July 23 – August 22	Leo
August 23 – September 22	Virgo
September 23 – October 22	Libra
October 23 – November 21	Scorpio
November 22 – December 21	Sagittarius

1. The Rat

The Yang water animal.

Lunar years ruled by the rat

1900	Jan 31, 1900 – Feb 18, 1901
1912	Feb 18, 1912 – Feb 5, 1913
1924	Feb 5, 1924 – Jan 24, 1925
1936	Jan 24, 1936 – Feb 10, 1937
1948	Feb 10, 1948 – Jan 28, 1949
1960	Jan 28, 1960 – Feb 14, 1961
1972	Feb 15, 1972 – Feb 2, 1973
1984	Feb 2, 1984 – Feb 19, 1985
1996	Feb 19, 1996 – Feb 7, 1997

The rat was welcomed in ancient times as a protector and a bringer of material prosperity.

THE RAT PERSONALITY

Anxious not to be a failure, the affable, elegant, and generous rat lives for today. When rat is being a charming socialite or a light-hearted gossip, this animal should never be underestimated. Attracted to whatever is clandestine, secretive, or a potential bargain, the rat is a very clever animal who enjoys taking the best possible advantage of all situations.

Characteristics

These are the general personality traits of those who are typical rats, both at their best and at their worst.

Positive	Negative
• intelligent	• calculating
• charming	• mean
• imaginative	• secretive
• placid	• restless
• opportunistic	• has ulterior motives
• passionate	• quick-tempered
• elegant	• a critical nitpicker
• sentimental	• a grumbler
• affectionate	• a gossip and a
• constructive critic	scandalmonger
• alert	• an obsessive hoarder
• honest	• overambitious
• practical	• busybody
• materialistic	
• quickly learns from experience	

Secret rat

Some rats suffer from a morbid guilt. Almost all fear failure, so are often in a rat race. The rat's calm exterior hides inner aggressive restlessness. Rats tend to be gullible, falling into rattraps, but they learn from experience so are constantly on guard.

Element

Rat is linked to the ancient Chinese element of water. Water endows rat with qualities of quiet restraint, persistence, diplomacy, and the ability to predict future trends, especially in business and the material world. Water rats can influence others but need to turn their inner restlessness into active leadership.

Balance

The rat itself is Yang, but it is associated with the element water, which is Yin, so rat people have a built-in potential for good balance. The Yin tendency of water, linked with night, darkness, and introversion, can make good use of the resources of Yang, which is linked with day, light, and extrovert initiative. For example, Yin has a natural inclination to respond to opportunities as they occur. Therefore, to thrive, rats have to work hard in response to situations not immediately under their control. This is stressful for rats, but their innate Yang tendency enables rats also to create opportunities for themselves, thus removing the stress and keeping labors to a minimum. Rats do not enjoy very hard work, especially that which is thrust upon them.

Best associations

Traditionally, the following are said to be associated with rats:

• Taste	salt
• Season	winter
• Birth	anytime in the summer
• Colors	white, black, blue
• Plants	savory, wormwood
• Flowers	orchid, thistle
• Food	peas, pork
• Climate	cold

THE MALE RAT

If a man has a typical rat personality, he will generally display the behavior listed below.

- attempts to profit from everyone
- has an alert eye for the best opportunities
- thrives on the rat race in his line of work
- lives by his wits
- has business acumen
- saves for his old age
- takes gambles
- enjoys spending money
- has a wide circle of acquaintances
- picks up gossip easily and hoards it
- is quick to calculate the odds in any situation
- is sentimental about his family
- has a very active imagination
- is suspicious of the ulterior motives of others
- is basically honest

THE FEMALE RAT

If a woman has a typical rat personality, she will generally display the behavior listed below.

- rules the nest
- appears placid
- profits from her many acquaintances
- is a very resourceful businesswoman
- communicates well
- is an inveterate gossip
- has quick wits
- never misses a sale or a special offer
- keeps plenty of things in stock
- is fashionable but always elegant
- is a superb homemaker
- rarely denies herself anything
- is passionate
- is direct and honest to a fault
- is intellectually creative
- is very good at getting other people working
- is generous to those she loves

THE RAT CHILD

If a child has a typical rat personality, he or she will generally display the behavior listed below.

- is adventurous
- always takes things apart
- can't bear to be left out of anything
- will often be in trouble
- gets into fights
- will be able to get wants fulfilled
- is constantly busy
- embarrasses parents
- is into everything
- is happy and carefree
- loves exploring

RAT AT HOME

Rats are not domestic people. They do, however, like to have somewhere that they can use rather like a retreat. The typical rat home is comfortable, well protected and well furnished. On special occasions, rats like to invite guests around. So a rat home will be a place fit for entertaining. Rats are good hosts and enjoy cooking for and entertaining guests. They are generous and have a flair for light-hearted pleasures. Rats like to enjoy the profits from their labors and are often sentimental at special times such as birthdays and anniversaries. Rats keep their homes tidy and are organized about chores. If they live in a shared house, rats will be the ones to introduce a cleaning rotation and a household kitty.

RAT AT WORK

Rats have an aggressive drive that needs direction; they can be troublemakers if there is not enough to do. Although self-contained, rats can become neurotic about things at work. Rats need comfort and may seem lazy – they prefer others to be doing the really hard work. No matter how much a rat earns, the money is often soon spent. Some rats get a reputation for being a bit of a crook, but this is only because they have an uncanny knack of making a profit out of any situation. Rats prefer to use their minds and their wits, rather than take part in any kind of physical labor.

Some typical rat occupations

- critic
- financial advisor
- broker
- pawnbroker
- lawyer
- detective
- antique dealer
- auctioneer
- connoisseur
- confidential situations
- songwriter
- pathologist
- underground work

RAT PREFERENCES

Likes

- entertaining
- oddities and the unusual
- being the first to explore new places
- underground passages
- mysteries
- unearthing solutions
- money
- taking a gamble
- company
- good quality worldly possessions
- pleasure

Dislikes

- mundane everyday life
- alarm clocks
- rigid timetables
- agendas
- red tape
- bureaucracy
- having nothing to do
- any kind of failure
- being isolated

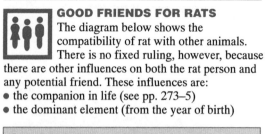

GOOD FRIENDS FOR RATS

The diagram below shows the compatibility of rat with other animals.

There is no fixed ruling, however, because there are other influences on both the rat person and any potential friend. These influences are:

- the companion in life (see pp. 273–5)
- the dominant element (from the year of birth)

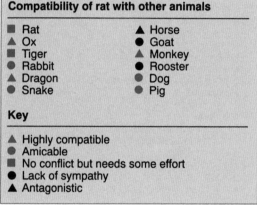

Compatibility of rat with other animals

■ Rat	▲ Horse
▲ Ox	● Goat
■ Tiger	▲ Monkey
● Rabbit	● Rooster
▲ Dragon	● Dog
● Snake	● Pig

Key

▲ Highly compatible
● Amicable
■ No conflict but needs some effort
● Lack of sympathy
▲ Antagonistic

Rat with rat This pairing can be very good or very bad. Two opportunistic rats can create double the trouble or double the benefit. At first, the relationship will be passionate but interest soon wanes when they finish exploring their similarities.

Ox with rat Even though these too have little in common, a match between them will be fortunate. Sensitive rat will appreciate ox's earnest nature. Ox will be attracted to rat's intelligence and sincerity. Rat can find a peaceful resting place with ox.

Tiger with rat The idealist tiger who doesn't care about material things and the materialist rat can be a good pair if they both make the effort. Together they could be volatile rebels with a cause, but rat will have to please tiger by letting tiger be the center of attention.

Rabbit with rat Yes, these two can get along together very well, but rat should be careful not to exploit rabbit, which would spoil the friendship. Business partnerships will be more successful than romantic ones.

Dragon with rat This is a very good match. Both are easily bored so plenty of activity can be expected, although rat may have to let dragon take the dominant role. The rat will admire the dragon; as dragons love admiration, a relationship could work.

Snake with rat These two make a friendly pair who both enjoy fine things and will gossip together for hours. Snake can blow hot and cold and may be possessive one moment and wander off to new pastures the next, but all this will be temporary.

Horse with rat A relationship between these two egotists is definitely to be avoided unless there are very positive influences. Horse and rat really do rub each other the wrong way. The rat will be annoyed by the horse's excessive outbursts.

Goat with rat There is not much mutual understanding between these two, but they are fine together for short periods for specific interests. In general, the carefree goat will be good for the rat and will enjoy rat's charm.

Monkey with rat On the whole, this combination will last because they have much in common. They will make an entertaining but cunning pair, constantly hatching new plans. The relationship may be marred by competitiveness, however, and rat may have to accept monkey's dominance.

Rooster with rat These two have very little common ground for more than a passing acquaintance. No serious relationships are likely to develop unless there are other strong influences. Rats will judge roosters on appearance and find them vain and superficial.

Dog with rat On the whole, these two live in different worlds, so, while they can be quite friendly toward each other, the long-term prospects are not good because dog's passion for fair play will clash with rat's tendency to exploit.

Pig with rat This sensual pair can be very good friends for a while, but trusting pig is rather vulnerable to rat's charms and may end up unable to say no when necessary.

RAT IN LOVE

All is romance and passion when a typical rat falls in love. Rat will be as sentimental about little things shared together as about anniversaries. The love partner of a rat can expect rat to be cautious and nervous at first until the relationship is better established, then rat's generosity will know no bounds. Rats are sensual people who will do much to please their partners. Unfortunately, once rats feel secure in a relationship, they have a tendency to be selfish and demanding. Unless they are strong-minded, rat partners may get depressed by this side of rat's nature.

RAT AND SEX

Rat is not backward when it comes to making sexual advances. They like to take the initiative and favor exciting intrigues over safe affairs. Both male and female rats want sex in a romantic spot, or, even better, in a secret place. Rats offer frequent nights of mad, passionate love. Rats are naturally faithful and, if they stray, it is by chance, and they will feel very guilty about it. If rat's partner is unfaithful, then rat will follow suit. The best way to seduce a rat is to find a setting for love that is secretive, mysterious, and has candles and good wine. If you want rat to abandon you, set the scene for a boring evening in the most mundane, unromantic setting you can find. Rat will soon leave, blaming you for the split.

HEALTH

Rat's element, water, is associated in ancient Chinese acupuncture with the kidneys and bladder, so it is these organs that should be kept in good balance. The rat's tendency to hide anxieties could lead to an imbalance. The more rats learn to talk about their problems, the better for their general health.

LEISURE INTERESTS

Rat people are most likely to enjoy puzzles and games of chance. Following the stock market, keeping up with fashions and bargain hunting for all kinds of antiques will please rat. Sports are not really rat's forte, except exploratory activities such as caving. Rats usually like to be associated with the current in-groups and enjoy all kinds of light-hearted socializing.

THE RAT YEARS AND THEIR ELEMENTS

The rat is a Yang water animal. Each of the rat years, however, is associated with an element which is said to have its own influence. These elements are wood, fire, earth, metal, and water. They influence rat in a regular sequence, which is repeated every 60 years. In the table opposite, for example, the rat year 1900 is a metal year. The next metal year is 60 years later in 1960, and the next will be 2020.

Rat's natural element is water. When the year is a metal year, the influences of water and metal are said to be combined. Those born in the year of the rat 1960 are **Rat Water–Metal** people. The possible effects of the year elements are listed below.

Lunar years ruled by the rat and their elements		
1900	Jan 31, 1900 – Feb 18, 1901	metal
1912	Feb 18, 1912 – Feb 5, 1913	water
1924	Feb 5, 1924 – Jan 24, 1925	wood
1936	Jan 24, 1936 – Feb 10, 1937	fire
1948	Feb 10, 1948 – Jan 28, 1949	earth
1960	Jan 28, 1960 – Feb 14, 1961	metal
1972	Feb 15, 1972 – Feb 2, 1973	water
1984	Feb 2, 1984 – Feb 19, 1985	wood
1996	Feb 19, 1996 – Feb 7, 1997	fire

Rat Water–Metal (1900, 1960)
This rat is endowed with integrity, ambition, and the ability to make a sustained effort to carry a project through to its conclusion. On the negative side, metal can be too inflexible, leading to rigid attitudes which threaten to stifle creative thought. This rat should try to be more malleable and open to compromise, although water does help to soften this tendency of metal.

Rat Water–Water (1912, 1972)
Rats born in water years are in their natural element. They are, therefore, doubly endowed with the ability to persuade diplomatically and have very acute

awareness of future trends. On the negative side, the double water rat may become swamped with too much information and keep too much hidden in their watery depths. Atypically, water rats are very sensitive and are too concerned about the opinions of others. This rat should try to be more forthcoming and take the lead occasionally.

Rat Water–Wood (1924, 1984)

Wood is a creative element, so rats born in these years may be artistic in some way. They are also endowed with self-confidence, a strong moral sense, and an ability to grow, expanding their activities widely. On the negative side, wood can create too many options, leading to a complexity that is unmanageable. Combined with indecisive water, this can mean trouble. These rats should try to control their inclination to bite off more than they can chew and, instead, concentrate their resources.

Rat Water–Fire (1936, 1996)

This rat is endowed with decisiveness, wisdom, and a capacity for innovation that leads to success. They can tolerate periods of rapid change and adjustment. On the negative side, they sometimes become too enthusiastic and passionate, which can lead to destruction of the very thing that they were about to achieve. This rat should try to control a sharp tongue and keep energies flowing in a positive direction.

Rat Water–Earth (1948, 2008)

Earth combined with water is a balancing combination for the rat. Earth rats are endowed with practicality, prudence, self-discipline, and the ability to work hard. On the negative side, they may move too slowly, losing the initiative and delaying making crucial decisions. This rat should use self-discipline to keep to a rigorously paced schedule, allowing the imagination more freedom.

RAT AND THE ZODIAC OF WESTERN ASTROLOGY

To work out your zodiac sign see p. 277. General character traits of rats of the 12 zodiac signs are given below. Bear in mind that the Western zodiac sign modifies the basic rat nature – especially in the area of personal relationships.

Aries rat Independent, enthusiastic and original, this combination has great potential unless there is opposition, in which case Aries rat can be extremely aggressive. Aries' lack of stamina is balanced by rat's staying power.

Taurus rat Conservative, resourceful, and artistically inclined, Taurean rats have great charm, love the good life but can be excessively indulgent. Taurus, however, will help rat to appreciate more fully the talents of others.

Gemini rat Social, great communicators, and collectors of interesting ideas, these rats have a touch of magic and are quick-change artists. Having nothing to do is a disaster for Gemini rats and can lead to depression. Their quick wits will help them to achieve their ambitions.

Cancer rat These rats are very emotional, sensitive to the needs of others, and protective. This combination can be overpowering, and care should be exercised to keep things in perspective. Cancer rats, however, are great dreamers but have a good business sense.

Leo rat Dignified, optimistic, and generous to a fault, Leo rats need to be in the limelight. This will have to be balanced with rat's preference for dark, secret places. These rats are great creative leaders, especially in the literary field.

Virgo rat Virgoan rats are meticulous, sensual, and logical. This combination is excellent at painstaking research. The Virgo attention to detail and the rat desire to hoard can be put to excellent use in building reserves, but these will never seem adequate.

Libra rat These rats are so charming, peaceable, and refined that aggression almost never occurs. They are well balanced, diplomatic, and value loyalty in personal relationships and in business. Libra rats seek companionship so are very romantic and must have music.

Scorpio rat Penetrative, investigative, and passionate, Scorpio rats have accurate instincts and are aware of the darker side of human nature. These rats can become great criminologists or criminals. Others should be wary since these rats like to work alone.

Sagittarius rat Energetic, bluntly honest, and disarmingly happy with life, these rats keep their sorrows and disappointments hidden. This combination can be successful in almost any project, provided variety and constant change are involved.

Capricorn rat Rats born under this sign are ambitious, controlling, and difficult to change. The rat personality, however, helps them to loosen up and enjoy a little fun from time to time.

Aquarius rat Energetic Aquarius combines to make this rat very intellectual and an authority in several areas of research. A tendency to eccentricity can work wonders or lead to neuroticism, but it will ensure that life will never be dull for Aquarius rat.

Pisces rat An intuitive, well-intentioned, and versatile combination, Pisces and rat can lead to confusion or the tendency to live in an illusory world. The rat's ability to gain from most situations, however, can result in success.

Some famous people born in the years of the rat and their zodiac signs

- Lucrezia Borgia
  Noblewoman
  Apr 18, 1480 Aries

- William Shakespeare
  Playwright
  Apr 26, 1564 Taurus

- Joseph Haydn
  Composer
  Mar 31, 1732 Aries

- Wolfgang Amadeus Mozart
  Composer
  Jan 27, 1756 Aquarius

- Jules Verne
  Writer
  Feb 8, 1828 Aquarius

- Leo Tolstoy
  Writer
  Sep 9, 1828 Virgo

- Auguste Rodin
  Sculptor
  Nov 12, 1840 Scorpio

- Claude Monet
  Artist
  Nov 14, 1840 Scorpio

- Henri Toulouse-Lautrec
  Artist
  Nov 24, 1864 Sagittarius

- Mata Hari
  Spy
  Aug 7, 1876 Leo

- Maurice Chevalier
  Actor/Singer
  Sep 12, 1888 Virgo

- Spencer Tracy
  Actor
  Apr 5, 1900 Aries

- Aaron Copland
  Composer
  Nov 14, 1900 Scorpio

- Gene Kelly
  Dancer/Actor
  Aug 23, 1912 Leo

- Richard Nixon
  US president
  Jan 9, 1913 Capricorn

- Doris Day
  Actress
  Apr 3, 1924 Aries

- Marlon Brando
  Actor
  Apr 3, 1924 Aries

- Lauren Bacall
  Actress
  Sep 16, 1924 Virgo

- Jimmy Carter
  US president
  Oct 1, 1924 Libra

- Charlton Heston
  Actor
  Oct 4, 1924 Libra

- Yves St Laurent
  Couturier
  Aug 1, 1936 Leo

- Vanessa Redgrave
  Actress
  Jan 30, 1937 Aquarius

- Boris Spassky
  Chessmaster
  Jan 30, 1937 Aquarius

- Prince Charles
  Heir to British throne
  Nov 18, 1948 Scorpio

2. The Ox

The Yin water animal.

Lunar years ruled by the ox

1901	Feb 19, 1901 – Feb 7, 1902
1913	Feb 6, 1913 – Jan 25, 1914
1925	Jan 25, 1925 – Feb 12, 1926
1937	Feb 11, 1937 – Jan 30, 1938
1949	Jan 29, 1949 – Feb 16, 1950
1961	Feb 15, 1961 – Feb 4, 1962
1973	Feb 3, 1973 – Jan 22, 1974
1985	Feb 20, 1985 – Feb 8, 1986
1997	Feb 8, 1997 – Jan 27, 1998

In China, many people do not eat beef as the ox is respected for the help it gives in working the land. The ox is associated with water, and figures of oxen were once thrown into rivers to prevent flooding.

THE OX PERSONALITY

Basically, oxen are honest, straightforward, kindhearted people – often described as down-to-earth. Oxen have great reserves of strength to call on and are very hardworking. They are normally easy to get along with because they have no duplicity in them. Oxen do exactly what they say, and mean what they say. Despite being respectable and conventional, oxen are very independent minded and not easily swayed by the opinions of others. They cannot take advice very well and can be intolerant and scathing to those they disagree with.

Characteristics

These are the general personality traits of those people who are typical oxen, both at their best and at their worst.

Positive	Negative
● conscientious	● slow
● patient	● stubborn
● hardworking	● intolerant
● reliable	● biased
● serious	● hot tempered
● gentle	● dogmatic
● strong	● conservative
● careful	● materialistic
● persistent	● complacent
● determined	● conformist
● clear-thinking	● gloomy
● capable	● dull
● practical	

Secret ox

The image of the ox is that of a placid person.
Mostly this is true. If, however, oxen are provoked
or their patience stretched too far, they can act like
bulls shown a red rag. This hot-tempered side of
ox's nature is well hidden but always present. Also,
despite their homely images, oxen are actually very
innovative and creative people.

Element

Ox is linked to the ancient Chinese element of water.
Water is linked to the arts and expressiveness. In
oxen, however, water is more likely to be stagnant
and passively, rather than actively, expressed. Bear
in mind, water can be both as nurturing as rain or as
destructive as a hurricane.

Balance

Oxen value their privacy highly. They very rarely
confide their feelings to anyone. Oxen go to great
lengths to keep their innermost secrets, and the
barriers they build to protect themselves can become
a prison. Unless people born in the year of the ox
learn to balance this need for privacy with a more
open and relaxed attitude to their emotions, they will
become neurotic and suffer from self-delusion, as
too much repression can direct the ox's quite
formidable energies inward.

Best associations

Traditionally, the following are said to be associated with oxen:

- Taste   sweet
- Season   winter
- Birth   summer night
- Colors   yellow, blue
- Plant   hemp
- Flower   orchid
- Food   ginger
- Climate   cold, wet

THE MALE OX

If a man has a typical ox personality, he will generally display the behavior listed below.

- is difficult to understand
- keeps doubts to himself
- appears to be a pessimist
- values his family life
- plans ahead for the future
- is not particularly quick-witted
- is disciplined and dutiful
- has a tendency to be authoritarian
- loves good food and drink
- will be lazy at home
- is likely to be a chauvinist

THE FEMALE OX

If a woman has a typical ox personality, she will generally display the behavior listed below.

- can be outspoken
- is lacking in the social graces
- is very good at organizing things
- is reticent but not shy
- will never forgive those who betray her
- is very industrious
- enjoys her home comforts
- is loyal to her family
- will always repay a debt
- is always dignified
- is a very private person
- is less inhibited than male oxen

THE OX CHILD

If a child has a typical ox personality, he or she will generally display the behavior listed below.

- is best left alone when in a temper
- enjoys collecting things
- is serious and thoughtful
- has few close friends
- likes to make and build things
- is often a bookworm
- needs encouragement to relax
- enjoys own company
- will organize themselves

OX AT HOME

Oxen enjoy the material things in life. An ox home will be comfortable but not necessarily luxurious, as Oxen are practical people. They prefer to live in a rural area rather than a large city, and the best location for an ox home is near water such as a river. If an ox is unable to live in the country, a garden is essential. It will be well maintained as oxen like to work with the earth and grow plants. If none of these options are possible, you are guaranteed to find many flourishing houseplants in an ox's home. An ox is likely to have a study or some area devoted to work in their house. It will be cluttered with old letters, photos, mementos and knickknacks collected over the years. There will, of course, be some organizing system – but only the ox will understand it.

OX AT WORK

Oxen can achieve something in most professions, as they will apply themselves and succeed through hard work and diligence. Before embarking on a project, they have to first be interested and convinced of its worth, then they will explore all facets of the situation, and finally decide on the best plan of action. In this calm and methodical way, logical oxen achieve a lot. They are, however, not suited to jobs that require negotiating skills. Working with food or in agriculture is often advantageous for an ox. Surprisingly, their ability to bring a carefully thought out and often highly unique solution to a problem makes oxen good candidates for the arts. Oxen are suited to musical careers, as they can apply themselves to the necessary practice as well as employ their creative capacities. As employers, oxen will be fair bosses and pay good wages but will expect loyalty to the company. As workers, oxen tend to blame others for their own mistakes. They are always punctual, though.

Some typical ox occupations

- composer
- landlord
- doctor
- religious leader
- estate management
- cook or chef
- farmer
- police or military officer

- soldier
- teacher
- philosopher
- judge
- banker
- insurance broker
- gardener

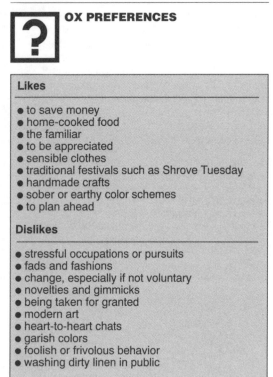

OX PREFERENCES

Likes

- to save money
- home-cooked food
- the familiar
- to be appreciated
- sensible clothes
- traditional festivals such as Shrove Tuesday
- handmade crafts
- sober or earthy color schemes
- to plan ahead

Dislikes

- stressful occupations or pursuits
- fads and fashions
- change, especially if not voluntary
- novelties and gimmicks
- being taken for granted
- modern art
- heart-to-heart chats
- garish colors
- foolish or frivolous behavior
- washing dirty linen in public

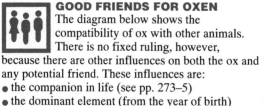

GOOD FRIENDS FOR OXEN

The diagram below shows the compatibility of ox with other animals. There is no fixed ruling, however, because there are other influences on both the ox and any potential friend. These influences are:

- the companion in life (see pp. 273–5)
- the dominant element (from the year of birth)

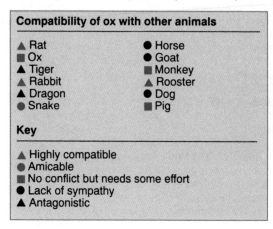

Compatibility of ox with other animals

▲ Rat	● Horse
■ Ox	● Goat
▲ Tiger	■ Monkey
▲ Rabbit	▲ Rooster
▲ Dragon	● Dog
● Snake	■ Pig

Key

▲ Highly compatible
● Amicable
■ No conflict but needs some effort
● Lack of sympathy
▲ Antagonistic

Rat with ox A partnership between these two could be auspicious – it will be strong and fortunate. Sensitive rat will appreciate ox's earnest nature. Ox will be attracted to rat's intelligence and sincerity. Rat can find a peaceful resting place with ox.

Ox with ox Two oxen could be very happy together, but one of them would have to make the first move. Otherwise the relationship would never get beyond acquaintanceship.

Tiger with ox Never! These two are natural enemies. Tiger's predilection for change and ox's need for orderliness do not go well together. There will definitely be arguments, fights even. Although tiger may seem more likely to dominate, ox will bulldoze tiger into defeat.

Rabbit with ox A harmonious match, as rabbit likes to feel secure, and ox can provide security. Refined rabbit may find ox a little too homely, and their straight-talking nature hard to handle.

Dragon with ox Willful dragon is too much for most oxen to cope with. Any relationship between these two will not be long-lived. Ox enjoys daily routine; dragon is always trying to escape from it. If they can compromise, dragon may learn the value of taking time to reflect; ox could learn to appreciate the unusual.

Snake with ox Ox is dependable and will give ambitious snake the support he needs. Both like to work toward long-term goals. Each will respect the other's need for privacy, and all should go well as long as snake does not reveal his manipulative nature to ox.

Horse with ox This will be an unhappy match for the pair. The two will only annoy each other. Lively horse will not get any excitement from ox; ox cannot give the flattery that vain horse requires. Also, horse is too independent to accept ox's authoritarian habits for long.

Goat with ox Goat and ox have discordant personalities. Goat's habit of acting without thinking will only annoy careful ox. They also have different priorities in life: goat is too capricious, and ox demands fidelity as the basis for a relationship.

Monkey with ox Mischievous monkey will tease serious ox, but usually gently and with love. Ox will be fascinated by monkey's sparkling personality, but these two are unlikely to settle down together. They may misunderstand each other, and monkey will not hang around long enough to sort any differences out.

Rooster with ox This is probably the best match for ox. These two are highly compatible. Sociable rooster complements ox's steady nature, and ox will allow rooster to show off. They both care about money and financial security.

Dog with ox Imaginative dog may not be happy with staid ox. Dog is likely to criticize ox for lacking a sense of humor. If they can learn to respect each other, however, they can get along, as both are realists and loyal.

Pig with ox Pig enjoys peace and quiet as much as ox but may find ox's responsible behavior wearisome. Pigs like to go out and enjoy themselves; oxen like to stay at home and relax. Pig may find ox too demanding; ox will find pig irritating.

OX IN LOVE

Oxen are wary about falling in love. They know that it destroys routines and brings new and unfamiliar experiences. Oxen rarely lose their heads, let alone their hearts, over another. They appear to be dispassionate and unromantic because their forthright natures do not understand the subtleties and game playing of romantic entrapments. But do not be deceived, oxen are still capable of deep feelings and will be faithful, loving, and devoted to their partners. Loyalty is very important to ox. Once betrayed, they will find it hard to enter a new relationship. Ox will probably neglect anniversaries, as ox is not particularly sentimental. Although oxen try not to be hurtful, they do need to learn how to respect their partner.

OX AND SEX

Oxen are usually considerate to others but can be timid in matters of love. They are unlikely to initiate lovemaking and find it hard to create a romantic atmosphere. Secretly, ox likes to be fussed over and even bossed around. Oxen are never jealous of their partner but will be jealous of their "rights" – especially fidelity. Responsibility and trust are more important to an ox than good sex. Lovers of oxen can feel taken for granted, as physically undemonstrative ox can be clumsy and tongue-tied when it comes to expressing emotions. A subtle approach to them may not work as oxen cannot read between the lines. Furthermore, they will definitely be angered by outright criticism.

HEALTH

Ox's element, water, is associated with the kidneys, so ox should pay particular attention to keeping these organs in working order. Water is also associated with the ears and bladder. Drink plenty of water and do not allow your body to get lazy. Oxen should also guard against neuroses by learning to express their emotions.

LEISURE INTERESTS

Oxen enjoy exercise and like to keep themselves in shape. They prefer traditional sports – rugby, football, or hockey, for example. Fighting sports are good for oxen as they allow them to vent their aggression in a controlled environment. Oxen are well suited to activities, such as martial arts, that require patience, practice, and hard work to become skilled at.
For holidays, oxen do not like to travel more than they have to and definitely not alone. They are happier to go in a group. Nevertheless, oxen are capable of extremes and may decide to sail single-handedly around the world.

THE OX YEARS AND THEIR ELEMENTS

The ox is a Yin water animal. Each of the ox years, however, is associated with an element which is said to have its own influence. These elements are water, fire, earth, metal, and wood. They influence ox in a regular sequence, which is repeated every 60 years. In the table

below, for example, the ox year 1901 is a metal year.
The next ox metal year is 60 years later in 1961, and
the next will be 2021. Ox's natural element is water;
the influence of this combines with those of the
element of the year of birth. The possible effects of
the year elements are listed below.

Lunar years ruled by the ox and their elements			
1901	Feb 19, 1901	– Feb 7, 1902	metal
1913	Feb 6, 1913	– Jan 25, 1914	water
1925	Jan 25, 1925	– Feb 12, 1926	wood
1937	Feb 11, 1937	– Jan 30, 1938	fire
1949	Jan 29, 1949	– Feb 16, 1950	earth
1961	Feb 15, 1961	– Feb 4, 1962	metal
1973	Feb 3, 1973	– Jan 22, 1974	water
1985	Feb 20, 1985	– Feb 8, 1986	wood
1997	Feb 8, 1997	– Jan 27, 1998	fire

OxWater–Metal (1901, 1961)

Metal strengthens some of the ox's qualities, so
metal oxen are even more stubborn and
hardworking. They are also incredibly self-sufficient
and resourceful. Conversely, metal also makes the
ox less objective and more intuitive, while the ox's
own strong character makes them the warmest of all
metal people. Metal oxen are artistic and eloquent,
and they have both logic and vision. This produces
charismatic people who inspire others with their
inevitable achievements. These oxen can be
domineering, however, and are prone to taking
themselves too seriously.

OxWater–Water (1913, 1973)

Water ox is in his natural element. Water brings sensitivity to this ox who is more likely to listen and help others. Atypically, this ox is almost diplomatic. Water helps oxen focus and channel their energies, and water oxen find it easier to express their emotions. Therefore, they are less prone to neuroses. Although double water slows the ox down, it also allows them to be more flexible. Despite being very patient, they are intolerant of weakness or self-pity in others.

OxWater–Wood (1925, 1985)

The ox's natural water element allows the wood to flower. Wood oxen have physical strength combined with natural energy. They are the most innovative, creative, and eloquent of all the oxen. These oxen have a better developed sense of humor and, at times, are even witty. Good learners, oxen born in a wood year are exceptional as they are not afraid to try new things. Wood makes this ox more sociable but due to its flammable nature also more quick-tempered.

OxWater–Fire (1937, 1997)

Fire conflicts with water to produce an impatient ox who lacks the typical ox's placid approach to life. Fire oxen are combative and forceful characters. Although they often offend people, fire oxen do try not to cause unnecessary conflict. All oxen consider themselves superior to others, but they usually conceal this with modesty. Fire oxen, however, lack the ox's normal self-effacing manner and can appear proud and arrogant. In fact, they are basically kind and honest but lack the skills of tact and diplomacy.

Ox Water–Earth (1949, 2009)
The element earth is associated with many of the ox's innate qualities: reliability, resourcefulness, practicality, steadfastness, and patience, for example. So these people are stereotypical oxen. Earth oxen are hugely materialistic but will always earn their wealth. They have a high sense of justice and are generous to those who need help. Earth allows the ox to be relatively at ease in expressing love physically. Earth oxen are the least creative of all oxen, and they never take risks or shortcuts. These people are very homely and pleasant but perhaps a little dull.

 OX AND THE ZODIAC OF WESTERN ASTROLOGY
To work out your zodiac sign see p. 277. General character traits of oxen of the 12 zodiac signs are given below. Bear in mind that the Western zodiac sign modifies the basic ox nature – especially in the area of personal relationships.

Aries ox The combination of steadfast ox and volatile Aries makes these oxen both imaginative and persistent. They are interesting people who are both capable and spontaneous.
Taurus ox The bull and ox combine to accentuate the ox's character, good points and bad. They are very stable, reliable, and down-to-earth, yet more tender. But these oxen must learn to be flexible.

Gemini ox These oxen are less serious then their counterparts. Relatively quick-witted, they are lively conversationalists, but they can be too opinionated. Gemini oxen are very good company.

Cancer ox Cancer diminishes some of the ox's assets, such as reliability and determination. If they are not careful, Cancer oxen may never achieve their goals. Cancer can make the ox touchy but, deep down, they are very sensitive. These oxen are generally careful with money.

Leo ox Leo allows these people to get out of the traditional ox rut. They are more easygoing and fun-loving, unless opposed – Leonine oxen can be aggressive. Mostly, however, they are caring people who have great style.

Virgo ox Virgo brings precision to the patient ox, although others can find their perfectionism irritating and their manner too critical. Virgo oxen are often eccentrically conservative.

Libra ox Charming and popular, Libra oxen are at ease in social situations. They are sensual and love to indulge themselves. Atypically, these oxen don't mind talking about themselves; in fact, they feel a need to be understood.

Scorpio ox Ox determination combined with Scorpio depth make formidable characters who are still emotional and sensitive at heart. Dangerous when angry, however, they can be stubborn and are even violent at times. Scorpio oxen never compromise on anything.

Sagittarius ox Sagittarius brings balance to the ox. These oxen are the most open-minded of the breed.

All oxen are given to reflection, but Sagittarian oxen go to lengths philosophizing.

Capricorn ox These people seek status, power, and recognition. Eventually they will achieve them through perseverance. The most serious of all oxen, Capricornean ones do not suffer jokers.

Aquarius ox Ox born under this sign is more flexible than others. Aquarian oxen are very talkative but nervous, and they find it hard to say what they really mean. Still powerful, they disguise their strength with subtlety.

Pisces ox An unlikely combination of flighty Pisces with steady ox produces a relatively happy person. They are difficult to understand but are basically kind and loving. Piscean oxen should try a career in the arts.

Some famous people born in the years of the ox and their zodiac signs

- George F. Handel
  Composer
  Feb 23, 1685 Pisces

- J.S. Bach
  Composer
  Mar 21, 1685 Aries

- Napoleon Bonaparte
  Military leader
  Aug 15, 1769 Leo

- Antonín Dvořák
  Composer
  Sep 18, 1841 Virgo

- Vincent van Gogh
  Painter
  Mar 30, 1853 Aries

- William Butler Yeats
  Poet/Playwright
  Jun 13, 1865 Gemini

- Jean Sibelius
  Composer
  Dec 8, 1865 Sagittarius

- Charlie Chaplin
  Comic actor
  Apr 16, 1889 Aries

- Adolf Hitler
  Dictator
  Apr 20, 1889 Taurus

- Jawaharlal Nehru
  Statesman
  Nov 14, 1889 Scorpio

- Walt Disney
  Film producer
  Dec 5, 1901 Sagittarius

- Vivien Leigh
  Actress
  Nov 5, 1913 Scorpio

- Paul Newman
  Actor
  Jan 26, 1925 Aquarius

- Jack Lemmon
  Actor
  Feb 8, 1925 Aquarius

- Margaret Thatcher
  British politician
  Oct 13, 1925 Libra

- Warren Beatty
  Actor/Director
  Mar 30, 1937 Aries

- Jack Nicholson
  Actor
  Apr 28, 1937 Taurus

- Vladimir Ashkenazy
  Pianist
  Jul 6, 1937 Cancer

- David Hockney
  Artist
  Jul 9, 1937 Cancer

- Dustin Hoffman
  Actor
  Aug 8, 1937 Leo

- Robert Redford
  Actor
  Aug 18, 1937 Leo

- Jane Fonda
  Actress
  Dec 21, 1937 Sagittarius

- Juan Carlos I
  Spanish monarch
  Jan 5, 1938 Capricorn

- Meryl Streep
  Actress
  Jun 22, 1949 Cancer

3. The Tiger

The Yang wood animal.

Lunar years ruled by the tiger

1902	Feb 8, 1902	–	Jan 28, 1903
1914	Jan 26, 1914	–	Feb 13, 1915
1926	Feb 13, 1926	–	Feb 1, 1927
1938	Jan 31, 1938	–	Feb 18, 1939
1950	Feb 17, 1950	–	Feb 5, 1951
1962	Feb 5, 1962	–	Jan 24, 1963
1974	Jan 23, 1974	–	Feb 10, 1975
1986	Feb 9, 1986	–	Jan 28, 1987
1998	Jan 28, 1998	–	Feb 5, 1999

Associated with good fortune, power, and royalty, tigers are viewed with both fear and respect. Their protection and wisdom is sought after. The Chinese see the tiger, and not the lion, as the king of animals.

THE TIGER PERSONALITY

Tigers are contrary creatures. The striped coat reflects tiger's ambivalent nature.

Tigers are creatures of great strength and ability; but how this is used can vary greatly. They are born leaders or rebels, and they are instinctively protective, though prone to taking risks, so it may not always be wise to follow one. Often critical, tigers make fine revolutionaries. Once involved in battle, they usually come out on top, though their impetuosity can be their downfall.

Characteristics

These are the general personality traits of those people who are typical tigers, both at their best and at their worst.

Positive	Negative
• loyal	• impetuous
• honorable	• disobedient
• wise	• arrogant
• protective	• impatient
• generous	• critical
• ambitious	• imprudent
• charismatic	• domineering
• daring	• aggressive
• fortunate	• selfish
• idealistic	• demanding
• courageous	• vain
• determined	• stubborn
• sensitive	• quarrelsome
• benevolent	

Secret tiger

On the surface, tigers may appear peaceful and controlled. Hidden underneath, however, there is often an aggressive and even belligerent nature. Also, surprisingly, when faced with difficult decisions, the seemingly decisive tiger has a tendency to retreat into procrastination.

Element

Tiger is linked to the ancient Chinese element of wood. The symbolism of wood is as ambivalent as that of the tiger. As a tree, wood's branches reach for the sky while its roots anchor it in the earth. This endows tiger with the ability (not necessarily used) to moderate his impulsive behavior. Yet wood also gives the tiger passion, which can either lend gentleness to their behavior or may make them violent and destructive.

Balance

The tiger itself is Yang; its striped coat, however, represents the union of both Yin and Yang forces – the balance of which confers great power. It is this contradiction that is at the heart of understanding the nature of tigers. So, while tigers have huge potential, it is a potential for both success or failure. Although usually fortunate, tigers are predisposed to dangerous situations. If they act wisely, tigers can take advantage of this and become very successful. Otherwise, they may fail on a grand scale. Whether a tiger is calm and wise or impetuous and hotheaded in the use of power depends on the individual's ability to learn from experience, heed advice, and channel their energy constructively.

Best associations

Traditionally, the following are said to be associated with tigers:

● Taste	acid
● Season	winter/spring
● Birth	night
● Colors	orange, dark gold
● Plant	bamboo
● Flower	heliotrope
● Food	bread, poultry
● Climate	windy

THE MALE TIGER

If a man has a typical tiger personality, he will generally display the behavior listed below.

- is good-natured
- is peaceful in appearance
- is confident of his good fortune
- possesses a very strong will
- needs to achieve power and recognition
- gives good advice
- seeks attention
- is quick to take the lead
- is usually well mannered
- is a smart and elegant dresser
- takes risks
- is outspoken against authority
- often champions good causes
- is protective toward those weaker than himself
- is a passionate lover

THE FEMALE TIGER
If a woman has a typical tiger personality, she will generally display the behavior listed below.

- is attracted to unusual places, things, and people
- tries to be honest
- dislikes authority
- hates, and will fight against, injustice
- is intense in her feelings of love
- lives an adventurous life
- is not easily impressed by the fashionable
- is very good with children
- likes to be independent
- does not feel remorse or guilt easily
- is often a daring dresser
- will try to avoid the mundane in life
- is a good storyteller
- may be easy to offend
- is strong spirited and intelligent
- can be demanding if she feels she is not valued
- is frank in her opinion of others
- tends to be authoritarian
- if bored, she will become aggressive and quarrelsome

THE TIGER CHILD

If a child has a typical tiger personality, he or she will generally display the behavior listed below.

- is prone to accidents and injuries
- will not be a sneaky child
- likes school
- needs to experience a feeling of danger
- is difficult to discipline
- acts before thinking
- will probably be a constant source of worry
- likes to be the center of attention
- is impatient and demanding
- will often get into scrapes
- is very energetic and playful
- likes to be treated maturely

TIGER AT HOME

A typical tiger home will be very comfortable. Probably expensive, the furnishings will be tasteful and deceptively simple in design. Having a taste for the unusual, tiger's home may be decorated in a unique, though still elegant, fashion, perhaps decorated with mementos from travels abroad, for tigers like to roam and are not happy in one place for long. Tigers are not fond of housework, but, anxious to keep up appearances, they will do their chores quickly with a minimum of fuss. Dotted around the tiger's home you will probably find the odd trophy of some sporting, academic, or other achievement. These are arrayed to impress guests.

TIGER AT WORK

Tigers are formidable business leaders. With their risk-taking natures and natural good luck, tigers make fine entrepreneurs. Tigers' creative minds are full of ideas of how to make money. Although they do not desire riches for their own sake, tigers love the chase. To be really successful, though, a tiger, may need the steadying influence of another. Dragons make ideal business partners for tigers, but a tiger will never be happy taking orders from someone else. This can create problems unless tiger's ego is regularly boosted. Even then, it won't take tigers long to work their way up the ranks to the top. Alternatively, tigers can often be found among the literary and artistic professions as noted writers, poets, or artists, for example. As they yearn for recognition they may feel the need to communicate their ideas to others – usually with great success.

Some typical tiger occupations

- entrepreneur
- military officer
- head of state
- politician
- publicist
- musician
- writer/poet
- advertising executive
- designer
- film/theater director
- stockbroker
- athlete
- film star
- union leader
- company director
- stunt person
- rebel leader
- explorer
- lion tamer
- teacher

TIGER PREFERENCES

Likes

- success
- to be their own person
- comfort, though not too sumptuous
- big parties
- appreciation and recognition of their prowess
- spending money
- honesty in others and themselves
- change and anything new or unusual
- to buy the best quality goods they can afford
- a challenge
- being in charge
- flattery
- surprises

Dislikes

- failure
- feeling caged in by circumstances or people
- rules and laws made by others
- everyday life and its responsibilities
- paying attention to detail
- scandalmongering
- taking orders or criticism
- nursing others
- jewels and trinkets
- being ignored
- established authority
- hypocrisy

GOOD FRIENDS FOR TIGERS

The diagram below shows the compatibility of tiger with other animals. There is no fixed ruling, however, because there are other influences on both the tiger and any potential friend. These influences are:

● the companion in life (see pp. 273–5)
● the dominant element (from the year of birth)

Also, for any relationship to succeed, the tiger must be the center of attention and at least appear to take the lead.

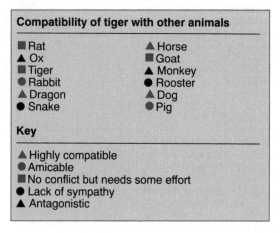

Compatibility of tiger with other animals

■ Rat	▲ Horse
▲ Ox	■ Goat
■ Tiger	▲ Monkey
● Rabbit	● Rooster
▲ Dragon	▲ Dog
● Snake	● Pig

Key

▲ Highly compatible
● Amicable
■ No conflict but needs some effort
● Lack of sympathy
▲ Antagonistic

Rat with tiger Although both passionate, the idealistic tiger and the materialistic rat can only be a good pair if they both make the effort. Tiger may find rat charming but a little insincere. Rat may be impressed by tiger's energy but will not appreciate his impulsiveness.

Ox with tiger Tiger's predilection for change and ox's need for orderliness do not go well together. In fact, their temperaments are so different that these two are often enemies.

Tiger with tiger Any relationship between two tigers will be fiery. During good times, the tigers' love of excitement and basic good nature will make for a wild relationship. They will not be able to stand each other, however, during bad times. Ultimately, as all tigers need to be the center of attention, two tigers is often one too many.

Rabbit with tiger Basically, these two understand each other very well. Rabbit is tactful enough to let tiger take the lead. Sometimes, however, rabbit will not take tiger seriously, and tiger will resent this. If the two share an interest, the bond will be stronger.

Dragon with tiger Very similar in temperament, both are impulsive and passionate, yet dragon provides a steadying influence on tiger. Any relationship between them will never be boring. As they are both frank, misunderstandings do not last for long.

Snake with tiger Snake and tiger approach life from opposite angles. Snake follows its head and tiger its heart; snake likes peace and quiet while tiger likes action and risk. Both would misunderstand and feel suspicious of the motivations of the other.

Horse with tiger There can be great attachment
between a tiger and a horse. Patient horse will enjoy
the company of energetic tiger and stick by tiger
when he's down. Even so, they will probably still
argue and need to take time out from the relationship
occasionally.

Goat with tiger A difficult but potentially mutually
rewarding partnership. Goat will admire tiger's
nerve and loyalty while tiger will appreciate goat's
fun-loving nature. To be more than fair-weather
friends, however, a little effort will be needed.

Monkey with tiger Tiger and monkey are both
competitive, and neither knows how to compromise.
Secretly, monkey may admire but cannot resist
mocking tiger; tiger cannot help retaliating, and the
relationship could quickly become destructive.
Unless there is great love on monkey's part and
moderation on tiger's part, no relationship will work.

Rooster with tiger Initially promising, tiger and
rooster are unable to have more than a brief
friendship. Although these two colorful characters
have much in common, they will quickly begin
misunderstanding and criticizing each other. Not
given to reflection, tiger will most likely fail to see
the thoughtful nature behind rooster's swaggering
facade.

Dog with tiger The different natures of these two
actually complement each other perfectly. Anxious
dog will curb tiger's excessive risk taking; tiger will
appreciate dog's loyalty. The relationship could
prove long-lasting and stable. Both are idealists and

can combine their talents to achieve great things for a good cause.

Pig with tiger These two can get on well together as they are both gregarious, tolerant, and independent. Tiger will protect pig from his enemies, and pig will prove loyal. Be warned, however, that tiger may be tempted to test pig's temper and find himself on the losing end of the stick.

TIGER IN LOVE

Thanks to their charismatic personalities, tigers are not short of admirers. Led by the heart, tiger is quick to fall in love. When in love, tiger will at first be intense and passionate. After the initial thrill has passed, however, tiger often loses interest. Therefore, the love life of a tiger may be hard to keep up with – full of ups and downs, bursts of passion, and many "conquests." If tiger's love partner is clever, they will let tiger know that they would be quite happy alone. This will ensnare tiger, who hates an easy prey. Tiger can make a romantic, affectionate, but sometimes inattentive partner.

TIGER AND SEX

Tiger's boundless energy, creative mind, and passionate nature make both the male and female imaginative and energetic lovers. Lovemaking will most likely come in short bursts as tigers are sprinters, not long-distance runners. To seduce a tiger, remember that luxurious or exotic settings are best; a touch of danger added to the encounter will be an irresistible lure. On the whole, tigers are faithful; if they do have an affair it will be to assert their independence. Tigers expect loyalty from their mates, so if the tiger's partner is unfaithful, the relationship will soon end. To get rid of unwanted tigers, don't ignore them! Simply become possessive, demanding, dependent – make them feel caged in, and they'll soon break away.

 HEALTH

Tiger's element, wood, is associated with the liver, so tigers should pay particular attention to keeping this organ in working order. Emotionally, tiger should let off steam occasionally by releasing any pent-up anger or passion. Otherwise tiger may become too anxious and obsessive.

 LEISURE INTERESTS

Tiger people tend to engage in the more energetic and daring varieties of any activity. So skiing, hang gliding, stock-car racing, or surfing are ideal sports for the tiger. For vacations, tigers like to travel to distant places. Package tours, though, are not their style; trekking, mountaineering, going on safaris, white-water rafting, and so on are more suitable. On a tamer level, tigers love a good party where they can cause a stir.

THE TIGER YEARS AND THEIR ELEMENTS

The tiger is a Yang wood animal. Each of the tiger years, however, is associated with an element which is said to have its own influence. These elements are wood, fire, earth, metal, and water. They influence tiger in a regular sequence, which is repeated every 60 years. In the table below, for example, the tiger year 1902 is a water year. The next tiger water year is 60 years later in 1962, and the next will be 2022. Tiger's natural element is wood; the influence of this combines with those of the element of the year of birth. The possible effects of the year elements are listed below.

Lunar years ruled by the tiger and their elements			
1902	Feb 8, 1902	– Jan 28, 1903	water
1914	Jan 26, 1914	– Feb 13, 1915	wood
1926	Feb 13, 1926	– Feb 1, 1927	fire
1938	Jan 31, 1938	– Feb 18, 1939	earth
1950	Feb 17, 1950	– Feb 5, 1951	metal
1962	Feb 5, 1962	– Jan 24, 1963	water
1974	Jan 23, 1974	– Feb 10, 1975	wood
1986	Feb 9, 1986	– Jan 28, 1987	fire
1998	Jan 28, 1998	– Feb 5, 1999	earth

Tiger Wood–Water (1902, 1962)

This reserved tiger is endowed with compassion and is more sensitive to the needs of others than a typical tiger. Full of noble ideas, combined with an ability to control passionate whims and look before leaping, this tiger can make a just and wise leader. A water tiger's life will be more calm than other tigers'. There is a tendency, though, for water tigers to be slightly pompous.

Tiger Wood–Wood (1914, 1974)

This sociable tiger is particularly charming and witty – a real party animal. Wood tigers are very enterprising and good at thinking up grand schemes; the details, however, will be left to others to sort out. Apparently superficial emotionally, double wood tigers can actually become quite anxious – so they should try to keep stress under control.

Tiger Wood–Fire (1926, 1986)

Tigers are already inherently Yang; fire is also Yang. This doubling of the Yang force makes fire tigers incredibly active people. They are animated, exciting yet changeable characters. Sensitive to perceived slights, the fire tiger often has a very quick temper and can soon become explosive. Fortunately, bursts of temper never last long with this tiger. To really enjoy life, fire tiger needs to try and relax and take things at a more controlled pace.

Tiger Wood–Earth (1938, 1998)

Unlike most other tigers, earth tiger is hardly impulsive at all, naturally less excitable, and not averse to stability and continuity. This tiger is very practical and fond of comfort. For such reasons, earth tigers tend to be more successful at long-term relationships than other tigers. There is a danger, however, that unless they give free rein to their dynamic Yang element, earth tigers can become real stick-in-the-muds. This should be avoided, and, instead, a more forward-looking mind should be cultivated.

TigerWood–Metal (1950, 2010)

This tough, outspoken tiger can sometimes be too bossy. Metal tiger is less ruled by the heart than typical tigers. Unfortunately, sometimes this only serves to make them unscrupulous. Metal tigers can be high achievers as they are very ambitious and self-disciplined. Advice to a metal tiger would be to try to listen to the wishes of others, practice tact, and be more flexible.

TIGER AND THE ZODIAC OF WESTERN ASTROLOGY

To work out your zodiac sign see p. 277. General character traits of tigers of the 12 zodiac signs are given below. Bear in mind that the Western zodiac sign modifies the basic tiger nature – especially in the area of personal relationships.

Aries tiger This is the most reckless and impetuous of all tigers. Aries tiger is well loved for sincerity, frankness, and kindheartedness. Although not very reflective, Aries tiger is very talented and often conscientious.

Taurus tiger Careful but bold, a realist but brave, passionate but reliable, Taurus tiger combines the attributes of these two signs to great effect. This tiger is practical and determined, so will often achieve great material prosperity.

Gemini tiger Impulsive tiger and mercurial Gemini make this person a mental and physical nomad. Hard to pin down to one idea or place, Gemini tigers are nonetheless highly creative people. What they lack in stamina, they make up for with inventiveness.

Cancer tiger The combination of these opposites makes an enigmatic and at times overly sensitive person. Cancer tigers are often eccentric but likable characters. Self-discipline is vital to ensure that tasks are achieved, as Cancer tigers have a tendency toward introspection.

Leo tiger Both Leos and tigers seek the limelight, a Leo tiger doubly so. Also, the Leo tiger is naturally arrogant, so at times this tiger can be unbearable. Nevertheless, they are generous, loyal, and charming people as well.

Virgo tiger Hesitant Virgo and foolhardy tiger actually go very well together. A Virgo tiger is trustworthy, self-disciplined, diligent, and resourceful – an unbeatable combination. On the negative side, this variety of tiger may be a snob.

Libra tiger Noble tiger's sense of justice is enhanced by the altruistic Libran sign. Libra tigers are often very attractive personalities. They combine a hardworking trait with a charming and compassionate nature.

Scorpio tiger These tigers display all the tiger traits in the extreme; they have fearsome tempers, huge amounts of energy, and are dangerously reckless. As a friend, loyal Scorpio tiger is a great advantage; as an enemy, beware!

Sagittarius tiger The Sagittarian tiger is an unpredictable dreamer. Basically gentle and easygoing, they can at times be infuriatingly changeable. Perhaps extroverted then withdrawn, generous then miserly – these people do not like to be taken for granted.

Capricorn tiger Capricorn endows these tigers with the ability to avoid their usual pitfalls – in particular thoughtlessness. Capricorn tigers are not as at ease socially as others, though, and tend to be moody. They are, however, dependable and good-natured.

Aquarius tiger This is the most idealistic of tigers. Intellectual Aquarius complements active tiger well; great things could be accomplished. Gullibility and lack of steadfastness can prove a problem. Aquarian tigers are fascinated by the latest gadgets.

Pisces tiger This tiger is sympathetic, loving, very creative, but often woefully indecisive. The Pisces tiger will only achieve inner peace when the tiger is fully under control.

Some famous people born in the years of the tiger and their zodiac signs

- William Wordsworth
  Poet
  Apr 7, 1770 Aries

- Karl Marx
  Social philosopher
  May 5, 1818 Taurus

- Emily Brontë
  Novelist
  July 30, 1818 Leo

- Oscar Wilde
  Writer
  Oct 16, 1854 Libra

- Arthur Rimbaud
  Poet
  Oct 20, 1854 Libra

- H G Wells
  Writer
  Sep 21, 1866 Virgo

- Isadora Duncan
  Dancer
  May 27, 1878 Gemini

- Ho Chi Minh
  Political leader
  May 19, 1890 Taurus

- Agatha Christie
  Writer
  Sep 15, 1890 Virgo

- Groucho Marx
  Comedian
  Oct 2, 1890 Libra

- Dwight D. Eisenhower
  US president
  Oct 14, 1890 Libra

- Charles de Gaulle
  French president
  Nov 22, 1890 Sagittarius

- John Steinbeck
  Novelist
  Feb 27, 1902 Pisces

- Georgette Heyer
  Novelist
  Aug 16, 1902 Leo

- Alec Guinness
  Actor
  Apr 2, 1914 Aries

- Pierre Balmain
  Fashion designer
  May 18, 1914 Taurus

- Dylan Thomas
  Poet/Writer
  Oct 27, 1914 Scorpio

- Hugh Hefner
  Publisher
  Apr 9, 1926 Aries

- Queen Elizabeth II
  Monarch
  Apr 21, 1926 Taurus

- Marilyn Monroe
  Actress
  Jun 1, 1926 Gemini

- Joan Sutherland
  Opera singer
  Nov 7, 1926 Scorpio

- Rudolf Nureyev
  Ballet dancer
  Mar 17, 1938 Pisces

- Germaine Greer
  Feminist
  Jan 29, 1939 Aquarius

- Stevie Wonder
  Singer
  May 13, 1950 Taurus

4. The Rabbit

The Yin wood animal.

Lunar years ruled by the rabbit	
1903	Jan 29, 1903 – Feb 15, 1904
1915	Feb 14, 1915 – Feb 2, 1916
1927	Feb 2, 1927 – Jan 22, 1928
1939	Feb 19, 1939 – Feb 7, 1940
1951	Feb 6, 1951 – Jan 26, 1952
1963	Jan 25, 1963 – Feb 12, 1964
1975	Feb 11, 1975 – Jan 30, 1976
1987	Jan 29, 1987 – Feb 16, 1988
1999	Feb 6, 1999 – Feb 4, 2000

The rabbit is associated with longevity and the moon. Some astrologers identify this sign as the cat, not rabbit, but Chinese astrologers always refer to it as the rabbit or hare.

THE RABBIT PERSONALITY

Seemingly unexceptional, rabbits provoke extreme reactions. They inspire either adoration or hate, but never indifference. Rabbits are mysterious yet practical, timid but ruthless, articulate but inscrutable, and virtuous as well as cunning. They like their lives to be secure, comfortable, and calm, yet they are fiercely independent. Sensitive and intuitive by nature, rabbits are easily influenced by their emotions.

Characteristics

These are the general personality traits of those people who are typical rabbits, both at their best and at their worst.

Positive	Negative
● diplomatic	● indecisive
● circumspect	● unpredictable
● peaceful	● hesitant
● sensitive	● fainthearted
● intuitive	● easily shocked
● discreet	● touchy
● moderate	● conservative
● reflective	● conformist
● well organized	● egotistical
● principled	● superficial
● refined	● cruel
● hospitable	● gossipy
● intelligent	● cunning
● expressive	● secretive
● honorable	● pedantic

Secret rabbit

Mistakenly, people often assume that rabbits' need for security and comfort combined with the urge to avoid confrontation means that they are weak. This is not true. Rabbits will use all their diplomacy, charm, and cunning to achieve their ends. The fact that they very rarely need to resort to outright battle to get their own way is proof of rabbits' strength, not weakness of character.

Element

Rabbit is linked to the ancient Chinese element of wood. Wood can be both flexible like a sapling or sturdy as an oak. How its energy is expressed depends on how well a wood person can both control and indulge their natural tendencies. For a rabbit, the tendencies to be wary of are the urge to avoid change or trouble at all costs, self-indulgence, and timidity.

Balance

The behavior of a rabbit can be unpredictable as it varies according to current circumstances. During peaceful times, rabbits will be at ease and relaxed. Sudden changes, unforeseen events, or conflicts will unbalance rabbits and make them irritable, confused, and even aggressive. Rabbit people will not be happy at such times until they are back in control of the situation. Also, rabbit personalities need to balance their self-preoccupied Yin natures and occasionally try to see things from another's point of view.

Best associations

Traditionally, the following are said to be associated with rabbits:

- Taste   acid
- Season   spring
- Birth   summer
- Color   white
- Plant   fig tree
- Flower   Queen Anne's lace
- Food   wheat, poultry
- Climate   windy

THE MALE RABBIT

If a man has a typical rabbit personality, he will generally display the behavior listed below.

- is not a victim of fashions
- is careful when spending money on necessities
- is extravagant with his money when buying luxuries
- is neat and well dressed
- has a tendency to be superficial
- is interested in the arts and culture
- is not a family-minded man
- is faithful and loving
- is a careful listener
- is happy and content
- has a traditional outlook
- is protective towards his peace and quiet
- is flamboyant
- is in touch with his feminine side but not effeminate

THE FEMALE RABBIT

If a woman has a typical rabbit personality, she will generally display the behavior listed below.

- is not overtly maternal
- is good at entertaining
- is sophisticated
- is tender and wistful
- is very determined
- is good at giving practical advice
- makes herself at home in most social circles
- is attentive to her material needs
- is able to strike a good bargain
- is naturally elegant and always stylishly dressed
- is wary of commitment
- has a sharp sense of humor
- is emotional
- prefers a comfortable to an adventurous life
- can be manipulative to get her own way
- prefers company to solitude
- is well mannered and conscious of etiquette

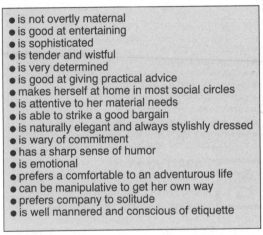

THE RABBIT CHILD
If a child has a typical rabbit personality,
he or she will generally display the
behavior listed below.

- is not argumentative
- is shy and sometimes nervous
- is obedient and well disciplined
- is happy at school
- enjoys team sports
- is usually more academic than athletic
- needs stimulation and motivation
- can be lacking in imagination
- is prone to nightmares
- succeeds through hard work
- enjoys fairy tales and fantasy stories

RABBIT AT HOME
Rabbits are sensitive to environments and
like to create cosy, intimate homes.
Furnishings will be beautiful and
comfortable; antiques or classic designs are
preferred. Rabbits are meticulous and cannot bear to
have an untidy or unclean home; a spill of red wine
could move a rabbit to hysteria. Rabbits prefer to
entertain at home rather than venture out into the
cold. They make fine hosts and hostesses as they go
to great lengths to make guests feel at home. Rabbits
put a lot of effort into arranging their environments.
Once established and satisfied with their homes,
rabbits hate the disruption of moving.

RABBIT AT WORK

Although rabbits are not authoritative, they can make good leaders and organizers as they are skilled diplomats. A rabbit can win a battle without anyone knowing one has been fought. Not being ambitious, rabbits rarely reach the top of their chosen professions. They excel in administrative or clearly defined positions. Once rabbits know what needs to be done, they are thorough and diligent in carrying out their tasks. They are good at team work, but often prefer to work alone or be self-employed. Job security is important, so stable professions are preferred. With their ability to charm, rabbits are good at wheeling and dealing. However, their basically honest nature stops them from taking too much advantage of this. In business, rabbits should try and use their instinctive good taste, careful nature, and ability to evaluate a situation well to good advantage.

Some typical rabbit occupations

- antique dealer
- diplomat
- administrator
- interior decorator
- politician
- historian
- art collector
- attorney
- tailor
- receptionist
- chemist
- landlord
- pharmacist
- beautician
- accountant
- librarian

? RABBIT PREFERENCES

Likes

- privacy
- conversation, including gossip
- routines
- to use their wits to solve a problem
- romantic films
- secrets and mysteries
- long hairstyles
- prefers company of good friends and family to going out
- comfortable surroundings
- beautiful paintings
- paying attention to detail

Dislikes

- arguments
- seeing or using violence
- drastic change
- taking risks
- surprises
- saying anything unpleasant
- being forced to make a decision
- complicated plans
- changing their mind
- witnessing suffering
- commitment
- open criticism

GOOD FRIENDS FOR RABBITS

The diagram below shows the compatibility of rabbit with other animals. There is no fixed ruling, however, because there are other influences on both the rabbit and any potential friend. These influences are:

- the companion in life (see pp. 273–5)
- the dominant element (from the year of birth)

Compatibility of rabbit with other animals

- ● Rat
- ▲ Ox
- ■ Tiger
- ■ Rabbit
- ● Dragon
- ▲ Snake

- ▲ Horse
- ▲ Goat
- ● Monkey
- ▲ Rooster
- ● Dog
- ● Pig

Key

- ▲ Highly compatible
- ● Amicable
- ■ No conflict but needs some effort
- ● Lack of sympathy
- ▲ Antagonistic

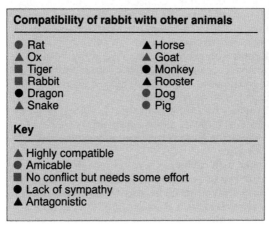

Rat with rabbit These two can get on very well. Rabbit should make sure, however, that rat does not exploit the relationship. Business partnerships will be more successful than romantic ones.

Ox with rabbit An ideal match, ox can provide rabbit with security and peace so that the two can live in harmony. Rabbit may find ox's straight-talking nature hard to handle, and at times may be tempted to stray to assert independence.

Tiger with rabbit Unexpectedly, these two actually understand each other very well. Perhaps too well for a lasting relationship, as rabbit has a tendency not to take tiger seriously.

Rabbit with rabbit Two rabbits can live together without ever arguing. Rabbits can be too passive, so the relationship may lack excitement unless one of them is a bit more adventurous.

Dragon with rabbit Unlikely to get along, dragons annoy rabbits with their madcap, untidy natures. A compromise could be achieved if both have their own space.

Snake with rabbit Both snakes and rabbits cultivate peace and security and share a love of the arts. Snake can help rabbit be more adventurous, as long as rabbit is tolerant of snake's less virtuous nature.

Horse with rabbit Moody horse makes a disruptive partner for rabbit, who may not tolerate this for long unless very much in love.

Goat with rabbit This may be the best match as both have good taste and a love of luxuries. Goat's imaginative nature appeals to rabbit's romantic side. In difficult times, however, neither will be able to look to the other for courage and support as both are anxious creatures.

Monkey with rabbit Devious monkey can bring out the worst, cunning side of rabbit. But, as lively monkey finds stable rabbit dull, they are not often together long enough for this to happen.

Rooster with rabbit On no account should these two attempt a serious relationship. Rooster's tendency to voice criticisms will send rabbit running, and rooster will find rabbit unsympathetic.

Dog with rabbit Loyal dog gets along well with rabbit, and the two can have a happy relationship, as long as they do not take each other for granted.

Pig with rabbit Pleasure-loving, tolerant pig is a good match for rabbit. Discreet rabbit may be a bit unnerved by sensual pig's public displays of affection, but this is a minor point.

RABBIT IN LOVE

Rabbits are wary of commitment as it involves change and making a major decision. This does not mean that they are fickle, just careful about choosing their partners. Rabbits would rather be alone than in unsatisfactory relationships; they prize their peaceful lives highly. Once committed, rabbits put a lot of effort into their relationships. Always willing to listen and loathe to argue, they make attentive, tender, and loving partners. Despite this, it is sometimes hard to know what rabbit partners are feeling or thinking as they are very private people. Rabbits listen better than they confide. This can be exasperating for others unless they learn how to read the signs. Rabbits need a lot of attention and love – but most are clever enough to have learnt that, if given, these will be returned.

RABBIT AND SEX

Not quick to jump into bed, courtships are lengthy with rabbits, and it may be left to others to take the initiative. Once involved, a rabbit will be a faithful lover. Traditional and sensitive by nature, rabbits are often romantics and are easily seduced by roses, candlelight dinners, and perhaps even poetry if it is not avant-garde. But do not assume that they will appreciate drama in their sex life – sophisticated rabbits are repulsed by raw emotion and tears. Rabbits can be unexciting lovers as they are inhibited people and restrained by their lack of imagination. They do listen well, however, and like to please, so a rabbit will be willing to learn what their partner likes in bed. If still a bit hesitant, try being demanding as rabbits hate confrontation and will do most things for a quiet life. Nothing kinky will be tolerated though, as rabbits are actually quite prudish.

HEALTH

Rabbit's element, wood, is associated with the liver, so rabbits should pay particular attention to keeping this organ in working order. Rabbits should make sure that they get enough exercise, otherwise their love of a quiet, comfortable life could damage their long-term health.

Psychologically, rabbits need to try not to be too self-absorbed and concerned with themselves. Also, they should take care that their methodical, tidy natures do not become obsessively fastidious.

LEISURE INTERESTS

Rabbits will enjoy a wide range of activities, as long as they are not responsible for organizing them. For this reason, package tours are perfect for rabbits. Although not especially sporty, they can make good team players. Being lovers of art and culture, rabbits can often be found visiting museums and art galleries. Even though they are usually music lovers, rabbits would rather listen to a good recording in the comfort of their own home than go to a crowded, live concert. Rabbits like to be alone at times and may go on long nocturnal walks to indulge this. Great lovers of the good things in life – fine wine, gourmet food, and conversation – rabbits like to throw dinner parties for friends. Entertaining at home is always preferred to wild parties.

THE RABBIT YEARS AND THEIR ELEMENTS

The rabbit is a Yin wood animal. Each of the rabbit years, however, is associated with an element which is said to have its own influence. These elements are wood, fire, earth, metal, and water. They influence rabbit in a regular sequence, which is repeated every 60 years.

In the table below, for example, the rabbit year 1903 is a water year. The next rabbit water year is 60 years later in 1963, and the next will be 2023. Rabbit's natural element is wood; the influence of this combines with those of the element of the year of birth. The possible effects of the year elements are listed below.

Lunar years ruled by the rabbit and their elements

1903	Jan 29, 1903	– Feb 15, 1904	water
1915	Feb 24, 1915	– Feb 2, 1916	wood
1927	Feb 2, 1927	– Jan 22, 1928	fire
1939	Feb 19, 1939	– Feb 7, 1940	earth
1951	Feb 6, 1951	– Jan 26, 1952	metal
1963	Jan 25, 1963	– Feb 12, 1964	water
1975	Feb 11, 1975	– Jan 30, 1976	wood
1987	Jan 29, 1987	– Feb 16, 1988	fire
1999	Feb 6, 1999	– Feb 4, 2000	earth

RabbitWood–Water (1903, 1963)
Water enhances rabbit's natural sensitive nature. Unfortunately, these rabbits can empathize with others so much that they become unproductive and shy away from harsh reality. All rabbits dislike conflicts, but water rabbits go to extremes to avoid confrontation. A natural passivity combined with a reflective nature can make them victims of remorse and "If Only" thoughts.

RabbitWood–Wood (1915, 1975)

Wood is rabbit's natural element, but it is a two-sided symbol. On the one hand, wood rabbits can be content to the point of placidity. Alternatively, they may be of the more adventurous type. In these cases, wood opens rabbits up to their emotions – which can also make them vulnerable. Double wood rabbits tend to be easygoing, generous people. They should beware of others trying to take advantage of them. Wood releases the creative powers of rabbit people and enhances their aesthetic taste; therefore, these people are artistic and creative.

RabbitWood–Fire (1927, 1987)

Wood and fire is a curious, flammable mixture that can make rabbit warm and friendly, or moody and bad tempered. Rabbits are naturally Yin, and fire is Yang. One balances the other, so fire can help rabbits use their skills to reach the top. It also helps them to be more expressive. Fire rabbits are more likely to become leaders as they have many admirers and inspire confidence. They should try to follow their true rabbit natures and let reason control passion.

RabbitWood–Earth (1939, 1999)

Earth endows this rabbit with a more realistic and pragmatic character. Earth rabbits are more able to deal with the downside of life than other rabbits, who typically try to hide from it. Better equipped to make decisions, the earth rabbit will do so carefully and after great deliberation. They tend to be humble and aware of their limitations. Independent and fond of solitude, earth rabbits can achieve much through hard work.

Rabbit Wood–Metal (1951, 2011)

Metal gives the naturally timid rabbit greater courage. Rabbits born in metal years will be forthright and self-confident, and some say even visionary. They are more ambitious and can be ruthless underneath their charming exteriors. Metal rabbits tend to be polite but cold, and they can be indifferent to the feelings of others. For these reasons, they are often loners. Metal lends strength to a character but can also make it rigid. It can make rabbit's naturally conservative nature inflexible to the point of being reactionary.

 RABBIT AND THE ZODIAC OF WESTERN ASTROLOGY

To work out your zodiac sign see p. 277. General character traits of rabbits of the 12 zodiac signs are given below. Bear in mind that the Western zodiac sign modifies the basic rabbit nature – especially in the area of personal relationships.

Aries rabbit Aries brings courage to rabbit, who adds grace to the equation. Aries rabbits are emotionally both expressive and vulnerable. Unlike other rabbits, however, they don't mind taking risks. Success is important to Aries rabbits.

Taurus rabbit Both Taureans and rabbits are peace-loving, calm, stay-at-home people; Taurus rabbits doubly so. Their liking for the good things in life can make them materialistic, and they should be wary of ostentatious behavior.

Gemini rabbit Mercurial Gemini and steady rabbit make an odd mixture. On the surface, a Gemini rabbit seems to be a superficial, turbulent kind of person; in fact, they are constantly on the alert and very analytical. These rabbits are persuasive and like to appear sophisticated and cultured.

Cancer rabbit The close similarities between these two signs can accentuate certain facets of rabbit's nature. Cancer rabbits are doubly cautious and can be weak. On the whole, they are nice, hospitable people who make good friends.

Leo rabbit At times deceptively calm, Leo rabbits are potentially great achievers. Open in expressing their desires, flamboyant and popular, these people find it hard to be self-restrained or objective. A tendency to be self-centered and pompous is offset by mild manners and a generous nature.

Virgo rabbit Analytical Virgo and careful rabbit combine to create a tendency to worry. These attributes can be beneficial though, and many Virgo rabbits are wise, considerate types. If their nervous energy is left unused, they can be fidgety.

Libra rabbit Sweet talking and melancholic, these rabbits may appear slightly effeminate. They have very inquiring minds and make good scholars or communicators. Libra rabbits like to surround themselves with the best of everything and can be extravagant; but they work hard to get what they want. A tendency to be snobbish should be watched.

Scorpio rabbit Scorpio rabbits are earnest people – they take themselves very seriously. Scorpio brings great willpower to the rabbit. They are secretive about intimate matters, but not dispassionate. In private, they can be passionate and have a high sex drive; but if they feel insecure, Scorpio rabbits can become deceitful and pedantic.

Sagittarius rabbit This combination makes for the most balanced and easygoing rabbit. Unusually interested in the more exotic side of life, these rabbits are exceptional in that they like to experience adventure. They are not as diplomatic or tactful as other rabbits but are loyal and loving people.

Capricorn rabbit Capricorn rabbits seem to be insensitive due to their brusque natures; underneath, however, they are kind and considerate, supportive and protective towards their family and loved ones. Physically graceful, these rabbits are surprisingly impractical.

Aquarius rabbit Thirsty for knowledge and eager for new experiences, these rabbits are true intellectuals – they often make good writers. Not so much in need of stability and security, Aquarian rabbits like to keep their distance.

Pisces rabbit The most difficult of all rabbits to read; spiritual and perceptive, Pisces deepens rabbit's inherently mysterious nature – such people can even be psychic. Accomplished in the arts, refined and companionable, Pisces rabbits have the ability to live happy, well-ordered lives. Their insecurities can make them appear stubborn at times.

Some famous people born in the years of the rabbit and their zodiac signs

- Adam Smith
  Economist
  Jun 5, 1723 Gemini

- Mary Wollstonecraft
  Feminist
  Apr 27, 1759 Taurus

- Queen Victoria
  British monarch
  May 24, 1819 Gemini

- Arturo Toscanini
  Conductor
  Mar 25, 1867 Aries

- Marie Curie
  Chemist
  Nov 7, 1867 Scorpio

- Albert Einstein
  Physicist
  Mar 14, 1879 Pisces

- Joseph Stalin
  Russian political leader
  Dec 21, 1879 Sagittarius

- Henry Miller
  Novelist
  Dec 26, 1891 Capricorn

- Barbara Hepworth
  Sculptor
  Jan 10, 1903 Capricorn

- Benjamin Spock
  Pediatrician
  May 2, 1903 Taurus

- Bob Hope
  Comedian/Actor
  May 29, 1903 Gemini

- George Orwell
  Writer
  Jun 25, 1903 Cancer

- Cary Grant
  Actor
  Jan 18, 1904 Capricorn

- Orson Welles
  Actor/Director
  May 6, 1915 Taurus

- Ingrid Bergman
  Actress
  Aug 29, 1915 Virgo

- Arthur Miller
  Dramatist
  Oct 17, 1915 Libra

- Frank Sinatra
  Singer
  Dec 12, 1915 Sagittarius

- Harry Belafonte
  Singer/Actor
  Mar 1, 1927 Pisces

- Ken Russell
  Film director
  Jul 3, 1927 Cancer

- Neil Simon
  Playwright
  Jul 4, 1927 Cancer

- Fidel Castro
  Cuban political leader
  Aug 13, 1927 Leo

- Neil Sedaka
  Singer/Songwriter
  Mar 13, 1939 Pisces

- David Frost
  TV personality
  Apr 7, 1939 Aries

- James Galway
  Flutist
  Dec 8, 1939 Sagittarius

5. The Dragon

The Yang wood animal.

Lunar years ruled by the dragon

1904	Feb 16, 1904 – Feb 3, 1905
1916	Feb 3, 1916 – Jan 22, 1917
1928	Jan 23, 1928 – Feb 9, 1929
1940	Feb 8, 1940 – Jan 26, 1941
1952	Jan 27, 1952 – Feb 13, 1953
1964	Feb 13, 1964 – Feb 1, 1965
1976	Jan 31, 1976 – Feb 17, 1977
1988	Feb 17, 1988 – Feb 5, 1989
2000	Feb 6, 2000 – Jan 23, 2001

The dragon is the only mythical animal in the Chinese zodiac. In China, dragons are associated with strength, health, harmony, and good luck; they are placed above doors or on the tops of roofs to banish demons and evil spirits.

THE DRAGON PERSONALITY

Dragons have magnetic, persuasive personalities and are capable of great success or spectacular failure. Normally, however, whatever they set their hearts on doing, they do well; the secret is their great faith in themselves. On the negative side, dragons are renowned for not finishing what they start. The frank and open way in which they approach people and situations can be disconcerting; but their innate sincerity and enthusiasm make up for this.

Characteristics

These are the general personality traits of those people who are typical dragons, both at their best and at their worst.

Positive	Negative
• visionary	• demanding
• dynamic	• impatient
• idealistic	• intolerant
• perfectionist	• gullible
• scrupulous	• dissatisfied
• lucky	• overpowering
• successful	• irritable
• enthusiastic	• abrupt
• sentimental	• naive
• healthy	• overzealous
• voluble	• eccentric
• irresistible	• proud
• exciting	• tactless
• intelligent	• short-tempered

Secret dragon

Despite their impressive appearance, deep down dragons are dissatisfied and discontent. The dragon's tireless search for excitement is not always fruitful. They need to be embarking on some new project, campaign, or love affair to feel truly alive. Inevitably, depression caused by the unavoidable daily routine will get most dragons down at some time.

Element

Dragon is linked to the ancient Chinese element of wood. Wood is an ambivalent element. As a crutch it lends support; as a spear it can be used as a weapon. Consequently, dragons are full of both positive and negative energies that will surface in, for example, strong emotions. For instance, emotionally, wood is associated with both anger and kindness. Wood is also responsible for growth and renewal, so dragons tend to be creative people.

Balance

Dragons spend a lot of time racing from one experience to another. Always set on the latest goal, they are blind to failures and try to forget any that occur. Only successes are considered significant. Dragons seem impressive only because they believe that they are, and this amazing self-confidence makes others believe in them also. You could say that the dragon's image is all done with mirrors. According to Chinese tradition, dragons must confront their image and recognize its illusory nature. Dragons will only be truly content when they accept their vulnerability and use it to balance their exuberance.

Best associations

Traditionally, the following are said to be associated with dragons:

- Taste   acid
- Season   spring
- Birth   anytime, except during a storm
- Color   yellow, black
- Plants   mandrake, sage
- Flower   lotus
- Food   wheat, poultry
- Climate   windy

THE MALE DRAGON

If a man has a typical dragon personality, he will generally display the behavior listed below.

- is a natural showman
- is seductively attractive
- will have many admirers
- has a few close friends
- believes he is irreplaceable
- is good at sports
- does not believe he can make mistakes
- is sentimental and passionate about loved ones
- can be impulsive but not a daredevil
- will harbor a grudge for years
- is good humored
- enjoys shopping
- has many hobbies and interests

THE FEMALE DRAGON
If a woman has a typical dragon personality, she will generally display the behavior listed below.

- will not be happy as a housewife
- is generous with both time and money
- can instill confidence in others
- desires perfection in herself and others
- is always attractive, even if not beautiful
- takes revenge on enemies, even if it takes years
- craves attention
- likes to be flattered
- hates to be manipulated or deceived
- tells good jokes
- likes children
- is very straightforward
- needs to feel irreplaceable

THE DRAGON CHILD

If a child has a typical dragon personality, he or she will generally display the behavior listed below.

- is prone to boredom
- dislikes authority
- needs motivating but potentially a good student
- dislikes demonstrations of affection
- is insolent with teachers
- enjoys and is good at sports
- is undemanding as far as attention is concerned
- dislikes timetables
- is inventive
- needs to be given ample freedom to blossom
- has a short attention span
- is gifted but difficult
- feels he or she is misunderstood (often true)

DRAGON AT HOME

Dragon people suffer from mild claustrophobia – they need space, fresh air, and freedom. To live in one place for long is a chore for a dragon. If they have settled down, dragons like to live in ultramodern houses, on board a houseboat, or near the coast, where they can hear the thunder of the ocean. If such options are not available, a dragon will at least try to redecorate frequently to keep boredom at bay. However pleasant their home environment though, dragons will spend more time out and about than sitting at home.

DRAGON AT WORK

Dragons are not power-hungry people, but they tend to end up at the top of their profession, simply because this is what they do best – lead. They are terrible at carrying out mundane tasks but excel at solving problems that others have found unsolvable. They make great directors and troubleshooters. Dragons inspire confidence in others and are good promoters or sellers; their integrity lends credibility to whatever they do. Dragons need to feel vital at work and be in a position that allows them to innovate or create.

Some typical dragon occupations

- managing director
- salesperson
- advertising executive
- president or prime minister
- prophet
- attorney
- film producer
- photojournalist
- architect
- professional speaker
- philosopher
- astronaut
- artist
- film star
- war correspondent

DRAGON PREFERENCES

Likes

- any sort of celebration such as parties and festivals
- to wear casual, comfortable clothes
- going on vacation and traveling
- to be taken seriously
- picnics
- jazz music
- amusement parks, especially the roller coaster
- watching fireworks
- being asked for help
- giving advice
- to feel irreplaceable
- to be in charge
- championing causes

Dislikes

- having to be calm and patient
- waiting for anything or anyone
- a lack of vision in others
- having nothing to do
- manipulative people
- listening to advice
- dishonesty and hypocrisy
- lack of energy or willpower in others
- being patronized
- compromise

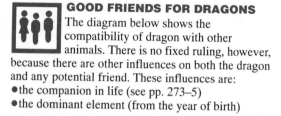

GOOD FRIENDS FOR DRAGONS
The diagram below shows the compatibility of dragon with other animals. There is no fixed ruling, however, because there are other influences on both the dragon and any potential friend. These influences are:

- the companion in life (see pp. 273–5)
- the dominant element (from the year of birth)

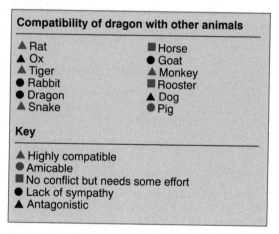

Compatibility of dragon with other animals

▲ Rat	■ Horse
▲ Ox	● Goat
▲ Tiger	▲ Monkey
● Rabbit	■ Rooster
● Dragon	▲ Dog
▲ Snake	● Pig

Key

▲ Highly compatible
● Amicable
■ No conflict but needs some effort
● Lack of sympathy
▲ Antagonistic

Rat with dragon Both are easily bored, so plenty of activity can be expected, although rat may have to let dragon take the dominant role. Dragons love admiration, so a relationship could work.
Ox with dragon Any relationship between these two will not be long-lived. Ox enjoys daily routine;

dragon is always trying to escape from it. If they can compromise, both could gain something positive from the experience.

Tiger with dragon These two are very similar in temperament, and both are energetic and courageous. Any relationship between them will never be boring but could become a struggle for dominance.

Rabbit with dragon Unlikely to get along, dragons annoy rabbits with their madcap, untidy natures. A compromise could be achieved if both have their own space. Rabbits can teach dragons tact.

Dragon with dragon Two dragons make a glittering partnership, although each of them may actually be more in love with themselves as a couple than with their partner as an individual. But dragons have to feel needed, and this cannot be satisfied by another equally demanding dragon.

Snake with dragon A well-matched couple, snakes are clever enough to let dragons think they are in charge. Dragons are pleased to associate with elegant snakes. Together, they can achieve a lot.

Horse with dragon Enthusiastic horse and energetic dragon can do well together if they share a common purpose and dragon does not invade horse's privacy too much. Self-preoccupied horses are not able to give dragons the attention they crave.

Goat with dragon Lack of understanding can blight any relationship between these two, unless both learn to accept and appreciate their differences. Business alliances will be more successful than personal ones, as dragons can help quiet goats realize their creativity.

Monkey with dragon Dragons are attracted to monkeys' charm and intelligence. The two inspire and complement each another without becoming rivals – they will have many friends and a busy social life.

Rooster with dragon Both these characters can be found in the limelight: roosters for reassurance; dragons as it is their natural habitat. This can bolster both their egos, but misunderstandings will occur.

Dog with dragon The intellectual but cynical dog will deflate a dragon's self-confidence. Dogs are able to see the dragon's image for the mirage it is – they are unable to admire a dragon.

Pig with dragon Pigs and dragons have little in common, but the two can be very compatible. Pig is easygoing and will enjoy dragon's showy nature. Dragon will sweep pig off his feet, and pig will adore and fuss over the dragon.

DRAGON IN LOVE

Dragons are never short of admirers and never suffer from unrequited love. They are passionate but never blinded by this. Dragons are very self-reliant and know that they could live without their partner. Although they are often loved, dragons fall in love rarely. Once in love, dragons are very loyal and loving. In fact, their partners are put on pedestals. If a dragon discovers that his or her partner is unworthy of their devotion, the dragon will be hurt and soon end the relationship. Otherwise, it is difficult to break a dragon's heart because first you have to damage their invulnerable egos.

DRAGON AND SEX

Sex is very important for dragons. They often embark on amorous adventures at an early age and see sexual expression as the key to their personal freedom. This is not necessarily a good thing for dragon bed partners because dragons have a tendency to view their lovers as instruments to bring about their great escape and not as individuals. Nevertheless, whatever dragons do, they perform well. They are not selfish or unimaginative lovers, just a bit impersonal maybe. Dragons in love will lavish affection on their partner and will do anything to please them.

HEALTH

Dragon's element, wood, is associated with the liver, so dragons should pay particular attention to keeping this organ in working order. Despite being associated with health and vitality, dragons often suffer from insomnia and respiratory problems. All dragons, however, take care of themselves to their best ability so they rarely get very sick. If they do, dragons normally recover quickly. When feeling vulnerable, dragons have a tendency to overeat and should watch out for this.

LEISURE INTERESTS

Dragons have many interests but often lack the staying power to learn the necessary skills. A typical dragon will be enthusiastically learning yoga one week, judo the next, and the saxophone for a while as well. Anything exciting, bold, or adventurous appeals. It cannot be something that involves too much training, but dragons will be keen to go on short breaks, where tuition or guidance is provided – a skiing vacation or safari, for example – and where they can still feel daring without taking many risks, as long as they can master the skills quickly and not spend too much time on the nursery slopes. Otherwise, they love to go backpacking somewhere like the Himalayas, where they feel at home in the lofty peaks.

THE DRAGON YEARS AND THEIR ELEMENTS

The dragon is a Yang wood animal. Each of the dragon years, however, is associated with an element which is said to have its own influence. These elements are wood, fire, earth, metal, and water. They influence dragon in a regular sequence, which is repeated every 60 years. In the table opposite, for example, the dragon year 1904 is a wood year. The next dragon wood year is 60 years later in 1964, and the next will be 2024. Dragon's natural element is wood; the influence of this combines with those of the element of the year of birth. The possible effects of the year elements are listed opposite.

Lunar years ruled by the dragon and their elements

1904	Feb 16, 1904	– Feb 3, 1905	wood
1916	Feb 3, 1916	– Jan 22, 1917	fire
1928	Jan 23, 1928	– Feb 9, 1929	earth
1940	Feb 8, 1940	– Jan 26, 1941	metal
1952	Jan 27, 1952	– Feb 13, 1953	water
1964	Feb 13, 1964	– Feb 1, 1965	wood
1976	Jan 31, 1976	– Feb 17, 1977	fire
1988	Feb 17, 1988	– Feb 5, 1989	earth
2000	Feb 5, 2000	– Jan 23, 2001	metal

Dragon Wood–Wood (1904, 1964)

Wood dragons are in their natural element. Wood, a symbol of growth and renewal, allows dragon to be a creative, innovative person fond of improvisation. They love harmony, elegance, and all beautiful things. Relaxed and at ease socially, these dragons do not like to offend people. Wood can bring pessimism to a character, but dragons temper this tendency with their dynamism. They are progressive people, and, untypically, curious of affairs not centered around them. Dramatic and generous, wood dragons are fun and considerate people.

Dragon Wood–Fire (1916, 1976)

Potentially a highly combustible combination of fire and wood, fire dragons are actually warmhearted and honest. They are temperamental and have no patience at all. Ambitious and proud, fire dragons tend to be authoritarian. They are perfectionists and will be highly critical if someone does not have the

same standards or even opinions as they. All dragons
are charismatic, fire dragons are inspirational –
many are famous or infamous people.

Dragon Wood–Earth (1928, 1988)

Like all dragons, earth dragons like to dedicate
themselves to a cause or project. Earth allows
dragons to be more cooperative and open to team
work than typical dragons, who are just as likely to
embark on a solitary quest. Earth dragons don't
mind paying attention to the details of a plan. Earth
brings patience to the dragon, so they are not in such
a hurry. Stability and security are important to these
dragons, who will probably equate them with
financial independence.

Dragon Wood–Metal (1940, 2000)

Metal strengthens many of dragon's qualities. Metal
dragons are very theatrical and have enormous egos.
Already resolute, they are argumentative to the point
of aggression, but always honest. If a metal dragon
believes in a cause, he or she will single-mindedly
champion it against all odds. Bordering on the
heroic, these dragons have the natures of gladiators.
Visionary but still practical, efficient and
hardworking, metal dragons are often successful.

Dragon Wood–Water (1952, 2012)

Normally, water would make a character calm and
reflective. On dragons, however, the opposite can be
true unless the dragon learns to balance the water
tendency with his innate dragon excessiveness.
Nevertheless, water dragons are more diplomatic
than average dragons and very creative. They are

pacifists and interested in social problems. This, combined with their intuitive wisdom, makes water dragons idealistic and compassionate.

DRAGON AND THE ZODIAC OF WESTERN ASTROLOGY

To work out your zodiac sign see p. 277. General character traits of dragons of the 12 zodiac signs are given below. Bear in mind that the Western zodiac sign modifies the basic dragon nature – especially in the area of personal relationships.

Aries dragon Two energetic signs make Aries dragons almost hyperactive. Their enthusiasm is infectious, but they need to learn to finish what they start. Selfish and impulsive, these dragons lead turbulent lives and tend to be excessively arrogant.

Taurus dragon Taurean dragons are more down-to-earth than typical dragons while still being forward-looking and creative. They have great staying power and are more likely to finish a project and achieve fame easily. Taurus dragons are sentimental and sensuous people.

Gemini dragon Airy Gemini and enthusiastic dragon combine to make a real character. These people have a razor-sharp wit and are verbally adroit. Gemini dragons are not fools; they use humor to make a serious point and are very principled.

Cancer dragon Cancer dragons are profound in their thoughts and feelings, but they can be too sensitive. Cancer tones down some of the dragon's qualities, making them less brash and reckless and more cautious. These dragons are very good at rousing and inspiring others to achieve their aims.

Leo dragon Leo dragons are exhausting, excessive, and superior – with good reason though. They are, however, noble at heart and basically good humored. Leo dragons love to bestow their generosity on others less fortunate than themselves. They are hospitable but need to be the center of everyone's attention.

Virgo dragon Analytical Virgo and brash dragon do not always make a harmonious combination. They are precise, cannot resist an intellectual challenge, and love solving puzzles. As dragons, these people are not so "make-believe"; they are more realistic. Underneath their harsh exteriors, however, they are well-meaning people.

Libra dragon Manipulative Libra allows dragon to be a more reassuring person, but deceptively so. Unusually diplomatic, they find it easy to rally support and take the lead. Libra dragons are refined and intelligent; style, taste, and quality are important to them.

Scorpio dragon Passionate and unpredictable, Scorpio dragons often provoke strong reactions and create intense dramas. They never compromise or give up. Dragons are suspicious anyway, but combined with Scorpio's jealous and vengeful nature, this is not a person to have as an enemy.

Sagittarius dragon Friendly and relatively quiet, Sagittarius dragons are fun-loving optimists. They are proud of their ability to get along with anyone and, unlike most dragons, they do not suffer from arrogance. Expressive but not sentimental, Sagittarius dragon is not afraid to take great risks.

Capricorn dragon Although eloquent about worldy matters, Capricornean dragons find it difficult to express their personal feelings. At times they seem hard and ambitious, but underneath they are really compassionate and sensitive.

Aquarius dragon Aquarius allows the dragon to be calm and lucid and even capable of self-criticism – unique among dragons. They have inquisitive and versatile minds but find it difficult to relax. Despite being popular and sociable people, at heart Aquarian dragons are pessimists.

Pisces dragon Watery Pisces dampens many of the dragon's fiery qualities. Pisces dragons are wise and inspired, but they are also enigmatic, making it hard to understand their motives. Often, they appear to have their head in the clouds but are in fact very shrewd people. On the whole, these dragons are loving and charming, but they will be defensive and demanding if insecure.

Some famous people born in the years of the dragon and their zodiac signs

- Charles Darwin
  Naturalist
  Feb 12, 1809 Aquarius

- Florence Nightingale
  Nurse
  May 12, 1820 Taurus

- Friedrich Nietzsche
  Philosopher
  Oct 15, 1844 Libra

- Sigmund Freud
  Neurologist
  May 6, 1856 Taurus

- George Bernard Shaw
  Playwright
  Jul 26, 1856 Leo

- Bing Crosby
  Singer
  May 2, 1904 Taurus

- Salvador Dali
  Painter
  May 11, 1904 Taurus

- Count Basie
  Jazz musician
  Aug 21, 1904 Leo

- Graham Greene
  Writer
  Oct 2, 1904 Libra

- Harold Wilson
  British politician
  Mar 11, 1916 Pisces

- Gregory Peck
  Actor
  Apr 5, 1916 Aries

- Yehudi Menuhin
  Violinist
  Apr 22, 1916 Taurus

- Kirk Douglas
  Actor
  Dec 9, 1916 Sagittarius

- Eartha Kitt
  Singer
  Jan 26, 1928 Aquarius

- Shirley Temple
  Actress
  Apr 23, 1928 Taurus

- Che Guevara
  Revolutionary
  Jan 14, 1928 Gemini

- Stanley Kubrick
  Filmmaker
  Jul 26, 1928 Leo

- Martin Luther King
  Civil rights leader
  Jan 15, 1929 Capricorn

- Ringo Starr
  Musician
  Jul 7, 1940 Cancer

- John Lennon
  Singer/Composer
  Oct 9, 940 Libra

- Cliff Richard
  Singer
  Oct 14, 1940 Libra

- Pelé
  Footballer
  Oct 23, 1940 Scorpio

- Joan Baez
  Folksinger
  Jan 9, 1941 Capricorn

- Pierce Brosnan
  Actor
  May 16, 1952 Taurus

6. The Snake

The Yin fire animal.

Lunar years ruled by the snake		
1905	Feb 4, 1905	– Jan 24, 1906
1917	Jan 23, 1917	– Feb 10, 1918
1929	Feb 10, 1929	– Jan 29, 1930
1941	Jan 27, 1941	– Feb 14, 1942
1953	Feb 14, 1953	– Feb 2, 1954
1965	Feb 2, 1965	– Jan 20, 1966
1977	Feb 18, 1977	– Feb 6, 1978
1989	Feb 6, 1989	– Jan 26, 1990
2001	Jan 24, 2001	– Feb 11, 2002

There are few animals with more symbolic associations than the snake. Chinese mythology holds that a half-human snake was the father of the Chinese emperors.

THE SNAKE PERSONALITY

In the West, the snake is often seen as evil. The snake of Chinese astrology, however, is associated with beauty and wisdom. Snakes may appear languid and serene, but they are always mentally active. Snakes are deep thinkers and give very good advice – but they cannot take it. Snakes are capable of lying to get out of a scrape. Linked with esoteric knowledge and spiritual discovery, snakes are sacred to many peoples. Snakes are often people who are "psychic," or who are interested in the psychic, the mystical, or the religious.

Characteristics

These are the general personality traits of those people who are typical snakes, both at their best and at their worst.

Positive	Negative
● distinguished	● extravagant
● elegant	● vengeful
● self-contained	● obstinate
● shrewd	● calculating
● profound	● mean with money
● perceptive	● cruel
● lucid	● self-doubting
● sophisticated	● suspicious
● wise	● crafty
● gregarious	● remote
● sensual	● possessive
● curious	● anxious
● reflective	● jealous
● organized	● dishonest

Secret snake

The typical image of a snake is one basking in the sun doing nothing. Many interpret this as laziness. In fact, snakes are very hardworking. If something needs to be done, snake will not shy away from it. The secret is their efficiency. Snakes will get the job done in the quickest, most economical way, which is why they always have plenty of time to relax.

Element

Snake is linked to the ancient Chinese element of fire. Fire is a dynamic, exciting sign, which is balanced by snake's innate Yin tendency. The energy of fire can be expressed positively and negatively. It brings warmth, comfort, and light, and it protects. But fire can also burn and destroy. For example, emotionally fire is associated with cruelty and intolerance as well as love and respect. Fire people are always attractive.

Balance

Snakes and dragons are especially karmic signs. Put simply, karma is a person's destiny. Each action performed affects the next and so on, into infinity. The Chinese believe that snakes particularly must deal with their karmic problems within their lifetime to achieve balance. This should not be too much of a problem as snakes are generally well-balanced people. Their natural wisdom grants them the ability to deal with life gracefully, and they are usually unperturbed by life's ups and downs. Tendencies to watch out for are their highly individual approach to morality and honesty – that is, snakes do or say whatever is most convenient for them.

Best associations

Traditionally, the following are said to be associated with snakes:

● Taste	bitter
● Season	summer
● Birth	warm, summer day
● Colors	green, red
● Plant	ferns
● Flowers	heather, thistle
● Food	rice, lamb
● Climate	hot, sunny

THE MALE SNAKE

If a man has a typical snake personality, he will generally display the behavior listed below.

- is a bad loser
- does not tolerate insults
- is influential
- does not understand fidelity
- will be handsome and well groomed
- is a hedonist
- may be a snob at times
- is romantic and passionate
- has a subtle sense of humor
- relies on first impressions
- is an unlucky gambler

THE FEMALE SNAKE

If a woman has a typical snake personality, she will generally display the behavior listed below.

- is witty and humorous
- takes failure personally
- gives good advice
- will be captivatingly beautiful
- is not prone to false modesty
- likes her home comforts
- is eager to please others
- will exact her revenge on enemies
- is more faithful than male snakes
- is uncannily perceptive

THE SNAKE CHILD

If a child has a typical snake personality, he or she will generally display the behavior listed below.

- is tranquil and problem free
- is basically happy
- needs to learn how to share toys
- is sensitive to family quarrels
- is good at art subjects at school
- performs erratically at school
- is calm – if family is settled
- seeks to please parents
- likes secrets and confidences
- does not mind responsibility
- is jealous of parents' attentions
- demands a lot of affection

SNAKE AT HOME

Home is snake's favorite place. They will try to create a calm and peaceful environment but in an imaginative way. Snakes can naturally combine colors and designs in a tasteful way. Furnishings are chosen to indulge the snake's sensuous nature – they will be sumptuously comfortable. The larder will always be well stocked with the finest foods and drinks, and there will be plenty of books to read. A snake home is likely to have expensive items such as antiques and works of art on display. If so, they will not be fakes. In some way, snakes' homes will reflect their perception of themselves. For example, snakes will make their surroundings elegant, witty, or austere depending on their personalities. Snakes' need to stamp their personality on their homes makes them difficult people to live with.

SNAKE AT WORK

Snakes are very efficient and adaptable people. They will do something quickly with the minimum of fuss and in the most cost-effective way. They are also quite capable of quietly eliminating the competition. Although they are willful and well organized, snakes are not so good at long-term planning. A snake is more likely to rely on chance and wits. This does not mean, however, that they take risks. Snakes are opportunistic and ambitious but combine this with deliberation not recklessness. Wisdom allows snakes to be objective about their goals and aspirations.

Snakes can be very determined and persevering if they are morally or materially inspired. If they are not motivated or have nothing to do, they will revert to their natural reflective pose – which others may interpret as laziness.

Some typical snake occupations

- professor
- linguist
- philosopher
- teacher
- psychiatrist
- psychologist
- ambassador
- anything related to the arcane

- astrologer
- clairvoyant
- personnel officer
- diviner
- public relations executive
- mediator
- interior designer

SNAKE PREFERENCES

Likes

- to please others
- ornaments
- dressing to impress
- confiding and hearing confessions
- deserts and wild landscapes
- to impress others with their knowledge
- to make gestures of good will
- a good debate
- to spend extravagantly on themselves
- abstract art
- applause
- harmony and stability
- to be asked for help

Dislikes

- people getting out of control
- to be found gullible
- prejudiced people
- to be made an example of
- disputes and violence
- to lend or give others money
- superficial people
- vulgarity
- to be abandoned
- fake anything

GOOD FRIENDS FOR SNAKES

The diagram below shows the compatibility of snake with other animals. There is no fixed ruling, however, because there are other influences on both the snake and any potential friend. These influences are:

- the companion in life (see pp. 273–5)
- the dominant element (from the year of birth)

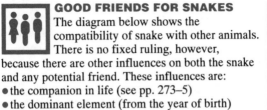

Compatibility of snake with other animals

- ● Rat
- ● Ox
- ● Tiger
- ▲ Rabbit
- ▲ Dragon
- ■ Snake

- ● Horse
- ● Goat
- ▲ Monkey
- ▲ Rooster
- ■ Dog
- ▲ Pig

Key

- ▲ Highly compatible
- ● Amicable
- ■ No conflict but needs some effort
- ● Lack of sympathy
- ▲ Antagonistic

Rat with snake This is a friendly pair who both enjoy fine things and will gossip together for hours. Snake can blow hot and cold and may be possessive one moment and wander off to new pastures the next, but all this will be temporary.

Ox with snake Oxen are dependable and will give snakes the support they need. Both like to work toward long-term goals, and ox can help snake do this effectively. Each will respect the other's need for privacy, and all should go well as long as the snakes do not reveal their manipulative sides.

Tiger with snake Snake and tiger approach life from opposite angles. Snakes follow their heads, and tigers follow their hearts; snakes enjoy relaxing with a book while tigers like action and risk. Both would misunderstand and feel suspicious of the other's motivations.

Rabbit with snake This can be a good match. Both snakes and rabbits cultivate peace and security and share a love of the arts. Snake can help rabbit be more adventurous, as long as rabbit is tolerant of snake's less virtuous nature.

Dragon with snake A well-matched couple, snakes are clever enough to let dragons think they are in charge. Dragons are pleased to be with elegant, seductive snakes. Together, they can achieve a lot.

Snake with snake A good combination for work and friendship, but not for a long-term relationship. In business, they will be ruthless and ambitious. For two snakes to live together, one would eventually be smothered by the other, and no snake likes to be dominated.

Horse with snake At first, there will be a mutual attraction of opposites between the outgoing horse and the more reticent snake. The horse will soon tire of thoughtful snake who, in turn, will tire of horse's lack of mental concentration.

Goat with snake Both the goat and the snake love art, beauty, and harmony. The snake appreciates goat's imagination and creativity. As long as life is good, these two will rarely argue as it is too much trouble. Otherwise, the goat may find snake too serious, and snake will think goat weak.

Monkey with snake The monkey is intelligent in a quick-witted sort of way, the snake in a more profound fashion. This can lead to competition or a perfect business relationship. In love, however, the monkey finds snake boring and will not settle down.

Rooster with snake This is the most ideal couple of Chinese astrology. They balance each other like mind and matter. Snake and rooster both flatter and understand the other.

Dog with snake Idealistic dog is attracted to snake's wisdom and depth and will ignore the snake's selfish, ambitious streak. Snakes admire the dog's honesty and, as long as snakes do not mind being idealized, this relationship could work out.

Pig with snake This is a case of opposites that do not attract. Snake sees the pig as naive and innocent, but the pig is wise to snake's true nature. Both are very sensual creatures and this can unite them. If a relationship does endure, it is likely to be thanks to the pig's giving nature.

SNAKE IN LOVE

Snakes are intense and passionate people. They have to feel they are the center of their lover's life. Often, this will smother a relationship. Snakes, however, will not curb their naturally flirtatious habits – they like to check that their sex appeal is still operational. Before they settle down, snakes will have many love affairs, liaisons, and intrigues; this may not stop once they are married. Snakes expect fidelity but may not be faithful themselves. Partners of snake people should try and remain a little independent to gain the snake's respect. Snakes will not like this but will admire them for it and will try harder to be faithful.

SNAKE AND SEX

Witty, passionate, and sensual, snakes are exciting and imaginative lovers. Like dragons, snakes use sex as a means of self-discovery. They will blossom in a relationship that is physically compatible. Snakes enjoy being intimate both physically and emotionally, but they are not as faithful as the dragon. Highly seductive, they enchant others by being almost hypnotically attentive to them, and they cannot abide to be resisted. Snakes do not undertake a seduction lightly – so do not toy with snake people's affections or they may show you their more dangerous, vengeful side.

HEALTH

Snake's element, fire, is associated with the heart and the small intestine, so snakes should pay particular attention to keeping these organs in working order. They should have regular medical checkups for their heart. Stomachaches are a common snake complaint, so try to cut down on rich, indigestible foods. Snakes need to learn to control their passions and indulgent natures. Sensitive and highly strung, snakes have a tendency to nervous disorders.

LEISURE INTERESTS

Snakes like nothing better than to curl up with a good book in their favorite chair with some classical music in the background. Relaxing in the country on the weekend is another favorite snake pastime. When they go out, snakes like to frequent the theater and love opera. These pursuits allow them to indulge their love of dressing up as well as their enjoyment of the "finer" things in life. Snakes are great strategists, and they excel at games like backgammon and chess. At home, if they are not relaxing, snakes will undertake home improvements such as painting and decorating or just rearranging the ornaments.

THE SNAKE YEARS AND THEIR ELEMENTS

The snake is a Yin fire animal. Each of the snake years, however, is associated with an element which is said to have its own influence.

These elements are wood, fire, earth, metal, and water. They influence snake in a regular sequence, which is repeated every 60 years. In the table below, for example, the snake year 1905 is a wood year. The next snake wood year is 60 years later in 1965, and the next will be 2025. Snake's natural element is fire; the influence of this combines with those of the element of the year of birth. The possible effects of the year elements are listed below.

Lunar years ruled by the snake and their elements

1905	Feb 4, 1905 – Jan 24, 1906	wood
1917	Jan 23, 1917 – Feb 10, 1918	fire
1929	Feb 10, 1929 – Jan 29, 1930	earth
1941	Jan 27, 1941 – Feb 14, 1942	metal
1953	Feb 14, 1953 – Feb 2, 1954	water
1965	Feb 2, 1965 – Jan 20, 1966	wood
1977	Feb 18, 1977 – Feb 6, 1978	fire
1989	Feb 6, 1989 – Jan 26, 1990	earth
2001	Jan 24, 2001 – Feb 11, 2002	metal

SnakeFire–Wood (1905, 1965)
Fire and wood can sometimes be a flammable combination. Normally, however, wood snakes are laid-back, easygoing and not as ruthless or vindictive as other snakes. Unusual for snakes, they can even be sympathetic and will work for the benefit of others, not just themselves. Wood is a creative element and allows the snake's imagination to run free. Wood snakes are often inventive or

creative people who work to combine beauty of form with space. Many are poets, painters, or musicians.

SnakeFire–Fire (1917, 1977)

Snakes born in fire years are in their natural element. Double fire means double Yang, so they are very dynamic, almost unstoppable people of action. Fire inflames the energies but can be destructive. They are passionate in the intensity of their feelings towards both their lovers and their enemies. In other animal signs, fire can be destructive, but snakes are Yin and, therefore, have the wisdom to control their excesses and use their energies positively. Like all fiery people, fire snakes are dramatic, appealing, and very sexy. These snakes are not as profound as other snakes.

SnakeFire–Earth (1929, 1989)

Earth is a very good element for the snake. They undergo a deep transformation that allows a ripening of many of the snake's qualities. Snakes born in earth years are less mysterious and easy to get to know. Friendly and calm, these snakes try to see the best in people and are not so quick to use others for their own ends. Earth snakes prefer harmony to status. They are not as ambitious as other snakes – they will still achieve their goals, but these will not be so grand. Earth can make these snakes introverted; they are so busy recalling dreams or remembering the past that they do not look to the future.

SnakeFire–Metal (1941, 2001)

Metal brings strength of character to any animal sign. In the snake, this strength wavers between

beauty and destruction. Metal snakes are energetic
and self-disciplined people, often perfectionists.
They have a very strong sense of self and are the
most independent of all snakes. Always reflective,
metal makes these snakes very serious people; the
rigidity of metal can incline them to fanatical
thinking, though. These snakes are intolerant, proud,
and ruthless, but, unlike other snakes, metal ones are
always honest.

Snake Fire–Water (1953, 2013)

Reflective water combines with mysterious snake to
produce one of the most enigmatic of all signs. Both
water and snake are intuitive, so this snake can be
intuitive to the point of clairvoyancy. The Yin of
water balances the Yang of fire but water snakes
should not let this element douse their inner fires.
Snake's natural element, fire, stops these water
people being too passive, although the water does
express itself as a pacifist streak. A case of still
waters run deep, these snakes are calm, wise, and
reflective. They are more just and honest than other
snakes but still practical and intelligent.

 **SNAKE AND THE ZODIAC OF
WESTERN ASTROLOGY**

To work out your zodiac sign see p. 277.
General character traits of snakes of the
12 zodiac signs are given below. Bear in mind that
the Western zodiac sign modifies the basic snake
nature – especially in the area of personal
relationships.

Aries snake Two fire signs, talented Aries and intelligent snake, combine to make a more powerful, pythonesque snake. They are more impulsive and less reserved than other snakes.

Taurus snake Taurus brings industriousness to the snake. Unusually faithful, they are still charming. Do not be fooled by their decadent air though, as snake's wisdom and Taurean practicality keeps them down-to-earth.

Gemini snake Quick-witted Gemini and profound snake combine the two traits in their conversation – dazzling others with eloquence on any sophisticated or intellectual subject. They should beware of being too clever and missing obvious truths.

Cancer snake Cancerians are prone to depression, but snake relieves this trait. These snakes can recognize their own weaknesses and thus avoid indulging them. Although Cancer snakes can be temperamental, they are basically well-meaning.

Leo snake Both fire signs, they combine to make an energetic and well-balanced individual. Noble lion makes this snake more generous and open. Leo snakes are endearing and have a lusty and adventurous approach to life but they can be self-righteous and competitive.

Virgo snake Virgo snakes are both analytical and intuitive. Often theatrical, but always sophisticated and stylish, they can appear intimidating or calculating to others. More cautious about romance, Virgo snakes are serious about matters of the heart.

Libra snake Idealistic Libra and wise snake make a magnetic combination. They are polite and great diplomats. Do not be deceived by their placid appearance though. All snakes dislike vulgar outbursts, but if a Libra snake is roused then beware.

Scorpio snake Suspicious Scorpio accentuates the snake's crafty, scheming side. They are always competitive, even at times when it is inappropriate. This makes their lives unnecessarily complicated.

Sagittarius snake Honorable snakes who have a sense of morality that other snakes lack, they feel more social responsibility and are generous with money. They are not as bothered with their appearance as other snakes, which makes them more approachable.

Capricorn snake Resolute Capricorn and ambitious snake make highly materialistic and status-seeking people. They are good providers and like to create a solid family base. They are even more profound than typical snakes but are too reserved. Capricornean snakes should relax a bit.

Aquarius snake Born under two intuitive signs, these snakes are almost too visionary and esoteric. Very individualistic, Aquarian snakes appear eccentric, but they are not bothered by others' opinions and make friends quickly.

Pisces snake On the surface, Piscean snakes are self-composed and appear cool. Underneath, they are kind but not courageous. The snake's great intellect is unfocussed in those born under Pisces; these snakes are dreamers and idealists and are consequently often disillusioned.

Some famous people born in the years of the snake and their zodiac signs

- Franz Schubert
  Composer
  Jan 31, 1797 Aquarius
- Edgar Allan Poe
  Writer
  Jan 19, 1809 Capricorn
- Alfred Lord Tennyson
  Poet
  Aug 6, 1809 Leo
- Johannes Brahms
  Composer
  May 7, 1833 Taurus
- Alfred Nobel
  Inventor
  Oct 21, 1833 Libra
- Mohandas K. Gandhi
  Indian political leader
  Oct 2, 1869 Libra
- Henri Matisse
  Painter
  Dec 31, 1869 Capricorn
- Béla Bartók
  Composer
  Mar 25, 1881 Aries
- Cecil B. De Mille
  Filmmaker
  Aug 12, 1881 Leo
- P.G. Wodehouse
  Writer
  Oct 15, 1881 Libra
- Pablo Picasso
  Artist
  Oct 25, 1881 Scorpio
- Mao Tse-Tung
  Chinese political leader
  Dec 26, 1893 Capricorn

- Henry Fonda
  Actor
  May 16, 1905 Taurus
- Jean-Paul Sartre
  Philosopher
  Jun 21, 1905 Cancer
- Greta Garbo
  Actress
  Sep 18, 05 Virgo
- John F. Kennedy
  US president
  May 29, 1917 Gemini
- Robert Mitchum
  Actor
  Aug 6, 1917 Leo
- Indira Gandhi
  Indian stateswoman
  Nov 19, 1917 Scorpio
- Gamal Abdel Nasser
  Egyptian statesman
  Jan 15, 1918 Capricorn
- André Previn
  Conductor
  Apr 6, 1929 Aries
- Audrey Hepburn
  Actress
  May 4, 1929 Taurus
- Jackie Kennedy Onassis
  Wife of J.F.Kennedy
  Jul 28, 1929 Leo
- Grace Kelly
  Actress
  Nov 12, 1929 Scorpio
- Bob Dylan
  Singer/Songwriter
  May 24, 1941 Gemini

7. The Horse

The Yang fire animal.

Lunar years ruled by the horse		
1906	Jan 25, 1906	– Feb 12, 1907
1918	Feb 11, 1918	– Jan 31, 1919
1930	Jan 30, 1930	– Feb 16, 1931
1942	Feb 15, 1942	– Feb 4, 1943
1954	Feb 3, 1954	– Jan 23, 1955
1966	Jan 21, 1966	– Feb 8, 1967
1978	Feb 7, 1978	– Jan 27, 1979
1990	Jan 27, 1990	– Feb 14, 1991
2002	Feb 12, 2002	– Jan 31, 2003

The horse is associated with grace, elegance, bravery, and nobility. In China, the horse is the symbol of freedom.

THE HORSE PERSONALITY

Horses approach life with contagious enthusiasm. They are usually happy and will have many friends. They love to chat, converse, or orate. Horses have good images – others see in their zest for life bravery and independence – but they are actually quite cowardly. Although they love freedom, horses are not truly independent as they rely on others for support and encouragement that is vital to their well-being.

Characteristics

These are the general personality traits of those people who are typical horses, both at their best and at their worst.

Positive	Negative
• loyal	• unstable
• noble	• temperamental
• cheerful	• impatient
• enthusiastic	• insecure
• enterprising	• hot tempered
• flexible	• irresponsible
• sincere	• superficial
• frank	• ambitious
• versatile	• careless
• talkative	• spendthrift
• gregarious	• contradictory
• generous	• vain
• unselfish	• easily panicked
• realist	• vulnerable
• energetic	• anxious

Secret horse

On the surface, horses appear to be very self-assured and fearless. Underneath, however, horses are weak and fragile creatures. They are easily scared and let themselves get carried away by their emotions.

Element

Horse is linked to the ancient Chinese element of fire. Fire is a dynamic, exciting sign, which is enhanced by the horse's innate Yang tendency. The energy of fire can be expressed both positively and negatively. It brings warmth, light, and protection as well as the ability to burn and destroy. In horses, fire expresses itself erratically, making them both dynamic and temperamental.

Balance

Horses are both fire and Yang. Therefore, they naturally have great reserves of strength. Yet people born under this sign, although seemingly self-confident, are too easily affected by the opinions of others. Criticism or hostility, no matter how slight, shatters their vulnerable egos. Horses will only have access to their full strengths when they have learned to balance their need for approval with faith in themselves.

Best associations
Traditionally, the following are said to be associated
with horses:

● Taste	bitter
● Season	summer
● Birth	winter
● Color	orange
● Plant	palm tree
● Flower	hawthorn
● Food	rice, lamb
● Climate	hot, sunny

THE MALE HORSE
If a man has a typical horse personality,
he will generally display the behavior
listed below.

- is not very good with money
- is secretly a pessimist
- will always try to look good
- is egocentric
- will offend others without realizing it
- is independent
- needs approval
- likes the sound of his own voice
- appears to be cheerful and easygoing
- is sloppy at home

THE FEMALE HORSE
If a woman has a typical horse
personality, she will generally display the
behavior listed below.

- does not like authority
- will never tolerate a subordinate role
- has no time for the problems of others
- craves flattery and attention
- is elegant and well groomed
- is always late
- enjoys dramatic scenes
- needs her own space
- is a good persuader

THE HORSE CHILD
If a child has a typical horse personality,
he or she will generally display the
behavior listed below.

- is prone to temper tantrums
- is independent
- has a lazy tendency
- is impetuous
- gives up difficult tasks quickly
- is carefree and lively
- dislikes responsibility
- is untidy and disordered
- prefers playing to learning
- is easy to love
- is difficult to discipline

HORSE AT HOME

Horses are not great home lovers. Often, they prefer to spend time at other people's houses. Nevertheless, a stable home base is actually very important to the horse. They need one to bolster their fragile self-confidence. Horses will appreciate their homes more if they go away occasionally. Horses like to be proud of their home environments, but decorations in the house of a horse are unlikely to be imaginative or original. Also, they are not very good at housework. The home of a horse will be clean but untidy. Horses are not particularly materialistic people. They will decorate their homes with things of sentimental rather than real value.

HORSE AT WORK

Horses tend to be talented people rather than particularly intelligent. They need to have a job with variety to keep them interested and to exploit their versatile natures. Horse people are fast-talking and fast-thinking but are not good at long-term planning or organization. They are not suited to bureaucratic positions as horses hate routine and are unable to pay attention to details. They are skilled communicators, however, and very imaginative. Horses are great to have at brainstorming sessions as they will come up with many ideas – but don't expect them to carry out the ideas. Impatient for results, they are better at initiating projects than performing them. Initially, horses inspire confidence in others as they appear to be supremely confident and enthusiastic about their work. This enthusiasm crumbles at the least mishap, though, and the colleagues of horse will soon lose their faith in these inconstant creatures.

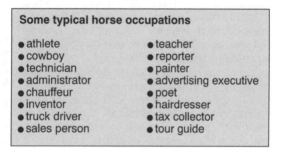

Some typical horse occupations

- athlete
- cowboy
- technician
- administrator
- chauffeur
- inventor
- truck driver
- sales person

- teacher
- reporter
- painter
- advertising executive
- poet
- hairdresser
- tax collector
- tour guide

HORSE PREFERENCES

Likes

- beginning a new project
- to be complimented
- dancing
- to make people laugh (but not at their own expense)
- a change of scenery
- going on a voyage
- meeting new people
- any conversation, chat, or gossip
- to feel like a pioneer
- to discuss his or her emotions
- to eat at expensive restaurants

Dislikes

- silence
- schedules and timetables
- disapproval
- bureaucrats
- unenthusiastic or disinterested people
- uncommunicative people
- being told what to do
- having too many material possessions
- listening to others
- criticism or complaint
- solitude
- being bored

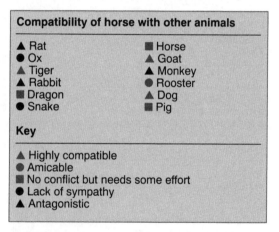

GOOD FRIENDS FOR HORSES
The diagram below shows the compatibility of horse with other animals. There is no fixed ruling, however, because there are other influences on both the horse and any potential friend. These influences are:
- the companion in life (see pp. 273–5)
- the dominant element (from the year of birth)

Compatibility of horse with other animals

▲ Rat   ■ Horse
● Ox   ▲ Goat
▲ Tiger   ▲ Monkey
▲ Rabbit   ● Rooster
■ Dragon   ▲ Dog
● Snake   ■ Pig

Key

▲ Highly compatible
● Amicable
■ No conflict but needs some effort
● Lack of sympathy
▲ Antagonistic

Rat with horse This is a partnership definitely to be avoided. Horse and rat rub each other the wrong way.
Ox with horse This will be an unhappy match for the pair. They will only annoy one another. Lively horse will not get any excitement from the ox; oxen

cannot give the flattery that vain horses require.
Also, horses are too unorthodox to accept the ox's
authoritarian habits for long.

Tiger with horse There can be great attachment
between a tiger and a horse. Patient horse will enjoy
the company of energetic tiger and stick by him
when he's down. Even so, they will probably argue
and need to take time out from the relationship.

Rabbit with horse Moody horse makes a disruptive
partner for rabbit, who may not tolerate this for long
unless very much in love.

Dragon with horse Enthusiastic horse and energetic
dragon can get along well together if they share a
common purpose and the dragon does not invade the
horse's privacy too much. Otherwise, daily life will
split them up. Self-preoccupied horses are not able
to give dragons the attention they need.

Snake with horse At first, there will be a mutual
attraction of opposites between the outgoing horse
and the more reticent snake. The horse will soon tire
of thoughtful snake who, in turn, will tire of horse's
lack of mental concentration.

Horse with horse This is a potentially enjoyable
combination but is likely to be unstable. Two restless
horses may have a lot in common but they will find
it doubly hard to settle down together.

Goat with horse Goats and horses complement each
other. The goat will feel secure with horse but the
relationship will still be exciting. Both are unstable
and irresponsible people who dislike routine.

Monkey with horse A relationship between these two will be plagued by misunderstandings. Horse will find monkey's lively intelligence calculating; monkey will think the horse's enthusiasm is based on naivety or even stupidity.

Rooster with horse These two can get on quite well together. The horse will initiate things, and the rooster can complete them. They are, however, both sensitive to the opinions of others while being tactless themselves. This could create problems and bruised egos.

Dog with horse This is a case of opposites that attract. The horse appreciates the dog's loyal and generous nature and their ability to see things as they really are. In turn, dogs take great pleasure in the company of lively horses and will ignore their waywardness.

Pig with horse At first, these two can get along. The pig will find the horse exciting, and the horse will enjoy pig's kind and loving nature. Eventually, however, selfish horse will test the pig's patience to the limit, or the horse will get bored with the pig.

HORSE IN LOVE

Horses love to be in love. In fact, they can be more in love with the idea of being in love than with the actual recipient of their affections. Horse people are the type to fall in love at first sight. Once smitten, they put all their energies into seducing that person. As partners, horses are exciting but difficult. They are moody and like their freedom while still demanding support. They are highly romantic and live at the mercy of their emotions. For love, a horse will change everything: buy a house, change job or emigrate, for example. They are flighty people, however, and will fall out of love as quickly as they fell in love. To keep horses interested, partners should try ignoring them. Any lasting relationship with a horse will be punctuated by major crises. Strangely enough, these actually help to prolong the relationship as they keep the horse interested – horse people thrive on dramatic scenes.

HORSE AND SEX

Horses are the epitome of sex appeal and are very sensual. A horse will be impatient to consummate a relationship and will employ whatever means are necessary to seduce the object of his or her passion. Horses are passionate and energetic lovers. They are sprinters, however, and not marathon runners, so don't expect all-night performances. Horses are enthusiastic about sex and expect their partners to share this. Their enthusiasm may quickly wane, however, as horses can run hot one minute and cold the next. Sadly, horses are likely to be unfaithful. They are generally weak people who cannot resist temptation. Unreasonably, perhaps, they will expect to be forgiven as easily as they forget. Usually, horse people's total immersion in love makes it easier for others to forgive their indiscretions and egocentric behavior.

HEALTH

Horse's element, fire, is associated with the heart and small intestine, so horses should pay particular attention to keeping these organs in working order, in particular by watching their diets and establishing healthy eating patterns. Horses are highly strung and need to expend their energies in some kind of exertion. This nervous energy will otherwise affect the horse both physically and mentally, therefore making them prone to psychosomatic disorders – those brought about by mental stress – such as anxiety attacks, insomnia, and eating disorders.

LEISURE INTERESTS

Horses enjoy all kinds of sport and especially competitive ones. Although they are not very good at cooperating, team sports such as football or hockey appeal to horses. This is because they allow the horse to shine while still providing the necessary support that the horse needs to succeed. Horses also love most outdoor pursuits – basically anything that gets them out of the house. On vacation, camping is enjoyed by horses as it allows them to feel independent and pioneering without actually being too daring. Hiking and canoeing appeal to their carefree natures.

THE HORSE YEARS AND THEIR ELEMENTS

The horse is a Yang fire animal. Each of the horse years, however, is associated with an element which is said to have its own influence. These elements are wood, fire, earth, metal, and water. They influence horse in a regular sequence, which is repeated every 60 years. In the table below, for example, the horse year 1942 is a water year. The next horse water year is 60 years later in 2003, and the next will be 2063. Horse's natural element is fire; the influence of this combines with those of the element of the year of birth. The possible effects of the year elements are listed below.

Lunar years ruled by the horse and their elements

1906	Jan 25, 1906 – Feb 12, 1907	fire
1918	Feb 11, 1918 – Jan 31, 1919	earth
1930	Jan 30, 1930 – Feb 16, 1931	metal
1942	Feb 15, 1942 – Feb 4, 1943	water
1954	Feb 3, 1954 – Jan 23, 1955	wood
1966	Jan 21, 1966 – Feb 8, 1967	fire
1978	Feb 7, 1978 – Jan 27, 1979	earth
1990	Jan 27, 1990 – Feb 14, 1991	metal
2002	Feb 12, 2002 – Jan 31, 2003	water

HorseFire–Fire (1906, 1966)

Fire horses are exceptional people. To be born during the year of the fire horse is considered either very advantageous or disastrous. In China, many people try to avoid giving birth during fire horse years as they do not want to risk bringing bad luck into the family. Fire multiplies both the good and bad attributes of the horse. These people are extreme and excessive. More adventurous, passionate, unruly, and talented than other horses, they will lead thrilling lives. Fire horses are destined for great success or spectacular failure.

HorseFire–Earth (1918, 1978)

Earth brings stability to the horse. The capability and resourcefulness of this element makes earth horses less flighty. They are more able to see a project through to the end. These horses are more responsible and cautious, yet they are not as much fun as typical horses. Normally, earthy types are very conventional, but horse breathes fresh air into this element and prevents inflexibility. Earth horses will express their nervous energies by paying attention to details and by displaying minor eccentricities.

HorseFire–Metal (1930, 1990)

Metal is quite a good element for horse. It compensates for some of the horse's failings. They can be more resolute and persevering than other horses – but only if they are motivated. Metal horses need a lot of stimulation to stop them getting bored. Metal horses are headstrong and irrepressible. Metal can also restrain horses, smothering their passionate natures. This is not necessarily a good thing as horses need to give vent to their emotions.

HorseFire–Water (1942, 2002)

Water facilitates the horse's dormant creativity and

brings these people success in the arts. Elusive water and easily distracted horse combine to produce people with very short attention spans. Water is a communicative element and enhances the horse's already verbose nature. It allows them to be humorous and witty in their conversation. Although inconsiderate and self-centered, water horses endear themselves to others by being charming. They cultivate daredevil personae that allow others to excuse their shortcomings. Water exploits the horse's nervous energy and these horses keep active and like to live by their wits.

HorseFire–Wood (1954, 2014)

Wood has a calming influence on the horse. Wood horses are more cooperative and helpful than other horses. They should watch out for others trying to take advantage of them though, as wood diminishes the horse's perceptive abilities, making them too gullible at times. Wood helps to settle the horse's nervous energies. Emotionally, therefore, this horse is not so prone to depression and bad moods and will be mostly happy and good-tempered.

HORSE AND THE ZODIAC OF WESTERN ASTROLOGY

To work out your zodiac sign see p. 277. General character traits of horses of the 12 zodiac signs are given on the next page. Bear in mind that the Western zodiac sign modifies the basic horse nature – especially in the area of personal relationships.

Aries horse Aries exacerbates the horse's wild side. These horses are aggressively competitive and very enterprising. Aries horses are more capable of devotion than other horses and are good company.

Taurus horse Pragmatic Taurus allows the horse to plan ahead. These horses are less temperamental and more stable but they can be too rigid. Taurean horses are not averse to taking advice from others.

Gemini horse These two signs share many similar traits which are, therefore, multiplied under this sign. Gemini horses are even more enthusiastic, curious, rebellious, and sociable than usual.

Cancer horse Cancer makes this horse able to appreciate the needs and wishes of others. Being more sensitive, these horses are very dependent on the love and support of close family and friends.

Leo horse To these horses, the world is their playground. The Leo horse loves adventure, craves admiration, and is not beset by the self-doubts that normally plague the horse.

Virgo horse Virgoan horses are well-balanced people. Virgo cures some of the horse's shortcomings, such as lack of precision, lack of self-discipline, irresponsibility, and unruliness.

Libra horse Libran horses are levelheaded and realistic yet surprisingly indecisive. Not as independent as other horses, they are honest about how important their loved ones are to them.

Scorpio horse Headstrong, stubborn, and wild, these horses never compromise. They direct their considerable energies into fulfilling their desires – which govern the lives of Scorpio horses.

Sagittarius horse The symbol of Sagittarius is itself a horse. In many ways, these people are almost stereotypical horses. Easygoing and carefree, they are fun people but typically unpredictable.

Capricorn horse Capricorn makes these horses relatively materialistic. A Capricorn horse is not afraid of working hard to achieve financial security. They are more serious in their demeanor than one would expect from a horse.

Aquarius horse Two unpredictable signs combine to produce an eccentric but talented horse. More than any other horses, Aquarian horses love the company of new friends.

Pisces horse Self-conscious Pisces heightens the horse's basic insecurities. When they are not being anxious, Piscean horses are loving, eager to please, and warmhearted.

Some famous people born in the years of the horse and their zodiac signs

- Rembrandt
  Painter
  Jul 15, 1606 Cancer

- Isaac Newton
  Scientist
  Dec 25, 1642 Capricorn

- Antonio Vivaldi
  Composer
  Mar 4, 1678 Pisces

- Davy Crockett
  Frontiersman
  Aug 17, 1786 Leo

- Frédéric Chopin
  Composer
  Feb 22, 1810 Pisces

- Edgar Dégas
  Artist
  Jul 19, 1834 Cancer

- Theodore Roosevelt
  US president
  Oct 17, 1858 Libra

- Giacomo Puccini
  Composer
  Dec 22, 1858 Capricorn

- Vladimir Lenin
  Russian political leader
  Mar 4, 1870 Pisces

- Igor Stravinsky
  Composer
  Jun 17, 1882 Gemini

- Otto Preminger
  Film director
  Dec 5, 1906 Sagittarius

- Leonid Brezhnev
  Russian political leader
  Dec 19, 1906 Sagittarius

- Mickey Spillane
  Writer
  Mar 9, 1918 Pisces

- Ella Fitzgerald
  Singer
  Apr 25, 1918 Taurus

- Rita Hayworth
  Actress
  Oct 17, 1918 Libra

- Alexander Solzhenitsyn
  Novelist
  Dec 11, 1918 Sagittarius

- Anwar Sadat
  Egyptian statesman
  Dec 25, 1918 Capricorn

- Clint Eastwood
  Actor
  May 31, 1930 Gemini

- Ted Hughes
  Poet
  Aug 16, 1930 Leo

- Sean Connery
  Actor
  Aug 25, 1930 Virgo

- Ray Charles
  Singer
  Sep 23, 1930 Libra

- Barbra Streisand
  Actress/Singer
  Apr 24, 1942 Taurus

- Paul McCartney
  Musician/Songwriter
  Jun 18, 1942 Gemini

- Jimi Hendrix
  Rock singer
  Nov 27, 1942 Sagittarius

8. The Goat

The Yin fire animal.

Lunar years ruled by the goat

1907	Feb 13, 1907 – Feb 1, 1908
1919	Feb 1, 1919 – Feb 19, 1920
1931	Feb 17, 1931 – Feb 5, 1932
1943	Feb 5, 1943 – Jan 24, 1944
1955	Jan 24, 1955 – Feb 11, 1956
1967	Feb 9, 1967 – Jan 29, 1968
1979	Jan 28, 1979 – Feb 15, 1980
1991	Feb 15, 1991 – Feb 3, 1992
2003	Feb 1, 2003 – Jan 21, 2004

The goat is associated with harmony, creativity, peace, and pleasure. In China, the goat is seen as a harbinger of peace.

THE GOAT PERSONALITY

Charming, amiable, and sympathetic, goats are genuinely nice people. They hate to criticize and always look for the best in people – including themselves. A goat will prefer to forget grievances rather than brood over them and will bottle up resentments to keep the peace. Goat people live in the present, which they enjoy to the best of their abilities. Thanks to their sensitive natures, goats are one of the most artistic and creative of all the Chinese horoscope signs.

Characteristics

These are the general personality traits of those people who are typical goats, both at their best and at their worst.

Positive	Negative
● creative	● eccentric
● imaginative	● illogical
● ingenious	● vulnerable
● honest	● irresponsible
● capricious	● irrational
● sensitive	● naive
● faithful	● unsatisfied
● sincere	● disorganized
● peaceful	● impulsive
● adaptable	● lazy
● independent	● gullible
● ardent	● fickle
● elegant	● careless
● gentle	● anxious
● easygoing	● impractical

Secret goat

From their description, people may think that goats are weak creatures who are easy to take advantage of. In reality, however, they will fight violently if something important to them is threatened. Fortunately, as goats assign value according to very personal criteria, what they would defend to the last is not often something that others covet.

Element

Goat is linked to the ancient Chinese element of fire. Fire is a dynamic, exciting, and energetic sign. In the case of goats, fire expresses itself in their imaginative and creative abilities. Normally, fire people are as fiery as the sign suggests. The easygoing and carefree nature of the goat, however, dampens their fiery sides, which are kept well hidden until times of crisis.

Balance

Normally, people are advised to look to themselves to balance the strengths and weaknesses of their characters. For example, the goat would be advised to try and take more care of the practical side of life – such as paying the bills – and not rely on others to support them as they pursue their own interests. Chinese tradition, however, holds that goats are mostly unable to change this aspect of their natures. Therefore, they will need to find a patron to take care of the "administration" of their life and allow them the freedom to make the most of their creative talents. This role could be filled by, for example, a devoted husband or wife, a manager, or even a loyal accountant!

Best associations

Traditionally, the following are said to be associated with goats:

- Taste   bitter
- Season   summer
- Birth   rainy day
- Color   sky-blue
- Plants   wormwood, anise
- Flower   honeysuckle
- Food   rice, lamb
- Climate   hot

THE MALE GOAT

If a man has a typical goat personality, he will generally display the behavior listed below.

- is dependent on his family
- will be a fun but irresponsible parent
- is fretful and indecisive
- has a highly developed aesthetic sense
- is unusually sensitive for a man
- has a natural flair for hospitality
- is reflective and gentle
- will remember birthdays and anniversaries
- is easily put off by obstacles

THE FEMALE GOAT

If a woman has a typical goat personality, she will generally display the behavior listed below.

- is indifferent to conventions
- is angered by injustice
- is talented
- leads a carefree existence
- is never hostile
- is impressionable and easily led
- likes to be the center of attention
- fears rejection and criticism
- needs security to blossom
- likes to be noticed

THE GOAT CHILD

If a child has a typical goat personality, he or she will generally display the behavior listed below.

- is delicate and sickly
- needs to be indulged
- is fickle and unstable
- is timid and uncertain at times
- blossoms with a supportive family
- must be allowed to find their own way
- enjoys creating things
- makes up fantasies and fairy tales
- will give away their toys to friends

GOAT AT HOME

Goats love the creature comforts of life but are not practical enough to go out and get them. It is usually left to their partner or family to decorate and furnish the home. Nonetheless, goats are very acquisitive – they are attracted to beautiful or novel things. A goat house will be full of knickknacks, souvenirs, and odd bits of furniture that have caught the goat's fancy. They love junk shops, charity shops, and markets where they can find new and interesting goods at low prices. If they have enough money, they will indulge themselves by rummaging round the better department stores as if they were flea markets. At heart, though, goats are indifferent to material possessions and will be as happy in another's home that is full of beautiful objects as their own. A goat may have one beautiful item, perhaps made by themselves, installed in their home that negates the drab surroundings.

GOAT AT WORK

Goats would never work if they had the choice, if only money was not a necessity. They are not especially active or hardworking and will be lazy and erratic at work. Despite this, if goats do undertake a job, they will carry it out properly or not at all. Goats can be both scrupulous and perfectionists. They have a profiteering side and hate to support themselves – they will try to profit from the hard work of others. This does not mean that they are ambitious, as they will not better themselves at the expense of others. If they do have some money, goats will be better off seeking advice on how to invest it wisely rather than using it to start their own business. Goats are inspired by the arts and love anything concerned with harmony and beauty. They come into their own in art if they have a mentor or patron who can recognize and encourage their talents.

Some typical goat occupations

- actor/actress
- story writer
- painter
- musician
- landscape gardener
- weaver
- potter
- courtesan

- television presenter
- gigolo
- dancer
- tramp!
- fortune-teller
- escort
- investor
- shareholder

GOAT PREFERENCES

Likes

- to please others
- beauty
- to make people curious
- tranquillity
- to forgive and forget
- parks with fountains
- marble statues
- costume dramas
- to be taken care of
- beautiful people

Dislikes

- to be made to choose
- unwanted responsibility
- routines
- to be involved in others' problems
- obligations
- hostile atmospheres
- to offend others
- emotional scenes
- doing the accounts
- taking the initiative

GOOD FRIENDS FOR GOATS
The diagram below shows the compatibility of goat with other animals. There is no fixed ruling, however, because there are other influences on both the goat and any potential friend. These influences are:
● the companion in life (see pp. 273–5)
● the dominant element (from the year of birth)

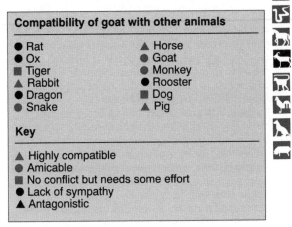

Compatibility of goat with other animals

● Rat	▲ Horse
● Ox	● Goat
■ Tiger	● Monkey
▲ Rabbit	● Rooster
● Dragon	■ Dog
● Snake	▲ Pig

Key

▲ Highly compatible
● Amicable
■ No conflict but needs some effort
● Lack of sympathy
▲ Antagonistic

Rat with goat There is not much mutual understanding between these two but they are fine together for short periods for specific interests. In general, carefree goat will be good for rat, and enjoy rat's charm.

Ox with goat Goats and oxen have discordant personalities. Goat's habit of acting without thinking will only annoy careful ox. They also have different priorities in life: goat is too capricious, and ox demands fidelity as the basis for a relationship.

Tiger with goat Difficult, but potentially mutually rewarding. Goat will admire tiger's nerve and loyalty while tiger will appreciate goat's fun-loving nature. To be more than fair-weather friends, however, a little effort will be needed.

Rabbit with goat This may be the best match as both have good taste and a love of luxuries in common. Goat's imaginative nature appeals to rabbit's romantic side. In difficult times, however, neither will be able to look to the other for courage and support as both are anxious creatures.

Dragon with goat A lack of understanding can blight any relationship between these two, unless they both learn to accept and appreciate their differences. Business alliances will be more successful than personal ones as dragons can help quiet goats realize their creativity.

Snake with goat Both goat and snake love art, beauty, and harmony. As long as life is good, these two will rarely argue as it is too much trouble. Otherwise, goat may find snake too serious and snake will think goat weak.

Horse with goat Goats and horses complement each other. The goat will feel secure with horse but the relationship will still be exciting, as both are unstable and irresponsible people who dislike routine.

Goat with goat Two goats can have an idyllic

relationship if they have enough money to not worry about paying the bills. Otherwise, neither can rely on the other for moral support. They can be friends only if they apply their tolerant natures to ignoring the other's faults.

Monkey with goat Goat and monkey will never be bored together. With monkey's quick wits and goat's imagination there will always be plenty to do, and they can be great friends. As lovers, monkeys may not be able to provide the constant reassurances that goats need.

Rooster with goat These two have very little in common and do not understand each other. Although rooster will be able to support goat financially, goat will not give rooster moral support in return.

Dog with goat Goat and dog can be friends if they apply their tolerant natures to ignoring the other's differences. Normally, however, whimsical goat and realistic dog just irritate each other.

Pig with goat This is a good alliance for both signs. Both value tranquillity and harmony and are able to make the concessions necessary to achieve them. Goat should take care not to stretch the pig's tolerance too far, however, by acting too irresponsibly.

GOAT IN LOVE

Goats cannot be objective, and they think that the world revolves around them and their loved ones. Effectively it does, as they will simply blind themselves to matters not concerning them. Emotional and sensitive, goats

have great expectations of romance but they will
also give a lot in return. A goat will adapt to please a
loved one and does not mind making concessions to
keep the peace. They are polite and affectionate
partners. Although goats are sympathetic, they are
not particularly compassionate, so partners should
not expect to burden the goat with their problems.
Goats do not like to be depended on. Conversely, the
goat will expect their partner to be always there for
them and never even to be tempted by another.
Above all else, partners must accept goats as they
are and not try to change them.

GOAT AND SEX

Goats are curious rather than passionate
people. They cannot be logical or
objective about their emotions. To a goat,
feelings and emotions are as important as the sexual
act itself. They are not capable of one-night stands
and will be hurt and confused if they embark on a
physical relationship only to find the other person
does not feel anything for them. Goats begin sexual
relationships with delicacy and elegance. They love
long drawn-out seductions with all the trimmings of
romance. The subtleties and game playing of
courtships intrigue them. Initially, though, they may
be timid and uncertain with new lovers. Goats are
not demanding lovers provided they think they are
the only one for their mate.

HEALTH

Goat's element, fire, is associated with the heart and small intestine, so goats should pay particular attention to keeping these organs in working order. Being of the Yin tendency, goats are advised to try and prevent, rather than cure, illnesses. It is probably the case that most goats, being nervous about their health, are already practicing this by having regular check-ups with the doctor. Yin people tend to have delicate constitutions. Goats should make sure they keep warm during the winter months and remember to relax occasionally. Meditation would probably be beneficial for goats as it would help them focus their energies and develop an inner sense of well-being.

LEISURE INTERESTS

Goats are not particularly energetic people. They would rather visit an art gallery than go swimming. Parks, botanical gardens, historic houses, and flower gardens will all have many goat visitors. Goats love anything in which they can find beauty and harmony. Alternatively, goats spend a lot of their time visiting friends. They are never short of invitations as goat people bring a pleasant ambience to any gathering. On the whole, goats are better as guests than hosts. As guests, they only have to be their agreeable selves, but as hosts they would have to organize and plan the event – not goat strong points.

THE GOAT YEARS AND THEIR ELEMENTS

The goat is a Yin fire animal. Each of the goat years, however, is associated with an element which is said to have its own influence. These elements are wood, fire, earth, metal, and water. They influence goat in a regular sequence, which is repeated every 60 years. In the table below, for example, the goat year 1907 is a fire year. The next goat fire year is 60 years later in 1967, and the next will be 2027. Goat's natural element is fire; the influence of this combines with those of the element of the year of birth. The possible effects of the year elements are listed below.

Lunar years ruled by the goat and their elements

1907	Feb 13, 1907 – Feb 1, 1908	fire
1919	Feb 1, 1919 – Feb 19, 1920	earth
1931	Feb 17, 1931 – Feb 5, 1932	metal
1943	Feb 5, 1943 – Jan 24, 1944	water
1955	Jan 24, 1955 – Feb 11, 1956	wood
1967	Feb 9, 1967 – Jan 29, 1968	fire
1979	Jan 28, 1979 – Feb 15, 1980	earth
1991	Feb 15, 1991 – Feb 3, 1992	metal
2003	Feb 1, 2003 – Jan 21, 2004	water

Goat Fire–Fire (1907, 1967)

Fire is the goat's natural element. Double fire goats are blessed with courage and intuition. These goats are dramatic and innovative, yet they have a knack for making their wild ideas seem safe and logical.

They do, however, have a tendency to be reckless and of not looking before they leap. Goats are never very good at managing their money, and double fire goats are even worse. Money almost burns holes in their pockets. As with all fire types, these goats are attractive and appealing people. They are gentle and sympathetic but intolerant of those they consider fools.

GoatFire–Wood (1955, 2015)

Wood is a creative element associated with growth, renewal, and innovation. Combined with the goat's imagination, this makes wood goats highly artistic. It also heightens the goat's sensitive nature. Unlike water goats, however, wood makes goats very compassionate people and not worriers. These people are generous with their time and money for good causes that they believe in; but they are more likely to be working in the local charity shop than far away in a refugee camp.

GoatFire–Earth (1919, 1979)

Earth grounds the goat. It brings them down to earth and keeps their heads out of the clouds for too long. Earth bestows steadfastness and the ability to work hard on the goat. These goats are more materialistic than the rest of the breed. Atypically, earth goats are capable of fulfilling their own material needs and are not so dependent on others to organize them. Earth goats are basically cheerful and optimistic people but when wronged they can complain too much. Earth signs can, at times, be so cautious and practical that they stagnate.

Goat Fire–Metal (1931, 1991)

Metal strengthens the goat. It brings determination and perseverance to an otherwise work-shy type of person. Fire combines with metal to give these people more presence than typical goats. Metal goats are still sensitive but not as vulnerable as usual. In fact, other people do not realize how sensitive and affectionate these goats really are underneath their harsh exteriors. As with all metal types, these are very ambitious people; but their ambitions will be directed toward typically goatlike goals – achieving in the arts, for example.

Goat Fire–Water (1943, 2003)

Fluid water makes the goat even more capricious than usual. Water goats are incredibly sensitive people and very perceptive emotionally. This can hamper them as they will internalize other people's problems and may become worriers. Fire aligned with water makes these people able to get their own way – but very subtly. Surprisingly, water goats are conservative people; they are fearful of change and do not like to take risks.

GOAT AND THE ZODIAC OF WESTERN ASTROLOGY

To work out your zodiac sign see p. 277. General character traits of goats of the 12 zodiac signs are given below. Bear in mind that the Western zodiac sign modifies the basic goat nature – especially in the area of personal relationships.

Aries goat The goat and the ram share many traits. So those born under both these signs are almost stereotypical goats. Yet they are more independent and are even headstrong. Aries makes the goat stubborn and, unlike other goats, these people hold grudges and will exact revenge on their enemies.

Taurus goat Taurean goats crave domestic and financial security. They are cautious and never take risks. Although still easygoing, if pushed to the limit a Taurus goat will soon break into a fury.

Gemini goat Mercurial Gemini and capricious goat combine to make easily distracted people. They are intelligent and curious and always have something on their minds.

Cancer goat Moody Cancer serves to make the goat temperamental as well as fickle. These goats are very concerned about what others think of them. If they feel secure, then Cancerian goats will be kind and gentle; if they feel neglected, they can be vindictive and stubborn.

Leo goat Leo brings a much-needed measure of common sense to the goat. Leo goats are both sensitive and resolute. They are the most charismatic of all the goats, and it is easy for them to find willing supporters of their latest idea or scheme.

Virgo goat Virgo goats are perfectionists and apply this in their drive to help others. Although they can be too critical, Virgoan goats are basically well meaning. They are more intellectual than other goats and need a job that exploits this to prevent boredom.

Libra goat Libra goats are intelligent and refined. They like to make a good impression and will take care of their appearance. Capable of making great compromises to keep people's affection, these goats need constant companionship.

Scorpio goat Scorpio endows the goat with huge reserves of willpower. Their sensitive natures take second place to their ambitions. Yet these goats are not practical. They are erratic and eccentric but have bursts of wisdom and are very gifted artistically.

Sagittarius goat Sagittarian goats have enough self-confidence to support themselves and do not need to look for others to care for them. They are more adventurous yet less sensitive than other goats.

Capricorn goat Capricorn goats are practical and opportunistic. Financial wealth and status are important to them, and they are usually successful in their chosen careers. These goats do find it difficult to be open emotionally with others though.

Aquarius goat Visionary Aquarius and imaginative goat combine to give great potential. These people are gifted planners, oblivious to criticism, and often idiosyncratic. Aquarian goats are innovative but need to learn to evaluate risks.

Pisces goat Born under two sensitive signs, Pisces goats are almost too sensitive for their own good. Their emotions will reflect the atmosphere of their surroundings. These goats are inspired people but need a stable home base before they can express their creativity.

Some famous people born in the years of the goat and their zodiac signs

- Michelangelo
  Artist
  Mar 6, 1475 Pisces
- Jane Austen
  Novelist
  Dec 16, 1775 Sagittarius
- Alexander Pushkin
  Writer
  Jun 6, 1799 Gemini
- Mark Twain
  Writer
  Nov 30, 1835 Sagittarius
- Arthur Conan Doyle
  Novelist
  May 22, 1859 Gemini
- Marcel Proust
  Novelist
  Jul 10, 1871 Cancer
- Franz Kafka
  Novelist
  Jul 3, 1883 Cancer
- Benito Mussolini
  Italian dictator
  Jul 29, 1883 Leo
- Coco Chanel
  Fashion designer
  Aug 19, 1883 Leo
- Rudolph Valentino
  Actor
  May 6, 1895 Taurus
- Laurence Olivier
  Actor
  May 22, 1907 Gemini
- Simone de Beauvoir
  Novelist
  Jan 9, 1908 Capricorn

- Margot Fonteyn
  Ballerina
  May 18, 1919 Taurus
- Iris Murdoch
  Novelist
  Jul 15, 1919 Cancer
- Doris Lessing
  Novelist
  Oct 22, 1919 Libra
- Anne Bancroft
  Actress
  Sep 17, 1931 Virgo
- John Le Carré
  Novelist
  Oct 19, 1931 Libra
- Diana Dors
  Actress
  Oct 23, 1931 Scorpio
- Mick Jagger
  Rock singer
  Jul 26, 1943 Leo
- Robert de Niro
  Actor
  Aug 17, 1943 Leo
- Chevy Chase
  Actor
  Oct 8, 1943 Libra
- Catherine Deneuve
  Actress
  Oct 22, 1943 Libra
- Joni Mitchell
  Singer/Songwriter
  Nov 7, 1943 Scorpio
- John Denver
  Singer
  Dec 31, 1943 Capricorn

9. The Monkey

The Yang metal animal.

Lunar years ruled by the monkey		
1908	Feb 2, 1908 – Jan 21, 1909	
1920	Feb 20, 1920 – Feb 7, 1921	
1932	Feb 6, 1932 – Jan 25, 1933	
1944	Jan 25, 1944 – Feb 12, 1945	
1956	Feb 12, 1956 – Jan 30, 1957	
1968	Jan 30, 1968 – Feb 16, 1969	
1980	Feb 16, 1980 – Feb 4, 1981	
1992	Feb 4, 1992 – Jan 22, 1993	
2004	Jan 22, 2004 – Feb 8, 2005	

In some parts of China, the monkey is worshipped as the "Great Sage Equal to Heaven." Monkeys are also associated with adultery, justice, and, emotionally, with sorrow.

THE MONKEY PERSONALITY

Highly competitive and insatiably curious, monkeys are very shrewd. They are intelligent and ingenious and try to make the best of any situation. Monkeys are quick-witted and never at a loss for words. They have a reputation for trickery. Although monkeys can be scheming and are good at manipulating people, they use these skills wisely. Despite this, monkeys are quick to stop others who manipulate them. Monkeys try to be honest but will tell a lie if it is convenient.

Characteristics

These are the general personality traits of those people who are typical monkeys, both at their best and at their worst.

Positive	Negative
● independent	● opportunistic
● astute	● restless
● sociable	● manipulative
● vivacious	● scheming
● enthusiastic	● unpredictable
● tolerant	● secretive
● lively	● deceitful
● quick-witted	● mischievous
● sensitive	● vain
● generous	● fickle
● optimistic	● dishonest
● entertaining	● selfish
● audacious	● cunning
● gregarious	● opinionated
● inventive	● devious

Secret monkey

In public, monkeys always appear lighthearted and carefree. In private, however, they may be nursing deep feelings of insecurity. Monkeys get very hurt if they feel rejected or shut out – but they will make light of the situation and cover their true feelings.

Element

Monkey is linked to the ancient Chinese element of metal. This is a very strong element. It can be seen positively as a valuable resource, such as gold; or negatively as a weapon, such as a sword. In monkeys, the energy of metal expresses itself as their imaginative, ambitious, and independent streaks.

Balance

Monkeys are curious people who find something of interest anywhere. They are attracted to the new and unknown. This can make them broad-minded and knowledgeable people, but their energies can be dissipated by these many interests. Monkeys need to learn how to channel their energies into one particular goal at a time. If they can balance their need to search for fresh pastures by bringing some routine or stability into their life, they will find that they can achieve considerable success.

Best associations

Traditionally, the following are said to be associated with monkeys:

- Taste — pungent
- Season — fall
- Birth — summer
- Color — white
- Plant — Chinese wolfberry
- Flower — bird of paradise
- Food — cloves
- Climate — dry

THE MALE MONKEY

If a man has a typical monkey personality, he will generally display the behavior listed below.

- breaks the rules
- lacks self-discipline
- likes to gamble
- is accommodating
- appears to be shallow
- is very good with children
- gets on well with women
- likes to tease his friends
- can lie cheerfully
- is warmhearted and generous
- has a sharp sense of humor

THE FEMALE MONKEY
If a woman has a typical monkey personality, she will generally display the behavior listed below.

- provokes jealousy
- is flirtatious
- needs to be independent
- is witty
- likes to have her own space
- prefers not to marry
- is very good with children
- does not have conventional morals
- is more honest than the male
- is very practical
- is good at fixing things

THE MONKEY CHILD
If a child has a typical monkey personality, he or she will generally display the behavior listed below.

- has a tendency to become overexcited
- needs to be encouraged to calm down
- is impatient and hotheaded
- has a lively imagination
- adapts easily to new environments
- is very critical of peers
- will not suffer bullying for long
- has a short attention span
- can stand up for himself or herself

MONKEY AT HOME

Monkeys are not stay-at-home types. Nevertheless, a stable home environment is important. It gives them a sound base from which to venture forth on their latest adventure. Monkeys hate the status quo. They will always be planning to move to a better house or, if this is not possible, then they will be organizing a major redecoration of their home. Monkeys are real do-it-yourself enthusiasts; they are practical people and enjoy making, repairing, and decorating. Even when restricted by funds, a monkey will find ingenious ways to furnish and decorate a house. For example, tables and chairs will be made from odds and ends and lots of brightly colored objects of interest displayed as ornaments.

MONKEY AT WORK

Monkeys can always find work as they are versatile and quick-thinking. They are highly flexible people who can turn their hand to virtually anything. Monkeys hate routine. For monkeys to stay in a job, it must provide them with plenty of variety as well as challenge. If they are overstimulated, however, their minds will wander. When this happens, or alternatively, if they are bored, the monkey's notoriously short attention span will cause them to change career. Also, a monkey will feel trapped in a predictable career. So, one year a monkey may be teaching English and the next driving a bus. Whatever their job though, monkeys are at their best when they are breaking or stretching the rules. To be happy at work, monkeys need a position where they are allowed to use their discretion and need to use their wits.

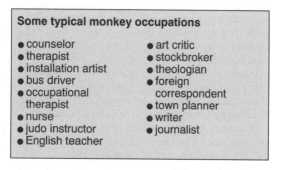

Some typical monkey occupations

- counselor
- therapist
- installation artist
- bus driver
- occupational therapist
- nurse
- judo instructor
- English teacher
- art critic
- stockbroker
- theologian
- foreign correspondent
- town planner
- writer
- journalist

MONKEY PREFERENCES

Likes

- a challenge
- to listen to other's problems and worries
- to care for people
- charting horoscopes
- alternative belief systems
- to travel
- practical jokes
- decorating the house
- reading tarot cards
- visiting friends
- ethnic art
- games of chance
- nightclubs

Dislikes

- routine
- bars and alcohol
- established religions
- being manipulated
- depending on others
- doing without money
- purely physical work
- the achievements of others
- conventional people
- compromising their independence

GOOD FRIENDS FOR MONKEYS

The diagram below shows the compatibility of monkey with other animals. There is no fixed ruling, however, because there are other influences on both the monkey and any potential friend. These influences are:

- the companion in life (see pp. 273–5)
- the dominant element (from the year of birth)

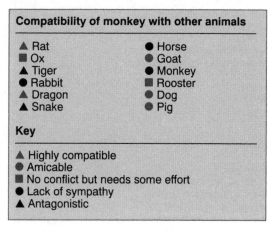

Compatibility of monkey with other animals

▲ Rat	● Horse
■ Ox	● Goat
▲ Tiger	● Monkey
● Rabbit	■ Rooster
▲ Dragon	● Dog
▲ Snake	● Pig

Key

▲ Highly compatible
● Amicable
■ No conflict but needs some effort
● Lack of sympathy
▲ Antagonistic

Rat with monkey An entertaining but cunning pair. On the whole, this combination will last because they have much in common. Rat may have to accept monkey's dominance.

Ox with monkey Mischievous monkey will tease the serious ox, but gently and with love. Oxen are fascinated by the monkey's sparkling personality but these two are unlikely to settle down together. They may misunderstand each other, and monkey will not hang around long enough to sort out any differences.

Tiger with monkey Tiger and monkey are both competitive and neither knows how to compromise. Secretly, monkeys may admire tigers, but cannot resist mocking them; tigers cannot help retaliating, and the relationship could quickly become destructive. Unless there is great love on monkey's part and moderation on tiger's part, no relationship will work.

Rabbit with monkey Devious monkey can bring out the worst, cunning side of rabbit. But as lively monkey finds stable rabbit dull, they are not often together long enough for this to happen.

Dragon with monkey Dragon is attracted by monkey's charm and intelligence. The two inspire and complement each other without becoming rivals – they will have many friends and a busy social life. Others may find them superficial, but they will be immune to criticism.

Snake with monkey Monkey is intelligent in a quick-witted sort of way, snake in a more profound fashion. This can lead to competition or a perfect business relationship. In love, however, monkey finds snake boring and will not settle down.

Horse with monkey A relationship between these two will be plagued by misunderstandings. Horse will find monkey's lively intelligence calculating; monkey will think horse's enthusiasm is based on naivety or even stupidity.

Goat with monkey A goat and a monkey will never be bored together. With monkey's quick wits and goat's imagination there will always be plenty to do, and they can be great friends. As lovers, monkeys may not be able to provide the constant reassurances that goats need.

Monkey with monkey Monkey relishes the company of another monkey. They can appreciate the other's intelligence and audacity. The two could quickly become rivals though, as they are both competitive types. Unless they can communicate calmly, they will taunt each other with constant cynicism.

Rooster with monkey Clever monkey and frank rooster can work well together. Yet they will judge each other on appearance alone, and both will find the other superficial. If they can learn not to criticize, these two can make a handsome and sociable couple.

Dog with monkey These two can be great friends. Dog is attracted by monkey's liveliness, and the monkey appreciates dog's stability and broad-mindedness. Although there will be a good mutual understanding, both are cynical, and the idealistic dog will be suspicious of realistic monkey's motives.

Pig with monkey As both are outgoing and friendly, this can be a well-balanced relationship. Monkey can help curb generous pig's excessive spending. Honest pig can appreciate monkey's plans and schemes.

MONKEY IN LOVE

Monkeys approach love in their typically vivacious and enthusiastic way. In the beginning, they are heady with passion and will be infatuated with their new-found love. As the novelty wears off, however, their excitement fades, and monkeys may instead start to criticize their partner. The relationship has to be lively to keep a monkey interested. If happy and stimulated, a monkey can be a tolerant and understanding partner, although tears are just as likely as laughter in a relationship with a monkey – they are excitable and unpredictable people. Monkeys are usually charming and love to please. In return, they expect their partner to be alert and attentive to their needs.

MONKEY AND SEX

Not at all prudish, monkeys have healthy appetites for sex. They are inventive and imaginative lovers. Even so, it is important that a monkey's lover is entertaining company as well as passionate in bed. Monkeys soon tire of purely physical relationships. Unless they are well balanced, monkeys have a problem with fidelity. Always believing that the grass is greener on the other side of the fence, they have

trouble appreciating what they already have. At the
first sign of trouble, the instinct of a monkey is to
run rather than to stay and sort it out.

HEALTH

Monkey's element, metal, is associated
with the lungs and large intestine, so
monkeys should pay particular attention
to keeping these organs in working order. Also,
monkeys should take care of their kidneys by not
consuming too much coffee and salt. Despite the fact
that they are not great athletes or health-club fans,
monkeys are usually surprisingly fit and healthy
people well into their old age. They tend to be
naturally slight people. Monkeys should not neglect
their diets – either through distraction or illness – as
they may become too thin.

LEISURE INTERESTS

The leisure interests of monkeys are
typically varied. Friendly and gregarious,
monkeys inevitably spend a lot of time
socializing. Either visiting or entertaining at home, a
monkey can always be found at the hub of any social
activity. For entertainment, they like to see the latest
film or play the latest game. Monkeys like games of
chance but will probably cheat! For exercise, they
are attracted to all sports that involve speed,
especially water sports. Monkeys indulge their taste
for the unusual and the exotic by visiting exhibitions
of art from different cultures. Many monkeys are

keen amateur photographers. This gives them an
excuse to explore new places and acts as a cover for
their curious natures.

THE MONKEY YEARS AND THEIR ELEMENTS

The monkey is a Yang metal animal.
Each of the monkey years, however, is
associated with an element which is said to have its
own influence. These elements are wood, fire, earth,
metal, and water. They influence monkey in a
regular sequence, which is repeated every 60 years.
In the table below, for example, the monkey year
1908 is an earth year. The next monkey earth year is
60 years later in 1968, and the next will be 2028.
Monkey's natural element is metal; the influence of
this combines with those of the element of the year
of birth. The possible effects of the year elements are
listed below.

Lunar years ruled by the monkey and their elements

1908	Feb 2, 1908	– Jan 21, 1909	earth
1920	Feb 20, 1920	– Feb 7, 1921	metal
1932	Feb 6, 1932	– Jan 25, 1933	water
1944	Jan 25, 1944	– Feb 12, 1945	wood
1956	Feb 12, 1956	– Jan 30, 1957	fire
1968	Jan 30, 1968	– Feb 16, 1969	earth
1980	Feb 16, 1980	– Feb 4, 1981	metal
1992	Feb 4, 1992	– Jan 22, 1993	water
2004	Jan 22, 2004	– Feb 8, 2005	wood

Monkey Metal–Earth (1908, 1968)

Earth is a sympathetic and balancing element for the metal-dominated monkey. It grounds these otherwise flighty people. Atypically, earth monkeys are studious, dutiful, hardworking, and thorough. They are patient and scientific in their approach to solving problems. Earth enhances the monkey's natural intelligence, making them more intellectual. Earth monkeys have cutting tongues. They can be harsh in their criticisms of others. For this reason, these monkeys may have difficulties in their personal relationships.

Monkey Metal–Metal (1920, 1980)

Metal is the monkey's natural element. Double metal multiplies the monkey's intelligence but also increases aggressiveness. Metal monkeys are extremely independent people, simply because they feel superior to their peers. Metal monkeys are materialistic and, fortunately, have a knack for making money. With their nerves of steel, metal monkeys like to take risks and can be successful gamblers as they are fortunate people.

Monkey Metal–Water (1932, 1992)

Water and metal are a harmonious combination. Water monkeys are cooperative and understanding people. They are almost too sensitive and will see implied criticism where none is meant. Water enhances the monkey's already gregarious nature. Yet water monkeys are complex characters. Enigmatic and secretive, they keep their true feelings well hidden. These monkeys are prone to mood swings and are notoriously fickle.

Monkey Metal–Wood (1944, 2004)

Wood is a fortunate element for monkeys. It helps to focus and stabilize them. Wood monkeys are friendly and approachable people. Coupled with metal, wood makes the monkey very resourceful and a great problem solver. In fact, wood monkeys are remarkable people. Wood is a creative element, so monkeys born in these years are likely to be artistic. They are also gifted communicators who have a strong sense of ethics.

Monkey Metal–Fire (1956, 2016)

Strong metal combined with passionate fire creates powerful and dominant but aggressive people. Fire also makes this monkey the most competitive of all monkeys. They are driven to succeed. Yet fire and metal bring conflict to the monkey. Fire monkeys have great potential but they tend to overstretch themselves. They do not always respond to challenges in the best way. These monkeys need to accept their own limitations and act accordingly.

MONKEY AND THE ZODIAC OF WESTERN ASTROLOGY

To work out your zodiac sign see p. 277. To work out your zodiac sign see p. 277. General character traits of monkeys of the 12 zodiac signs are given below. Bear in mind that the Western zodiac sign modifies the basic monkey nature – especially in the area of personal relationships.

Aries monkey Aries monkeys are some of the most talkative and forthright people around. They are uncannily perceptive and people can always recall the words of an Aries monkey. Both enterprising and opportunistic, they are also very successful.

Taurus monkey Determined Taurus facilitates the monkey's remarkable mental abilities. These people are capable and resourceful. Unusually persevering, they can apply themselves successfully to one task at a time.

Gemini monkey Mercurial Gemini and the trickster monkey have a lot in common. People born under both these signs are incredibly quick-witted but lack focus and direction. They are the mental gymnasts of the Chinese zodiac.

Cancer monkey Cancer brings extra sensitivity to the monkey. In fact, Cancer monkeys are moody as well as unpredictable. If they feel secure, then they can become more like the typical, happy-go-lucky monkey personality.

Leo monkey Leo monkeys are direct and candid people. They are very witty and are great raconteurs. Happy when they are the center of attention, Leo monkeys get irritable when they are ignored.

Virgo monkey Analytical Virgo and clever monkey combine to make very profound people. Virgo monkeys can be too calculating and emotionally distant, however. Busy looking for hidden agendas, they can miss the more obvious facts.

Libra monkey Eloquent and sociable, these monkeys have the "gift of the gab." They pride themselves on their ability to get along with anyone. But Libran monkeys can be manipulative and tend to exploit weaker people.

Scorpio monkey Mystery-loving Scorpio and devious monkey are a dangerous combination. They are secretive people who are suspicious of everyone. Always planning and scheming, these monkeys assume that others are equally ambitious.

Sagittarius monkey Sagittarian monkeys are almost stereotypical monkeys. They are broad-minded and curious people. They love to travel and explore new horizons. If they are not stimulated, these monkeys will act mischievously.

Capricorn monkey This sign brings conflict to the monkey. Austere Capricorn and witty monkey combine to produce seemingly debonair people. In fact, Capricornean monkeys are often hiding great personal anguish beneath their smooth exteriors.

Aquarius monkey This sign is very good for monkeys. It allows their creativity to blossom and Aquarius lends a visionary aspect to their work. They may appear independent, but, at heart, Aquarius monkeys need to be loved and appreciated.

Pisces monkey Pisces is spiritual; the monkey is clever. Together, they create intuitive and impressionable people. Pisces monkeys often appear eccentric, when, in fact, they just have rather unique thought processes.

Some famous people born in the years of the monkey and their zodiac signs

- René Descartes
  Philosopher
  Mar 31, 1596 Aries

- John Milton
  Poet
  Dec 9, 1608 Sagittarius

- Christopher Wren
  Architect
  Oct 20, 1632 Libra

- Marquis de Sade
  Writer
  Jun 2, 1740 Gemini

- Lord Byron
  Poet
  Jan 22, 1788 Aquarius

- Charles Dickens
  Writer
  Feb 7, 1812 Aquarius

- Paul Gauguin
  Painter
  Jun 7, 1848 Gemini

- Amedeo Modigliani
  Artist
  Jul 12, 1884 Cancer

- F. Scott Fitzgerald
  Novelist
  Sep 24, 1896 Libra

- Joan Crawford
  Actress
  Mar 23, 1908 Aries

- Bette Davis
  Actress
  Apr 5, 1908 Aries

- James Stewart
  Actor
  May 20, 1908 Taurus

- Ian Fleming
  Novelist
  May 28, 1908 Gemini

- Lyndon Johnson
  US president
  Aug 27, 1908 Virgo

- Claude Lévi-Strauss
  Anthropologist
  Nov 28, 1908 Sagittarius

- Yul Brynner
  Actor
  Jul 11, 1920 Cancer

- Walter Matthau
  Actor
  Oct 1, 1920 Libra

- Elizabeth Taylor
  Actress
  Feb 27, 1932 Pisces

- John Updike
  Writer
  Mar 18, 1932 Pisces

- Omar Sharif
  Actor
  Apr 10, 1932 Aries

- Peter O'Toole
  Actor
  Aug 2, 1932 Leo

- Diana Ross
  Singer
  Mar 26, 1944 Aries

- Bjorn Borg
  Tennis player
  Jun 6, 1956 Gemini

- Sebastian Coe
  Athlete/Politician
  Sep 29, 1956 Libra

10. The Rooster

The Yin metal animal.

Lunar years ruled by the rooster		
1909	Jan 22, 1900	– Feb 18, 1910
1921	Feb 8, 1921	– Jan 27, 1922
1933	Jan 26, 1933	– Feb 13, 1934
1945	Feb 13, 1945	– Feb 1, 1946
1957	Jan 31, 1957	– Feb 17, 1958
1969	Feb 17, 1969	– Feb 5, 1970
1981	Feb 5, 1981	– Jan 24, 1982
1993	Jan 23, 1993	– Feb 9, 1994
2005	Feb 9, 2005	– Jan 28, 2006

In China, the rooster is associated with the five virtues: fortune, courage, goodness, confidence, and military honor.

THE ROOSTER PERSONALITY

Roosters are flamboyant people. Appearance is very important to them, and roosters are constantly improving themselves as they are never satisfied with how they look. Roosters are also friendly, pleasant, and obliging people. At times of crisis, they prove themselves to be resourceful and talented. Roosters have the wisdom to take life as it comes and keep their attitudes relaxed. They are genuinely independent and rely on none but themselves for moral support and for solutions to their problems.

Characteristics

These are the general personality traits of those people who are typical roosters, both at their best and at their worst.

Positive	Negative
• honest	• vain
• obliging	• thoughtless
• courageous	• self-preoccupied
• flamboyant	• arrogant
• resilient	• vulnerable
• enthusiastic	• critical
• relaxed	• superior
• cultivated	• argumentative
• loyal	• harsh
• sincere	• boastful
• capable	• dissipated
• generous	• ostentatious
• charitable	• pretentious
• entertaining	• embellishes the truth

Secret rooster

For all their bluff and bravado, in reality roosters are very sensitive and vulnerable people. They are susceptible to both flattery and criticism, and so are easily influenced by either. They hide this weakness behind their arrogant facades. Another little-known fact about roosters is that they like to read. They are actually very knowledgeable people but do not display this aspect of themselves. A rooster would rather be judged on appearance than intelligence.

Element

Rooster is linked to the ancient Chinese element of metal. This is a very strong element. It can be seen positively as a valuable resource, such as gold, or negatively as a weapon, such as a sword. For example, the energy of metal expresses itself supportively and inspirationally as well as destructively and inflexibly. Metal people are also intuitive and ambitious.

Balance

Chinese tradition holds that the lives of roosters will be filled with ups and downs. They will experience both the joys and sorrows that life has to offer; for example, sometimes poor and at other times rich. Roosters should aim to achieve emotional stability. They must balance their larger-than-life images with their vulnerable inner selves. Only then will their lives become calm and productive.

Best associations

Traditionally, the following are said to be associated
with roosters:

- Taste   pungent
- Season   fall
- Birth   spring
- Colors   yellow, white
- Plants   orange and palm trees
- Flower   sunflower
- Food   cereals
- Climate   dry

THE MALE ROOSTER

If a man has a typical rooster personality,
he will generally display the behavior
listed below.

- is charming
- is attracted to difficult situations
- has a tendency to be a braggart
- is brutally frank
- has a good memory
- is jealous of rivals
- appears indifferent
- is a real spendthrift
- may be a dandy
- tells great stories
- is entertaining and witty
- likes the company of women

THE FEMALE ROOSTER
If a woman has a typical rooster personality, she will generally display the behavior listed below.

- is not malicious
- does not tell white lies
- is reasonable
- is social and communicative
- applies herself totally to whatever she does
- is not as secretive as male roosters
- keeps her promises
- is secretly a jealous person
- appears frivolous
- is good at dealing with catastrophes
- is generous with friends

THE ROOSTER CHILD
If a child has a typical rooster personality, he or she will generally display the behavior listed below.

- is alert and curious
- responds to reasoning
- has many interests and hobbies
- is rebellious if discouraged
- is easy to live with
- will be a daredevil
- is secretive
- likes being independent
- is good with brothers and sisters
- dislikes solitude
- is well organized

ROOSTER AT HOME

A typical rooster is very adaptable and can feel at home anywhere. If they can, roosters will indulge their extravagant tastes in their homes. Although expensive, furniture is likely to be simple in design. On the whole, roosters will try to create a harmonious and comfortable home. They love gadgets and novelties. Anything that makes life easier or more comfortable, roosters will install in their home. Roosters are obsessive about cleanliness and order in their home, and they keep even little-used cupboards neat and tidy. Ideally, roosters should have a room, den, or at least a corner of a room set aside for their sole use. Roosters need a space purely for themselves, where they can gather their wits.

ROOSTER AT WORK

As they are not blessed by good fortune, roosters have to work hard to achieve success. This is not a problem as roosters give their all to their work and are conscientious. Roosters can succeed in any profession that requires nerve, self-confidence, and charisma. Therefore, they are suited to anything concerned with selling and also commercial professions. Roosters are too conspicuous to be doing anything discreet and too tactless to be diplomats. They are interested in topical events and dislike routine. Roosters would enjoy working in the media, perhaps on a news-based television show or as a journalist for a newspaper. Roosters are reasonably ambitious and

do not like subordinate positions. They are more
likely to be head of a department than managing
director though, as roosters prefer to avoid undue
stress.

Some typical rooster occupations

- TV anchor
- salesperson
- sales director
- restaurant owner
- hairdresser
- public relations officer
- actor
- farmer
- aesthete
- critic
- manicurist
- teacher

- town crier
- waiter
- journalist
- travel writer
- beautician
- dentist
- surgeon
- soldier
- fireman
- security guard
- police officer

❓ ROOSTER PREFERENCES

Likes

- seductions
- receiving admiring looks
- serious conversations
- ostentatious displays of wealth
- putting on a show
- tidiness
- occasional periods of solitude
- flattery
- to dream
- to give advice
- spending money
- to make an entrance

Dislikes

- losing their composure
- to be asked direct, personal questions
- poorly dressed people
- to display their knowledge
- interference in their affairs
- keeping their opinions to themselves
- to confide in anyone
- practical jokes played on them

GOOD FRIENDS FOR ROOSTERS

The diagram below shows the compatibility of rooster with other animals. There is no fixed ruling, however, because there are other influences on both the rooster and any potential friend. These influences are:

- the companion in life (see pp. 273–5)
- the dominant element (from the year of birth)

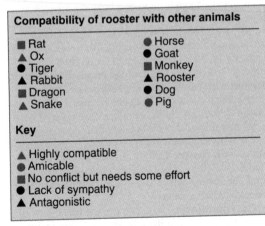

Compatibility of rooster with other animals

- ■ Rat
- ▲ Ox
- ● Tiger
- ▲ Rabbit
- ■ Dragon
- ▲ Snake
- ● Horse
- ● Goat
- ■ Monkey
- ▲ Rooster
- ● Dog
- ● Pig

Key

- ▲ Highly compatible
- ● Amicable
- ■ No conflict but needs some effort
- ● Lack of sympathy
- ▲ Antagonistic

Rat with rooster These two have very little in common. No serious relationship is likely to develop unless there are other strong influences. Competitive rat finds rooster's attention-grabbing behavior annoying.

Ox with rooster These two are highly compatible. Sociable rooster complements ox's steady nature, and ox will allow rooster to show off. They both care for money and financial security.

Tiger with rooster Initially promising, tiger and rooster are unable to have more than a brief friendship. They have much in common, but will quickly fall to misunderstanding and criticizing each other. Not given to reflection, tiger will most likely fail to see the thoughtful nature behind rooster's swaggering facade.

Rabbit with rooster On no account should these two attempt a serious relationship. Rooster's tendency to voice criticisms will send rabbit running, and rooster will find rabbit unsympathetic.

Dragon with rooster The Chinese believe that dragon inspires rooster. Both can be found in the limelight: roosters for reassurance, dragons as it is their natural habitat. This bolsters their egos, but they may misunderstand the other's motives.

Snake with rooster This is the most ideal couple of Chinese astrology. They balance each other like mind and matter. Snake and rooster both flatter and understand one another.

Horse with rooster These two can get on quite well together. Horse will initiate things, and rooster can complete them. They are, however, both sensitive to the opinions of others while being tactless themselves. This could create problems and bruise egos.

Goat with rooster These two have very little in common and cannot understand each other.

Although roosters will be able to support goats financially, goats will not be able to give roosters the moral support they need in return.

Monkey with rooster Clever monkey and frank rooster can work well together. Yet they will judge each other on appearance alone, and both will find the other superficial. If they can learn not to criticize, these two can make a handsome and sociable couple.

Rooster with rooster Chinese legend holds that two roosters under the same roof make life intolerable for everyone else. They either get along very well or dislike each other intensely. Roosters cannot accept their own faults but are quick to point out those of others, so two roosters are guaranteed to argue.

Dog with rooster Idealistic dog and carefree rooster approach life from different angles. Dog will think rooster self-absorbed and unkind. Rooster hates to be judged by others and will be critical of dog's high moral stance.

Pig with rooster Pig and rooster can be very good friends and true, if not exciting, lovers. Pig can recognize rooster's well-hidden sensitivity and kindness, but rooster will be disarmed by understanding pig.

ROOSTER IN LOVE

To a rooster, love is a responsibility and a challenge, not a casual matter. The organized and analytical approach they have towards love makes them prey to disappointment. After all, things rarely happen as planned in a love affair. Roosters are intense and devoted to their loved ones, but they have a tendency to be domineering. Preoccupied with their own needs, desires and longings, roosters do not always make the most sympathetic of partners. They expect their partners to know what mood they are in and act accordingly – to know when to be silent or chatty, for example. The rooster's dislike of confidences is an obstacle to real intimacy. Also, the fact that roosters like to sort out their problems by themselves leaves little room for mutual support in a relationship.

ROOSTER AND SEX
Roosters are bold, ostentatious, and confident in bed. They are egocentric, however, and a rooster always comes first. Roosters are adept at seduction. First, they stun and impress their target with their flamboyance. Then, they make themselves indispensable to that person and finally make sure their partner is satisfied physically. In this way, roosters are usually successful in seducing and keeping lovers. Roosters are not faithful by nature and cannot resist temptation. They justify their infidelities by blaming their lovers – accusing them of neglect, for example. Partners should try making themselves exceptional in some way if they want to keep a rooster interested.

HEALTH
Rooster's element, metal, is associated with the lungs and the large intestine, so roosters should pay particular attention to

keeping these organs in working order. Roosters are often afflicted by respiratory problems and should make sure that they keep fit. This will improve both their health and their psychological balance. To maintain a healthy emotional life, roosters should put aside time to just relax and think, preferably on their own.

LEISURE INTERESTS

The favorite pastimes of roosters are socializing and reading. These very different pursuits are typical of the rooster, who is prone to extremes. Roosters have a busy social life as they are agreeable and entertaining guests. Occasionally, they like to get away from it all and visit some quiet, comfortable hideaway. This gives them a chance to replenish their energies and renew their vigor.

THE ROOSTER YEARS AND THEIR ELEMENTS

The rooster is a Yin metal animal. Each of the rooster years, however, is associated with an element which is said to have its own influence. These elements are wood, fire, earth, metal, and water. They influence rooster in a regular sequence, which is repeated every 60 years. In the table overleaf, for example, the rooster year 1909 is an earth year. The next rooster earth year is 60 years later in 1969, and the next will be 2029. Rooster's natural element is metal; the influence of this combines with those of the element of the year of

birth. The possible effects of the year elements are
listed below.

Lunar years ruled by the rooster and their elements		
1909	Jan 22, 1909 – Feb 18, 1910	earth
1921	Feb 8, 1921 – Jan 27, 1922	metal
1933	Jan 26, 1933 – Feb 13, 1934	water
1945	Feb 13, 1945 – Feb 1, 1946	wood
1957	Jan 31, 1957 – Feb 17, 1958	fire
1969	Feb 17, 1969 – Feb 5, 1970	earth
1981	Feb 5, 1981 – Jan 24, 1982	metal
1993	Jan 23, 1993 – Feb 9, 1994	water
2005	Feb 9, 2005 – Jan 28, 2006	wood

Rooster Metal–Earth (1909, 1969)
Steadfast earth and ambitious metal combine to
make very resourceful and determined people. These
people do not shy away from taking on
responsibilities and can quickly get to the root of a
problem. Earth, however, lessens the rooster's
immediate, dramatic appeal. On closer inspection
though, the rooster's penchant for finery reveals
itself in small touches – discreet but bizarre jewelry,
for instance. Earth roosters are not as talkative as
other roosters. This does not mean that they are less
outspoken, just not as verbose. The few words they
do say are guaranteed to be typically blunt.
Rooster Metal–Metal (1921, 1981)
Double metal roosters are trouble. They are the most
headstrong of all the roosters. Well organized and
precise, metal roosters are great sticklers for detail.

They have high expectations of themselves and others. These roosters can be harshly critical of those who fail to live up to their standards. The vitality of roosters can be constrained by the rigidity of double metal. Roosters are not naturally restrained, so metal roosters can, at times, feel confused and ill-at-ease with themselves. On such occasions, they need to seek out solitude to regain their harmony.

RoosterMetal–Water (1933, 1993)

Transparent water combines with clear-thinking metal to add clarity to the already considerable intellectual capabilities of the rooster. Water roosters are capable and adaptable people, proficient in many fields. Less authoritarian than others, they gain support by persuasion rather than by intimidation. Water also helps the rooster's innate sensitivity to surface. Roosters born in water years, therefore, are more sympathetic and easier to relate to than other roosters. The metal in their characters, however, stops them being overwhelmed by these sympathies and helps them to focus on worthwhile causes.

RoosterMetal–Wood (1945, 2005)

Wood roosters are enthusiastic and progressive people. Wood releases the rooster's dormant creativity and, with their fine imaginations, wood roosters can do well in arts such as poetry and painting. Wood is also, however, an element that is prone to excesses. Roosters are already aggressive and susceptible, and wood can serve to make these qualities more pronounced. On the positive side, both wood and metal are associated with integrity.

Wood tempers the moral rigidity of metal with kindness. Roosters born in wood years are completely trustworthy and are even capable of discretion.

Rooster Metal–Fire (1957, 2017)

Fire and metal combine to make strong, dramatic characters. Although eccentric, fire roosters are always convincing people. Rash, audacious, and argumentative, they are never inconspicuous. These roosters are high fliers. Fire roosters are often exceptional: people of action, leaders, heroes, or pioneers. Usually with great success, they single-mindedly pursue their goals. Fire enables the rooster to look ahead to the long-term future and not get lost in details on the way. Fire also strengthens the belligerent nature of roosters.

ROOSTER AND THE ZODIAC OF WESTERN ASTROLOGY

To work out your zodiac sign see p. 277. General character traits of roosters of the 12 zodiac signs are given below. Bear in mind that the Western zodiac sign modifies the basic rooster nature – especially in the area of personal relationships.

Aries rooster Aries and rooster are similar in many respects, so these roosters have the qualities and defects of typical roosters, but multiplied many times. Above all else, Aries roosters are courageous people who put all their talents into getting what they want out of life.

Taurus rooster Taurus brings stability to these roosters who are less flamboyant. Steady and dependable, they are always willing to help others. Taurus roosters are not as adaptable as other roosters but make up for this by being good planners.

Gemini rooster Mercurial Gemini and extravagant rooster combine to make these people both inconstant and hyperactive. Cultured and knowledgeable, they have a tendency to be intellectual poseurs.

Cancer rooster All roosters are susceptible to the opinions of others and are easily swayed by criticism or flattery. Cancer roosters take this tendency further and are ruled by their emotions. When feeling insecure, they are depressing, vain, and egotistical.

Leo rooster Leo roosters are honest, noble, proud, vain, and only happy when they are the center of attention. They are clever at disguising this egotism with acts of generosity, which are actually done to make the rooster feel good rather than the recipient.

Virgo rooster Precise and critical, Virgo roosters are argumentative perfectionists – their comments are usually accurate though. Underneath, Virgo roosters are full of self-doubt and lack confidence.

Libra rooster These roosters are talkative people, yet they are not outspoken – they are capable of diplomacy. Libran roosters are proud, indecisive, and have a highly developed aesthetic sense.

Scorpio rooster Scorpio roosters have the "gift of the gab" and are very persuasive people. Combined with their competitive natures, these are not people to get into a verbal sparring match with. They will be high achievers in any profession they choose.

Sagittarius rooster Sagittarius makes these roosters less ostentatious than their fellows. These roosters are still enthusiastic and excitable, of course, but not as pretentious. They have a more holistic approach to life and like to travel.

Capricorn rooster The least boastful of all roosters, Capricornean ones know that a conservative image is more suitable to achieve the material success they crave. They make loyal and devoted lovers, but their intellectual lives are fuller than their love lives.

Aquarius rooster More flamboyant and eccentric than any other rooster, Aquarian roosters are unique people. Despite this, they are not arrogant and despise this trait in others. These roosters are broad-minded idealists who are sincere and generous.

Pisces rooster Pisces makes the rooster more sensitive and vulnerable. Pisces roosters are lacking in self-confidence and cannot relax and be happy until they have reached a state of financial and domestic security.

Some famous people born in the years of the rooster and their zodiac signs

- Georg Philipp Telemann
  Composer
  Mar 14, 1681 Pisces

- David Livingstone
  Explorer
  Mar 19, 1813 Pisces

- Søren Kierkegaard
  Philosopher
  May 5, 1813 Taurus

- Richard Wagner
  Composer
  May 22, 1813 Gemini

- Giuseppe Verdi
  Composer
  Oct 10, 1813 Libra

- Johann Strauss
  Composer
  Oct 25, 1825 Scorpio

- August Strindberg
  Writer
  Jan 22, 1849 Aquarius

- William Faulkner
  Novelist
  Sep 25, 1897 Libra

- Joseph Goebbels
  Nazi official
  Oct 29, 1897 Scorpio

- James Mason
  Actor
  May 15, 1909 Taurus

- Errol Flynn
  Actor
  Jun 20, 1909 Gemini

- Katharine Hepburn
  Actress
  Nov 8, 1909 Scorpio

- Dirk Bogarde
  Actor/Writer
  Mar 28, 1921 Aries

- Peter Ustinov
  Actor/Producer/Writer
  Apr 16, 1921 Aries

- Deborah Kerr
  Actress
  Aug 30, 1921 Virgo

- Yves Montand
  Actor
  Oct 31, 1921 Scorpio

- Michael Caine
  Actor
  Mar 14, 1933 Pisces

- Philip Roth
  Writer
  Mar 19, 1933 Pisces

- Joan Collins
  Actress
  May 23, 1933 Gemini

- Roman Polanski
  Film director
  Aug 18, 1933 Leo

- Mary Quant
  Fashion designer
  Feb 11, 1934 Aquarius

- Eric Clapton
  Musician
  Mar 30, 1945 Aries

- Goldie Hawn
  Actress
  Nov 21, 1945 Scorpio

- Dolly Parton
  Singer/Actress
  Jan 19, 1946 Capricorn

11. The Dog

The Yang metal animal.

Lunar years ruled by the dog		
1910	Feb 10, 1910	– Jan 29, 1911
1922	Jan 28, 1922	– Feb 15, 1923
1934	Feb 14, 1934	– Feb 3, 1935
1946	Feb 2, 1946	– Jan 21, 1947
1958	Feb 18, 1958	– Feb 7, 1959
1970	Feb 6, 1970	– Jan 26, 1971
1982	Jan 25, 1982	– Feb 12, 1983
1994	Feb 10, 1994	– Jan 30, 1995
2006	Jan 29, 2006	– Feb 17, 2007

In China the dog is associated with justice and compassion. Dogs are often described as being the "champions of the underdogs."

THE DOG PERSONALITY

Essentially, dogs are honest and noble creatures. They are renowned for being champions of justice and have a tendency to see things in black and white. Dogs are respected for their lively minds and quick tongues, which they use in defense of their chosen cause. Yet dogs are cynics as well as idealists, which produces characters with high moral standards, but they are beset by doubts and anxieties.

Characteristics

These are the general personality traits of those people who are typical dogs, both at their best and at their worst.

Positive	Negative
• loyal	• cynical
• tolerant	• anxious
• idealistic	• pessimistic
• understanding	• suspicious
• dutiful	• timid
• moralistic	• strict
• faithful	• discouraging
• unselfish	• doubtful
• noble	• dissatisfied
• imaginative	• fatalistic
• honest	• obstinate
• courageous	• distrustful
• responsible	• shy
• witty	• introverted
• trustworthy	• unadventurous
• sensitive	• tasteless

Secret dog

Despite their courageousness and determination to do good, dogs need to be led. Left on their own, they can become confused and anxious. After all, there are so many deserving causes and not enough time to help everyone. Once they have been given instructions or help, they can move mountains to carry out a task.

Element

Dog is linked to the ancient Chinese element of metal. This is a very strong element. It can be seen positively as a valuable resource, such as gold, or negatively as a weapon, such as a sword. The energy of metal expresses itself in dogs as their strong-minded, idealistic traits. Metal people are usually ambitious; dogs, however, are not personally ambitious. Instead, they are more concerned with the advancement of the downtrodden.

Balance

The main character fault of dogs is their constant worrying and self-doubting natures. A certain amount of stress or anxiety can be useful as it helps motivate the dog, who lacks motivation. But dogs can worry to the extent that it stops them doing anything useful. This interferes with their ability to lead happy and productive lives. Anxious of the future and regretful of the past, dogs need to learn how to live in the present. If they can take each day as it comes, dogs will find that their anxieties lessen. They need to reach a balance between necessary and useful worrying and self-defeating anxiety.

Best associations

Traditionally, the following are said to be associated with dogs:

- Taste   pungent
- Season   fall
- Birth   daytime
- Colors   black, dark blue
- Plants   poppies, water lilies
- Flowers   orange blossoms, red poppy
- Food   oats
- Climate   dry

THE MALE DOG

If a man has a typical dog personality, he will generally display the behavior listed below.

- will be a protective father
- is loyal and faithful to friends and family
- can be unnecessarily defensive
- makes a good ally
- is slow to make close friends
- is quick to criticize the wrongdoings of others
- has an ironic sense of humor
- is prone to depression
- loves to gossip
- can be stubborn
- rarely shows his true feelings

THE FEMALE DOG

If a woman has a typical dog personality, she will generally display the behavior listed below.

- has a very black sense of humor
- is more ambitious than male dogs
- is gifted and creative
- is lacking in perseverance
- does not compromise
- is impatient
- is attractive
- likes conversation
- is more sociable than the male
- will be critical of those who do not have her high standards

THE DOG CHILD

If a child has a typical dog personality, he or she will generally display the behavior listed below.

- is sensitive and affectionate
- needs attentive and understanding parents
- is scared of the dark
- will be stable if parents are protective
- resents younger siblings at first
- is obliging and devoted
- has difficulty adapting to school
- is well behaved and obedient
- likes fantasy and monster stories

DOG AT HOME

Dogs are not renowned for their sense of taste. They are not materialistic people and would rather not spend all their time and money on perfecting their home. Dogs will decorate and furnish their homes according to personal preference, budget, and convenience. They are not ones to be dictated to by fashion, unless they actually like the latest design. This does not mean that the home of dog will be badly decorated and furnished. In fact, the overall effect is often welcoming, pleasant, and personal. It may not be the home of an interior designer, but it will have been put together with care and attention to detail.

DOG AT WORK

Dogs are very capable people. The only obstacle to their success is a lack of motivation. They lack the aggression and ambition needed to put their unique skills to work. Dogs can overcome this by choosing a profession that inspires their idealistic natures, something worthwhile and altruistic, for example, to which they can commit themselves. They will then prove themselves to be hardworking, conscientious, and honest. Dogs make good managers as they are able to wield authority with tact and will remain accessible to all their staff. They consider collective interests before personal concerns.

Some typical dog occupations

- priest
- missionary
- nun
- union leader
- teacher
- charity worker
- nurse
- doctor

- judge
- lawyer
- scientist
- researcher
- critic
- social worker
- legal aid lawyer
- community worker

DOG PREFERENCES

Likes

- anything arcane or concerned with the occult
- horror movies
- natural fabrics
- detective novels
- to remember birthdays
- writing letters to friends
- learning about other cultures
- silver jewelry
- reunions with old friends

Dislikes

- pedants
- hypocrites
- selfish behavior
- deceit and dishonesty
- family reunions
- smart cocktail parties
- superficial and ambitious people
- psychological game playing
- man-made fabrics
- counting the financial cost of an activity

GOOD FRIENDS FOR DOGS

The diagram below shows the compatibility of dog with other animals. There is no fixed ruling, however, because there are other influences on both the dog and any potential friend. These influences are:

- the companion in life (see pp. 273–5)
- the dominant element (from the year of birth)

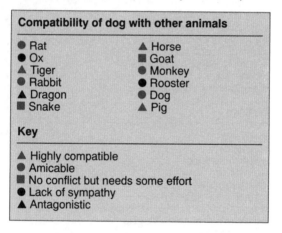

Compatibility of dog with other animals

● Rat	▲ Horse
● Ox	■ Goat
▲ Tiger	● Monkey
● Rabbit	● Rooster
▲ Dragon	● Dog
■ Snake	▲ Pig

Key

▲ Highly compatible
● Amicable
■ No conflict but needs some effort
● Lack of sympathy
▲ Antagonistic

Rat with dog These two live in different worlds. While they can be quite friendly toward each other, their prospects are not good. Dog's passion for fair play will clash with rat's tendency to exploit.

Ox with dog Imaginative dog will not be happy with staid ox. Dog is likely to criticize ox for lacking a sense of humor. If they can learn to respect each other, however, they can get along as both are loyal and faithful.

Tiger with dog The different natures of these two actually complement each other perfectly. Anxious dog will curb tiger's excessive risk taking; tiger will appreciate dog's loyalty. The relationship could prove long-lasting and stable. Both are idealists, and can combine their talents to achieve great things for a good cause.

Rabbit with dog Loyal dog gets along well with rabbit and the two can have a happy relationship as long as they do not take each other for granted.

Dragon with dog Intellectual but cynical dog will deflate dragon's self-confidence. Dogs are able to see through dragon's image for the mirage it is, so they are unable to admire dragon.

Snake with dog Idealistic dog is attracted to snake's wisdom and depth and can ignore snake's selfish, ambitious streak. Snake will admire dog's honesty and as long as snakes do not mind being idealized, this relationship could work out. It may be, however, that mutual respect will not be matched by a mutual passion.

Horse with dog This is a case of opposites that attract. Horses appreciate dogs' loyal and generous natures and their ability to see things as they really are. In turn, dogs take great pleasure in the company of lively horses and will ignore their waywardness.

Goat with dog Goat and dog can be friends if they apply their tolerant natures to ignoring the other's differences. Normally, however, whimsical goat and dutiful dog just irritate each other.

Monkey with dog This combination can work out well. Dog is attracted by monkey's liveliness, and monkey appreciates dog's stability and broad-mindedness. Although there will be a good mutual understanding, both are cynical, and idealistic dog will be suspicious of more realistic monkey's motives.

Rooster with dog Idealistic dog and carefree rooster approach life from different angles. Dog will think rooster self-absorbed and unkind. Rooster hates to be judged by others and will be critical of dog's high moral stance.

Dog with dog Dogs are genuine people and two together can have a warm and understanding, if not exciting, relationship. They will be very dependent on each other, and a sharp remark or criticism can easily trigger a major row.

Pig with dog Pleasure-loving pig brings optimism and a carefree aspect to any relationship between these two. This is very beneficial for dog, who will be happy and relaxed with pig. Both are also generous, kind, and honest people who, together, can build a lasting relationship.

DOG IN LOVE

Dogs are easy people to love. They are warm, kind, and generous. Dogs, however, are not quick to fall in love themselves. They are suspicious and distrustful of people at first. If they meet someone who lives up to their high ideals, dogs will allow themselves to slowly fall in love with that person. Once committed, a dog will want to share everything with their partner and will be affectionate and tender. In return, dogs expect their partners to be everything to them: lover, best friend, confidant, parent, and muse. Dogs are not always happy in love as they have such high expectations. Also, they are anxious people who need constant reassuring. Although they are stable characters themselves, their pessimism and anxiety makes it difficult for their partners to feel secure with them.

DOG AND SEX

Although dogs are sensual and passionate people, they value companionship and trust above physical intimacy. A dog cannot live without tenderness and prefers long relationships to brief flings. Nonetheless, dogs are anxious for approval and will try to please their lover. They are faithful by nature and know how to resist temptation. A dog will be destroyed by the infidelity of a lover, yet they can poison a relationship with unfounded suspicions. Compassionate and idealistic, dogs are easily seduced by vulnerable people who need rescuing.

HEALTH

Dog's element, metal, is associated with the lungs and large intestine, so dogs should pay particular attention to keeping these organs in working order. Dogs are anxious people and therefore prone to insomnia and stress-related illnesses. Dogs should try and maintain a balanced approach to life and not become eaten up by worry. Being Yang people, dogs are generally of sound physical health. They should make sure, however, that they watch their weight.

LEISURE INTERESTS

Dogs are sociable and enjoy spending time with friends. They are not particularly adventurous people: a dog is happier going to the movies or to a good restaurant than rock climbing. They enjoy visiting restaurants that serve foreign cuisine – although it has to be authentic – or just going for a coffee and a chat to the local café. Somewhere peaceful and friendly where they can discuss the wrongs of the world and how to put them right is preferred. For exercise, dogs like simple sports that they can incorporate into their lifestyle easily, swimming in the morning or bicycling to work, for example.

THE DOG YEARS AND THEIR ELEMENTS

The dog is a Yang metal animal. Each of the dog years, however, is associated with an element which is said to have its own influence. These elements are wood, fire, earth, metal, and water. They influence dog in a regular sequence, which is repeated every 60 years. In the table below, for example, the dog year 1922 is a water year. The next dog water year is 60 years later in 1982, and the next will be 2042. Dog's natural element is metal; the influence of this combines with those of the element of the year of birth. The possible effects of the year elements are listed below.

Lunar years ruled by the dog and their elements

1910	Feb 10, 1910	– Jan 29, 1911	metal
1922	Jan 28, 1922	– Feb 15, 1923	water
1934	Feb 14, 1934	– Feb 3, 1935	wood
1946	Feb 2, 1946	– Jan 21, 1947	fire
1958	Feb 18, 1958	– Feb 7, 1959	earth
1970	Feb 6, 1970	– Jan 26, 1971	metal
1982	Jan 25, 1982	– Feb 12, 1983	water
1994	Feb 10, 1994	– Jan 30, 1995	wood
2006	Jan 29, 2006	– Feb 17, 2007	fire

DogMetal–Metal (1910, 1970)
Dogs born in metal years are in their natural element. In China, metal dog years are approached warily as they will either be very bad or very good,

but never mediocre. In the same way, metal dogs
themselves are capable of extreme behavior. Dogs
are already idealistic, and double metal multiplies
this tendency twofold. Metal dogs are therefore very
principled to the point of being inflexible. This can
make metal dogs towers of strength, but their
inability to compromise may be their downfall.

DogMetal–Water (1922, 1982)
Dogs come into their own in this element. Yin water
balances with the dog's own innate Yang tendency.
Chinese tradition holds that water dogs are the most
beautiful and sensual of all the animal signs in the
Chinese zodiac. Water erodes the harder edges from
dogs, making them charming as well as sexy. These
dogs are more contemplative and intuitive than other
dogs. They are less rigid than their natural element,
metal, usually dictates and are instead very liberal.

DogMetal–Wood (1934, 1994)
Wood and metal together produce popular and
charismatic individuals. Wood allows the dog to
appraise situations with more open minds than
otherwise. They do not see everything in black and
white as most dogs do. They can devote themselves
to a cause without becoming obsessional. Wood
allows the dog's dormant creativity to blossom.
These people are interested in the arts even if they
are not creative themselves.

DogMetal–Fire (1946, 2006)
Yang fire enhances the dog's innate Yang tendency.
Fire quells their doubts and helps them to be
optimists rather than pessimists. Fire dogs are
unusually charismatic and flamboyant dogs, but in a

friendly and approachable way. These dogs are less egalitarian than other dogs and are not afraid to put themselves first. Fire dogs are enthusiastic and curious. They should make sure, however, that they control their excessive tendencies and do not become addictive personalities.

DogMetal–Earth (1958, 2018)
Earth dogs are well-balanced people. They are generally happy and stable. Earth gives dogs the ability to take each day as it comes and not to be so anxious about the future. These dogs are, of course, still idealists, but earth imparts efficiency which enables them to put their ideals to some practical use. Earth dogs are materialistic for dogs, but only relative to others of the breed.

DOG AND THE ZODIAC OF WESTERN ASTROLOGY
To work out your zodiac sign see p. 277. General character traits of dogs of the 12 zodiac signs are given below. Bear in mind that the Western zodiac sign modifies the basic dog nature – especially in the area of personal relationships.

Aries dog In some ways, Aries helps to balance the dog. Those born under this sign are more relaxed, less serious, and more energetic. In other ways, Aries accentuates some of the dog's traits. Arien dogs are incredibly strong minded and extremely idealistic.
Taurus dog Dogs born under this sign benefit from the sensible and constructive talents of Taurus.

These dogs, however, are the most materialistic of all, and the males can be chauvinistic.

Gemini dog Intellectual Gemini and ethical dogs are prone to theorizing about the causes of the world's problems. Gemini also increases the dog's already nervous disposition, and these people can be unstable.

Cancer dog Cancer dogs often appear cold and indifferent, but underneath they are among the most sensitive and vulnerable of all the animal signs. They are primarily family-orientated people.

Leo dog The most direct and honest of all the dogs, Leo ones despise being manipulated. They are spontaneous and energetic people who are unusually flamboyant and even egotistical, for dogs.

Virgo dog Critical Virgo adds bite to the dog's nature. These people are kind but not necessarily gentle. This applies to how they perceive themselves as well as others. Virgo dogs can be too critical of themselves, and this increases their anxiety.

Libra dog Refined and intelligent, Libran dogs are sociable animals. They are open to compromise as they are not aggressive enough to get their own way.

Scorpio dog Self-righteous and aggressive, Scorpio dogs are not sociable animals. They are nevertheless compassionate people at heart. These dogs find it hard to be faithful as they cannot resist temptation.

Sagittarius dog These dogs are intrigued by different cultures and other viewpoints. Although others may find their broad-mindedness a bit impersonal, they are still passionate about justice.

Capricorn dog Conservative and materially successful, Capricorn dogs are often pillars of the community. They have a strict sense of duty and responsibility and are very moralistic.

Aquarius dog Eccentric Aquarius and constant dog combine to produce highly individualistic people. They each have a uniquely personal outlook on life. All of them have well-developed communication skills.

Pisces dog Pisces dogs are a strange combination of strong minds with weak wills. All dogs are plagued by self-doubt, and Pisces dogs are at times incapacitated by this. They should beware of others taking advantage of this weakness.

Some famous people born in the years of the dog and their zodiac signs

- François Voltaire
  Philosopher
  Nov 21, 1694 Scorpio
- Benjamin Franklin
  Statesman
  Jan 17, 1706 Capricorn
- Victor Hugo
  Novelist
  Feb 26, 1802 Pisces
- Georges Bizet
  Composer
  Oct 25, 1838 Scorpio
- Claude Debussy
  Composer
  Aug 22, 1862 Leo
- Harry Houdini
  Escape artist
  Apr 6, 1874 Aries
- Guglielmo Marconi
  Physicist/Inventor
  Apr 25, 1874 Taurus
- Winston Churchill
  Statesman
  Nov 30, 1874 Sagittarius
- Bertolt Brecht
  Writer
  Feb 10, 1898 Aquarius
- Golda Meir
  Stateswoman
  May 3, 1898 Taurus
- George Gershwin
  Composer
  Sep 26, 1898 Libra
- René Magritte
  Artist
  Nov 21, 1898 Scorpio

- Judy Garland
  Actress
  Jun 10, 1922 Gemini
- Pierre Cardin
  Fashion designer
  Jul 7, 1922 Cancer
- Yuri Gagarin
  Astronaut
  Mar 9, 1934 Pisces
- Shirley MacLaine
  Actress
  Apr 24, 1934 Taurus
- Donald Sutherland
  Actor
  Jul 17, 1934 Cancer
- Sophia Loren
  Actress
  Sep 20, 1934 Virgo
- Elvis Presley
  Singer
  Jan 8, 1935 Capricorn
- Liza Minnelli
  Singer/Actress
  Mar 12, 1946 Pisces
- Cher
  Singer/Actress
  May 20, 1946 Taurus
- Barry Manilow
  Singer
  Jun 17, 1946 Gemini
- Sylvester Stallone
  Actor
  Jul 6, 1946 Cancer
- Michael Jackson
  Singer
  Aug 29, 1958 Virgo

12. The Pig

The Yin water animal.

Lunar years ruled by the pig	
1911	Jan 30, 1911 – Feb 17, 1912
1923	Feb 16, 1923 – Feb 4, 1924
1935	Feb 4, 1935 – Jan 23, 1936
1947	Jan 22, 1947 – Feb 9, 1948
1959	Feb 8, 1959 – Jan 27, 1960
1971	Jan 27, 1971 – Feb 14, 1972
1983	Feb 13, 1983 – Feb 1, 1984
1995	Jan 31, 1995 – Feb 18, 1996
2007	Feb 18, 2007 – Feb 6, 2008

In China, the pig is associated with fertility and virility. To bear children in the year of the pig is considered very fortunate, for they will be happy and honest.

THE PIG PERSONALITY

Pigs are among the most natural and easygoing personalities around. They are pleasure-loving characters who seek out the good and the fun things in life. Pigs are sympathetic and will always be there for friends at times of trouble. In turn, they look to their friends for advice and support when difficult decisions have to be made. Pigs still like to maintain their independence, though, and privacy is very important to them.

Characteristics

These are the general personality traits of those people who are typical pigs, both at their best and at their worst.

Positive	Negative
• eager	• indulgent
• optimistic	• impatient
• fortunate	• excessive
• tolerant	• spendthrift
• careful	• gullible
• sensual	• debauched
• courteous	• fierce
• uncomplaining	• fearful
• determined	• hesitant
• generous	• materialistic
• peaceful	• naive
• honest	• defenseless
• diligent	
• cheerful	

Secret pig

The Western view of pigs attributes to them various negative qualities such as greediness, laziness, filthiness, and stupidity. In fact, pigs are none of these things – although they do have a taste for good food. They are not overwhelming characters, but they are careful and determined people who are not easily stopped by obstacles.

Element

Pig is linked to the ancient Chinese element of water. Water is linked to the arts and inner expressiveness. Emotionally, water is associated with fear. It also endows sensitivity and understanding. In pigs, water expresses itself as their nurturing qualities and in their ability to compromise and avoid conflict.

Balance

The pig is a Yin animal that exemplifies the Yin principles of peace, rest, and harmony. On the whole, therefore, pigs are well-balanced people. Their lives will not suffer from the ups and downs typical of the more unbalanced animal signs such as the dragon and the horse. Indeed, the Chinese astrological symbol for the pig is a set of balanced scales.

Best associations

Traditionally, the following are said to be associated with pigs:

- Taste   salt
- Season   winter
- Birth   winter
- Color   black
- Plant   ginseng
- Flower   water lily
- Food   peas, meat
- Climate   cold, wet

THE MALE PIG

If a man has a typical pig personality, he will generally display the behavior listed below.

- is easily deceived
- has impeccable manners
- does not exact revenge on enemies
- is endowed with common sense
- enjoys good food and fine wines
- always sees the best in people
- is a pacifist
- will have a difficult youth

THE FEMALE PIG

If a woman has a typical pig personality, she will generally display the behavior listed below.

- is famous for her hospitality
- is often taken advantage of
- will always help her friends
- is naturally clever
- is always polite
- will not bear grudges
- is bright and alert
- is eager to learn
- forgives but does not forget

PIG CHILD

If a child has a typical pig personality, he or she will generally display the behavior listed below.

- is reasonable and peaceful
- daydreams
- is careless
- does not have tantrums
- will sulk if ignored
- needs gentle discipline
- enjoys privacy
- is enthusiastic when happy
- has a sweet tooth
- is even-tempered

PIG AT HOME

Pigs are very sensual as well as domestic people and their homes reflect this. Soft armchairs, deep-pile carpets and huge bathtubs are all favored by pigs. The home of a pig will not be ostentatious though. They do not decorate to impress – only to please themselves. Pigs like to be able to relax at home. They do not want to be inhibited by thoughts of leaving marks on expensive furniture. All pigs are prone to excesses. At home, they can be either extremely houseproud, tidy people or very slovenly, messy types. One thing is certain, however; the kitchen will be well stocked and well equipped. Pigs are gourmets when it comes to food. They love to be creative in the kitchen.

PIG AT WORK

Pigs are not lazy. They are very hardworking and will rarely be unemployed. Although money, status, and power are not particularly important to pigs, they do want to achieve a comfortable lifestyle. So, they will do their best to ensure their financial security. Pigs are suited to most kinds of technical, scientific, and practical work. They are careful and diligent – skills which are ideal for such occupations. Pigs also excel as managers. Attentive and understanding but not weak, they are good at dealing with people. Pigs can take advice, and indeed actually seek it out when faced by a decision. The decisions they make are, therefore, carefully thought out and never rash.

Some typical pig occupations

- researcher
- scientist
- chemist
- technician
- musician
- restaurateur
- shoemaker
- social worker
- fundraiser
- builder
- chef
- delicatessen owner
- personnel manager
- administrative officer
- gourmet
- Samaritan
- civil servant

? PIG PREFERENCES

Likes

- making presents for people
- to be comfortable
- organizing parties
- reading a good book
- famous people
- to gossip
- the sound of applause
- to work as part of a team
- to be in a relationship

Dislikes

- arguments
- making difficult decisions alone
- possessive people
- to be reproached
- talking to people they dislike
- living by their wits alone
- being deceitful
- to feel confused
- to argue with friends
- inhospitable people
- not knowing where they stand

GOOD FRIENDS FOR PIGS

The diagram below shows the compatibility of pig with other animals. There is no fixed ruling, however, because there are other influences on both the pig and any potential friend. These influences are:

- the companion in life (see pp. 273–5)
- the dominant element (from the year of birth)

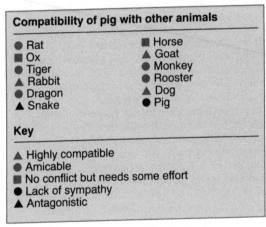

Compatibility of pig with other animals

- ● Rat
- ■ Ox
- ● Tiger
- ▲ Rabbit
- ● Dragon
- ▲ Snake

- ■ Horse
- ▲ Goat
- ● Monkey
- ● Rooster
- ▲ Dog
- ● Pig

Key

- ▲ Highly compatible
- ● Amicable
- ■ No conflict but needs some effort
- ● Lack of sympathy
- ▲ Antagonistic

Rat with pig This materialistic pair can be very good friends for a while, but trusting pig is rather vulnerable to rat's charms and may end up unable to say no when necessary.

Ox with pig Pig enjoys peace and quiet as much as ox but may find ox's responsible behavior wearisome at times. Pigs like to go out and enjoy themselves; oxen like to stay at home and relax. Pig may find ox too demanding, and ox may find pig irritating.

Tiger with pig These two can get along well together as they are both gregarious, tolerant, and independent. Tiger will protect pig from his enemies, and pig will prove loyal. Be warned, however, that tiger may be tempted to test pig's temper and find himself on the losing end.

Rabbit with pig Pleasure-loving, tolerant pig is a good match for rabbit. Discreet rabbit may be a bit unnerved by sensual pig's public displays of affection, but this is a minor point.

Dragon with pig Even though pigs and dragons have little in common, the two are actually very compatible. Pigs are easygoing and enjoy dragons' showy nature. Dragon will sweep pig off his feet who, in turn, will adore and fuss over dragon.

Snake with pig This is a case of opposites that do not attract. Snake sees pig as naive and innocent, but pig is wise to snake's true nature. Both are very sensual creatures, and this can unite them. If a relationship does endure, it is likely to be thanks to pig's forgiving nature. Pigs will not, however, allow themselves to be taken for granted for long.

Horse with pig At first, these two will get along. Pig will find horse exciting, and horse will enjoy pig's kind and loving nature. Eventually, however, selfish horse will test pig's patience to the limit, or horse will get bored with the pig.

Goat with pig This is a good alliance for both signs. Both value tranquillity and harmony and are able to make the concessions necessary to achieve them. Goat should take care not to stretch pig's tolerance too far, however, by acting irresponsibly.

Monkey with pig As both are outgoing and friendly, this can be a well-balanced relationship. Monkeys can help generous pigs curb their excessive spending. Honest pig can appreciate the monkey's planning and scheming.

Rooster with pig Pig and the rooster can be very good friends and true, if not exciting, lovers. Pig is one of the few animal signs that can recognize rooster's well-hidden sensitivity and kindness. Rooster will be disarmed by understanding pig.

Dog with pig Contented pig brings optimism and a carefree aspect to pessimistic dog. This is very beneficial for dog, who will be happy and relaxed with pig. Both are also generous, kind, and honest people who, together, can build a lasting relationship.

Pig with pig A pig can be a very good friend to another pig. There will be many misunderstandings, however, as they will bring out the worst, selfish side of each other. Also, the relationship may lack enough sparks to keep them both interested for long.

♥ PIG IN LOVE

Pig people are enthusiastic about love. Once they have met someone compatible, they fall in love quickly and deeply. It is obvious to everyone when a pig is in love, as they wear their hearts on their sleeves. Warmhearted and open people, pigs create peaceful and happy relationships. They will do anything to please the loved one. Pigs are sentimental and may overdo their displays of love and devotion. They should take care not to smother their partners, as not everyone appreciates constant attention. Conversely, pigs also like to maintain an aura of independence, even though at heart they are emotionally dependent on their partners. Pigs are vulnerable when they are in love. If they get hurt badly, then they may become bitter and will not risk the experience again.

PIG AND SEX

Pigs are both amorous and sensual people. They are not shy about sexual matters and know what they like. Even though pigs are romantic, they would rather express their feelings physically than emotionally. If the love of their life does not reciprocate, pigs will quite happily satisfy their desires elsewhere until they can get the person they want. Until they settle down, pigs will have many roller-coaster affairs that end badly – usually for them. But a pig is never depressed for long. Once committed, a pig will be faithful and loyal. To seduce a pig, cook a splendid meal, serve fine wines, and let nature take it course.

HEALTH

Pig's element, water, is associated with the kidneys and the bladder, so pigs should pay particular attention to keeping these organs in good working order. Watch out for the symptoms of urinary tract infections and drink plenty of water. Pigs cannot resist good foods, so many have a weight problem. They should try to establish healthy eating patterns and eat less rich foods. For a change, pigs could treat themselves with exotic fruits instead of high-fat foods.

LEISURE INTERESTS

Pigs love to read and write. They always keep in touch with old friends, often by letter if they live far away. To relax, pigs like to visit remote and wild landscapes. They can indulge their need for privacy and get involved in some outdoor sports. Rock climbing, canoeing, and windsurfing all appeal to pigs, who have an adventurous streak. Pigs also enjoy less daring activities such as long country walks. Rambling is ideal for the relaxed and sociable pig. Of course, all pigs enjoy preparing good food. Consulting the latest cookbook, they will try their hand at new and unusual dishes. The preparation is as enjoyable as the consumption for a pig.

THE PIG YEARS AND THEIR ELEMENTS

The pig is a Yin water animal. Each of the pig years, however, is associated with an element which is said to have its own influence. These elements are wood, fire, earth, metal, and water. They influence pig in a regular sequence, which is repeated every 60 years. In the table below, for example, the pig year 1911 is a metal year. The next pig metal year is 60 years later in 1971, and the next will be 2031. Pig's natural element is water; the influence of this combines with those of the element of the year of birth. The possible effects of the year elements are listed below.

Lunar years ruled by the pig and their elements

1911	Jan 30, 1911 – Feb 17, 1912	metal
1923	Feb 16, 1923 – Feb 4, 1924	water
1935	Feb 4, 1935 – Jan 23, 1936	wood
1947	Jan 22, 1947 – Feb 9, 1948	fire
1959	Feb 8, 1959 – Jan 27, 1960	earth
1971	Jan 27, 1971 – Feb 14, 1972	metal
1983	Feb 13, 1983 – Feb 1, 1984	water
1995	Jan 31, 1995 – Feb 18, 1996	wood
2007	Feb 18, 2007 – Feb 6, 2008	fire

Pig Water–Metal (1911, 1971)

Normally, the element metal makes a person rigid and pessimistic. The easygoing and optimistic pig, however, relieves these tendencies. Instead, metal pigs are blessed with immense fortitude and a great deal of perseverance. Metal makes these pigs more ambitious and stubborn than any other. They are extroverts as well as socialites. Unusually for pigs, those born in metal years have sharp wits and incisive intellects. Metal pigs are more brash than other pigs. For these reasons, they are prone to offending people.

Pig Water–Water (1923, 1983)

Pigs born in water years are in their natural element. Double water makes these people incredibly diplomatic and highly persuasive. Water pigs are very sympathetic and refuse to hear bad of anybody. They need to learn to be more realistic about others. All pigs are sensual and physically indulgent – water ones doubly so. These people need to find more constructive outlets for this side of their nature. Otherwise, they will become degenerates.

Pig Water–Wood (1935, 1995)

Wood and water is a fortunate combination for the pig. Water allows the creative wood element to blossom. These people are communicative and will gather respect and support in whatever field they operate. Consequently, wood pigs often rise to prominent positions. They are wise people who give very good, though not always welcome, advice. Wood pigs should take care not to associate with less scrupulous people who will take advantage of them.

Pig Water–Fire (1947, 2007)

Fire increases the excessive tendencies of pig people. Positively aspected, fire pigs are the most brave, adventurous, and optimistic of all pig people,

yet the huge energies they have are just as likely to
be concentrated on indulging their pleasure-loving
natures as plunged into some worthwhile cause. Pigs
born in fire years are capable of reaching great
heights of achievement or great depths of depravity.

PigWater–Earth (1899, 1959)
Earth steadies the fluid element of water. It is a
balancing medium for the pig. Those pigs born in
earth years are likely to lead safe, comfortable, and
secure lives. Most pigs suffer from fear and
excessive caution, but earth pigs are not beset by
such problems. Consequently, they are more self-
confident and assured than pigs usually are. Earth
pigs are hardworking and resourceful. They tend to
have great physical strength and stamina.

 **PIG AND THE ZODIAC OF
WESTERN ASTROLOGY**
To work out your zodiac sign see p. 277.
General character traits of pigs of the 12
zodiac signs are given below. Bear in mind that the
Western zodiac sign modifies the basic pig nature –
especially in the area of personal relationships.

Aries pig Impetuous Aries and carefree pig combine
to produce youthful, almost childlike people. They
are enthusiastic and innocent characters who are
well liked by everyone they meet. Aries pigs are also
brilliant at both art and management.
Taurus pig Taurus pigs are patient, materialistic,
and cautious. They can be found in the upper
echelons of society among the "beautiful people."

Pigs born under this sign are not snobs, however; they are generous, kind, and understanding to a fault.

Gemini pig Mercurial Gemini does not allow the pig to be as hesitant or indulgent as usual. Gemini pigs are more interested in cerebral matters than physical pleasure. They are outspoken and have a sardonic sense of humor.

Cancer pig Cancer pigs are amazingly self-sufficient. They have self-discipline and great insight. Unfortunately, this assurance can crumble when they feel insecure. Cancer pigs are prone to mood swings and bouts of depression.

Leo pig Leo pigs are larger-than-life characters. They are open, warmhearted, and very generous. A pig born under this sign positively enjoys helping others out. The only bad thing to be said about a Leo pig is that, at times, they are self-centered.

Virgo pig Virgo pigs can appear cold and calculating. They are still typically kind pig people, however, but just a little more discriminating than other pigs. Analytical Virgo makes them less ready with their favors. They will only help those who they feel really deserve help.

Libra pig Sophisticated Libra lends refinement to the pig. Libran pigs are talented and creative people. Dreamers as well, if they are not careful they will spend all their time with their heads in the clouds.

Scorpio pig Scorpio brings a measure of depth to the pig. Typically, pigs are credulous people, but not those born under this sign. Scorpio pigs are very suspicious. Pushy and outspoken, these people are driven by the need to secure their financial success.

Sagittarius pig Sagittarius pigs are happy-go-lucky adventurers. They have an enthusiastic and curious approach to life. Although they make loving partners, these pigs cannot stand to feel tied down.

Capricorn pig Capricornean pigs are authoritarian and opportunistic. They want to both succeed materially and impress their contemporaries. Despite this, they are loyal and protective, if a little overpowering, with loved ones.

Aquarius pig Honest and sincere, Aquarian pigs are popular people. They often appear eccentric, however. In fact, these pigs have such a unique perspective on life that they find it difficult to get close to anyone.

Pisces pig Charming, sweet-natured, and loving, Pisces pigs are truly nice people. They are renowned for their hospitality but can be unexpectedly mean with their money. Pisces pigs often have healing gifts.

Some famous people born in the years of the pig and their zodiac signs

- King Henry VIII
  British monarch
  Jun 28, 1491 Cancer
- Oliver Cromwell
  British statesman
  Apr 25, 1599 Taurus
- Otto von Bismarck
  German statesman
  Apr 1, 1815 Aries
- Carl Jung
  Psychologist
  Jul 26, 1875 Leo
- Fred Astaire
  Dancer
  May 10, 1899 Taurus
- James Cagney
  Actor
  Jul 17, 1899 Cancer
- Ernest Hemingway
  Writer
  Jul 21, 1899 Cancer
- Alfred Hitchcock
  Filmmaker
  Aug 13, 1899 Leo
- Jorge Luis Borges
  Writer
  Aug 24, 1899 Virgo
- Noël Coward
  Actor/Writer
  Dec 16, 1899 Sagittarius
- Humphrey Bogart
  Actor
  Dec 25, 1899 Capricorn
- Ronald Reagan
  Actor/US president
  Feb 6, 1911 Aquarius
- Jean Harlow
  Actress
  Mar 3, 1911 Pisces
- Tennessee Williams
  Writer
  Mar 26, 1911 Aries
- Georges Pompidou
  French statesman
  Jul 5, 1911 Cancer
- Ginger Rogers
  Dancer
  Jul 16, 1911 Cancer
- Lucille Ball
  Actress
  Aug 6, 1911 Leo
- Henry Kissinger
  US statesman
  May 27, 1923 Gemini
- Richard Attenborough
  Filmmaker
  Aug 29, 1923 Virgo
- Maria Callas
  Opera singer
  Dec 3, 1923 Sagittarius
- Dudley Moore
  Comedian/Actor
  Apr 19, 1935 Aries
- Jerry Lee Lewis
  Musician
  Sep 29, 1935 Libra
- Johnny Mathis
  Singer
  Sep 30, 1935 Libra
- Elton John
  Singer
  Mar 25, 1947 Taurus

Index

Aquarius 216-35
    and friends 230
    and love 225
    and partner 227
    and sex 226
    at home 222
    at work 223
    famous Aquarians 235
    female 220
    health 233
    leisure interests 232
    look 218
    male 219
    personality 217
    young 220
Aries 16-35
    and friends 29
    and love 26
    and partner 28
    and sex 27
    at home 23
    at work 24
    famous Ariens 35
    female 20
    health 32
    leisure interests 30
    look 19
    male 19
    personality 17
    young 21
Astrological symbols 15
Cancer 76-95
    and friends 90
    and love 86
    and partner 88

    and sex 87
    at home 83
    at work 84
    famous Cancerians 95
    female 80
    health 93
    leisure interests 90
    look 79
    male 79
    personality 77
    young 81
Capricorn 196-215
    and friends 210
    and love 206
    and partner 208
    and sex 207
    at home 203
    at work 204
    famous Capricorns 215
    female 200
    health 213
    leisure interests 212
    look 199
    male 199
    personality 197
    young 201
Companion in life 273-76
Dog 468-86
    and sex 479
    and zodiac 483
    at home 473
    at work 473
    child 472
    famous Dogs 486
    female 472

good friends 476
health 480
in love 479
leisure interests 480
male 471
personality 469
preferences 475
years and elements 481
Dragon 354-72
and sex 365
and zodiac 369
at home 359
at work 360
child 359
famous Dragons 372
female 358
good friends 362
health 365
in love 364
leisure interests 366
male 357
personality 355
preferences 361
years and elements 366
Gemini 56-75
and friends 70
and love 66
and partner 68
and sex 67
at home 63
at work 64
famous Geminis 75
female 60
health 73
leisure interests 70
look 59
male 59
personality 57
young 61

Goat 411-29
and sex 422
and zodiac 426
at home 416
at work 416
child 415
famous Goats 429
female 415
good friends 419
health 423
in love 421
leisure interests 423
male 414
personality 412
preferences 418
years and elements 424
Horse 392-410
and sex 403
and zodiac 407
at home 397
at work 397
child 396
famous Horses 410
female 396
good friends 400
health 404
in love 402
leisure interests 404
male 395
personality 393
preferences 399
years and elements 405
Leo 96-115
and friends 110
and love 106
and partner 108
and sex 107
at home 103
at work 104

famous Leos 115
female 100
health 113
leisure interests 110
look 99
male 99
personality 97
young 101
Libra 136-55
  and friends 150
  and love 146
  and partner 147
  and sex 147
  at home 143
  at work 144
  famous Libras 155
  female 140
  health 153
  leisure interests 152
  look 139
  male 139
  personality 137
  young 141
Lunar calendar 260-64
Monkey 430-505
  and sex 441
  and zodiac 445
  at home 435
  at work 435
  child 434
  famous Monkeys 448
  female 434
  good friends 438
  health 442
  in love 441
  leisure interests 442
  male 433
  personality 431
  preferences 437

years and elements 443
Ox 297-315
  and sex 308
  and zodiac 312
  at home 302
  at work 302
  child 301
  famous 315
  female 301
  good friends 305
  health 309
  in love 308
  leisure interests 309
  male 300
  personality 298
  preferences 304
  years and elements 309
Pig 487-505
  and sex 498
  and zodiac 502
  at home 492
  at work 492
  child 491
  famous Pigs 505
  female 491
  good friends 495
  health 499
  in love 498
  leisure interests 499
  male 490
  personality 488
  preferences 494
  years and elements 500
Pisces 236-55
  and friends 250
  and love 246
  and partner 248
  and sex 247
  at home 243

at work 244
famous Pisceans 255
female 240
health 253
leisure interests 252
look 239
male 239
personality 237
young 241
Rabbit 335-53
  and sex 346
  and zodiac 350
  at home 340
  at work 341
  child 340
  famous Rabbits 353
  female 339
  good friends 343
  health 346
  in love 345
  leisure interests 347
  male 338
  personality 336
  preferences 342
  years and elements 347
Rat 278-96
  and sex 289
  and zodiac 293
  at home 283
  at work 284
  child 283
  famous Rats 296
  female 282
  good friends 286
  health 290
  in love 289
  leisure interests 290
  male 281
  personality 279

preferences 285
years and elements 290
Rooster 449-67
  and sex 460
  and zodiac 464
  at home 454
  at work 454
  child 453
  famous Roosters 467
  female 453
  good friends 457
  health 460
  in love 459
  leisure interests 461
  male 452
  personality 450
  preferences 456
  years and elements 461
Sagittarius 176-95
  and friends 189
  and love 186
  and partner 188
  and sex 187
  at home 183
  at work 184
  famous Sagittarians 195
  female 180
  health 193
  leisure interests 190
  look 179
  male 179
  personality 177
  young 181
Scorpio 156-75
  and friends 170
  and love 165
  and partner 167
  and sex 167
  at home 162

at work 164
famous Scorpios 175
female 160
health 173
leisure interests 172
look 159
male 159
personality 157
young 161
Snake 373-91
and sex 384
and zodiac 388
at home 378
at work 378
child 377
famous Snakes 391
female 377
good friends 381
health 385
in love 384
leisure interests 385
male 376
personality 374
preferences 380
years and elements 385
Taurus 36-55
and friends 50
and love 46
and partner 47
and sex 47
at home 43
at work 44
famous Taureans 55
female 40
health 53
leisure interests 52
look 39
male 39

personality 37
young 41
Tiger 316-34
and sex 327
and zodiac 331
at home 321
at work 322
child 321
famous Tigers 334
female 320
good friends 324
health 328
in love 327
leisure interests 328
male 319
personality 317
preferences 323
years and elements 329
Virgo 116-35
and friends 130
and love 126
and partner 128
and sex 127
at home 123
at work 124
famous Virgos 135
female 120
health 133
leisure interests 132
look 119
male 119
personality 117
young 121
Yin and Yang 270-73